"An absorbing and exciting chronicle.
Milbourne Christopher...has brilliantly captured the egotism of the man....Above all, he
has made you feel some of the pity and terror
which Houdini aroused in his audiences."

—Maurice Zolotow
The New York Times Book Review

"The most informed biography of Houdini to
date."
—John Barkham
Saturday Review Syndicate

"Mr. Christopher's book moves as swiftly, and
holds as much fascination for an audience, as
Houdini slipping out of a set of Scotland
Yard's best manacles."

—Maurice Dolbier
Book World (Chicago Sun-Times)

"...newest, and best, biography of Harry
Houdini...as objective as it is thorough."
—Charles Cooke
Washington Star

HOUDINI: THE UNTOLD STORY
was originally published by
Thomas Y. Crowell Company.

Are there paperbound books you want but cannot find in your retail stores?

You can get any title in print in:
Pocket Book editions • Pocket *Cardinal* editions • Permabook editions or Washington Square Press editions. Simply send retail price, local sales tax, if any, plus 15¢ to cover mailing and handling costs for each book wanted to:

MAIL SERVICE DEPARTMENT
   POCKET BOOKS • A Division of Simon & Schuster, Inc.
   1 West 39th Street   •   New York, New York 10018
   Please send check or money order. We cannot be responsible for cash.
   Catalogue sent free on request.

Titles in these series are also available at discounts in quantity lots for industrial or sales-promotional use. For details write our Special Projects Agency: The Benjamin Company, Inc., 485 Madison Avenue, New York, N.Y. 10022.

MILBOURNE CHRISTOPHER

HOUDINI:
The Untold Story

PUBLISHED BY POCKET BOOKS NEW YORK

FOR MAURINE

who shut her eyes when I caught bullets between my teeth, cheered when I made a live elephant disappear, and who hopes I will never be handcuffed and submerged in an underwater box.

HOUDINI: THE UNTOLD STORY

Thomas Y. Crowell edition published March, 1969
Pocket Book edition published June, 1970
The Illustrations Are from the Christopher Collection.

This *Pocket Book* edition includes every word contained in the original, higher-priced edition. It is printed from brand-new plates made from completely reset, clear, easy-to-read type. *Pocket Book* editions are published by Pocket Books, a division of Simon & Schuster, Inc., 630 Fifth Avenue, New York, N.Y. 10020. Trademarks registered in the United States and other countries.

Standard Book Number: 671-77169-8.
Library of Congress Catalog Card Number: 69-11829.
Copyright, ©, 1969, by Milbourne Christopher. All rights reserved.
This **Pocket Book** edition is published by arrangement with Thomas Y. Crowell Company.

Printed in the U.S.A.

CONTENTS

Illustrations follow page 146.

THE INCREDIBLE HOUDINI

The special matinee at the London Hippodrome on March 17—St. Patrick's Day—1904 drew a capacity audience of 4,000. Five days earlier, Harry Houdini had been challenged by the *Daily Illustrated Mirror* to escape from what it believed was the strongest pair of handcuffs ever made. The manacles had six sets of locks and nine tumblers in each cuff. A Birmingham man had labored five years, and used five hundred dollars' worth of material, to make them. The *Mirror* was confident that this test would thoroughly deflate the American magician's claim that he could free himself from any device that the ingenuity of man could create.

The six acts that preceded Houdini might just as well never have gone on; the crowd was there to see the heavily advertised test. Harry, in a black frock coat, stiff collar and dark tie, was given a roof-shaking welcome. When he asked if the *Mirror* representative was present, the challenger walked down the aisle and up to the stage where he shook hands with the challenged. The request for a committee from the audience brought forty men from their seats.

The newsman displayed the Birmingham handcuffs, then closed them on Houdini's wrists. He inserted a key and turned it six times in each keyhole. The committeemen assured the audience that the cuffs were locked.

"Ladies and gentlemen," Harry said, "I am now locked up in a handcuff that has taken a British mechanic five years to make. I do not know whether I am going to get out of it or not, but I can assure you I am going to do my best."

It was 3:15 p.m. when he bent down to enter his small black cabinet. The committeemen surrounded it on all sides except the front. The theater orchestra struck up a rousing tune. Houdini's wife, Bess, waited anxiously in the wings.

Time slipped by. The man from the *Mirror* paced restlessly back and forth, one eye always on the small enclosure. Twenty-two minutes after he had vanished from view, Hou-

1

dini's head came up from the top of the cabinet. There were excited shouts: "He is free." But Houdini merely wanted more light on the cuffs. As he slipped from view again, the orchestra struck up another number.

After thirty-five minutes Harry came out of the cabinet. Perspiration ran down his face. His stiff collar had wilted and broken. He took a few brisk steps, bent his legs. "My knees hurt," he said, then he glanced at the man from the *Mirror*. "I'm not done yet." There were cheers. The newsman turned and spoke to the theater manager. The manager whispered to an usher. Soon a large pillow was in the *Mirror* representative's hands.

"The *Mirror* has no desire to submit Mr. Houdini to a torture test," he said graciously, "and if Mr. Houdini will permit me, I shall have great pleasure in offering him the use of this cushion." Houdini smiled and tugged the pillow inside his enclosure.

For twenty minutes more the music continued. Then up came Houdini. The tense audience was ready to cheer, but the manacles were still in place. He walked over to the man from the *Mirror:* "Will you remove the handcuffs for a moment?" He explained that he wanted to take off his coat.

The journalist hesitated. If he unfastened the cuffs Houdini would see how they were opened. He had seen them locked on his wrists, but not the opening sequence. "I am sorry . . . Mr. Houdini, but I cannot unlock these cuffs unless you admit you are defeated."

Most performers would have accepted the reply, shrugged their shoulders, and gone back to work on the cuffs. Not Houdini! He twisted his hands until he could reach a pocket-knife in his vest pocket, then pulled a blade open with his teeth. With contortions similar to those he went through to escape from a straitjacket he yanked his coat over his head so that it hung inside out between his manacled hands. Gripping the knife firmly between his teeth, he sliced the coat into shreds. The audience roared with sheer delight at this unexpected display of determination and agility. Houdini tossed the strips of his coat aside and went back through the curtains of the cabinet.

An hour had passed without complaints of boredom from the audience. The orchestra swept into a march. An hour and ten minutes. Houdini suddenly leaped from the cabinet.

His hands were free. He held the cuffs aloft. The crowd shouted, cheered, stamped their feet, waved their arms. Some of the committeemen lifted Houdini to their shoulders and paraded him around the stage. Then Houdini's reserve broke. Tears gushed from his eyes. Eventually he took a deep breath, wiped his face, and accepted the hearty handshake and the compliments of the man from the *Mirror*. The journalist said that the newspaper would present him with a trophy—a solid-silver replica of the Birmingham cuffs—as soon as it could be made. Harry assured the audience he had never been treated as fairly, or as gentlemanly, in a challenge test.

Bess had watched until shortly before the coat-cutting. Forty minutes of strain had forced her to leave the theater, knowing that she would collapse in public if she did not. She was overjoyed when she heard he had escaped. No one knew how she suffered during the difficult challenges, how she cried as she wiped away the blood from the cuts and scratches on Harry's swollen wrists and dabbed his wounds with ointments.

When Harry learned how upset she had been during the *Mirror* test, he told the reporter: "Eleven years ago she brought me luck and it has been with me ever since. I never had any before I married her."

Like many of Houdini's feats, the exact method by which he accomplished this one remained a mystery. Will Goldston, a British magician and friend of Houdini's, wrote in his *Sensational Tales of Mystery Men* that an unidentified man informed him that Bess had cajoled the key from the newspaperman while Houdini was struggling in the cabinet and smuggled it to her husband in a glass of water. Goldston said, that in his opinion, the story was "an exaggeration." Nonetheless, later writers offered this as the solution to the *Mirror* release. How little they understood Houdini and his methods. He would never accept a challenge, especially one as highly publicized as this one had been, without devising a surefire release long before the day of the test.

There was an amusing postscript to the *Mirror* episode. Houdini offered five hundred dollars to any handcuffs performer who could do what he had done. One man took him up on the offer. As he stood beside Houdini it was obvious that his small wrists could be pulled free from the cuffs without any effort on his part to open the twelve locks. Harry was equal to the situation. He locked the manacles, then tossed them to the man. "Get them open now!" His money was as safe as if it had been in the Bank of England.

More than forty years after his last performance in 1926, Houdini is still the world's best-known mystifier. He created the illusion that he could squeeze through the keyhole of a lock. No manacle, straitjacket, or jail could hold him. He was, and is, a symbol for man himself—the ingenious creature who overcomes seemingly impossible obstacles by sheer force of willpower.

Houdini staged his sensational feats with a sure sense of the dramatic that made good copy for the press. He was tied to the arm of a Dutch windmill, to escape, if he could, as it turned in the air. Russian secret police sought to restrain him in a metal-lined prison van. Lashed to the open barrel of a British cannon set with a time fuse, the master escapologist proclaimed he would free himself or "be blown to Kingdom Come."

Hundreds of thousands of fascinated spectators saw Houdini squirm free from straitjackets as he dangled in the air high above city streets, and watched entranced as he leaped from bridges to divest himself of handcuffs and chains in the rivers below.

In Chicago, Houdini escaped from a huge sealed envelope without breaking the paper. He released himself from the interior of a giant football laced with metal links and fastened with padlocks in Philadelphia. In Boston he penetrated the chained carcass of an embalmed "sea monster" and left no clue to his method.

Less imaginative competitors freed themselves from mere jails. Houdini, the peerless showman, escaped from the Sheffield prison which had held Charles Peace, "Britain's most notorious criminal"; and broke out of the cell of the United States Jail in Washington, where Guiteau, "the assassin of President Garfield, was confined until he was led forth to be hanged."

Houdini's blue-gray eyes sparkled behind the footlights, his smile was infectious. He moved with authority, radiated confidence and charm. Offstage he was less impressive, a shorter than average, stocky, clean-shaven man. His clothes always looked a little rumpled, his neckties were frequently askew.

There was not a trace of theatrical glamour—until he spoke. In Europe they called him "the syllable-accenting American." His voice could be heard in the last gallery row of the largest auditorium.

He enjoyed playing a role offstage as well as on, and he was a master of the dramatic entrance. When a temperamental singer complained, backstage in a Midwestern vaudeville theater, that her trunk had not been taken to her dressing room, a muscular man left the crate he was opening, hefted her baggage and lugged it up three flights of stairs. The singer offered him a tip. He shrugged it away with a pixyish expression. "Are you the propman?" she asked. "No," replied the star of the show, introducing himself with a Chaplinesque bow, "I'm Houdini."

His presentations generated maximum spectator excitement. When he was nailed inside a crate made for the occasion by challenging carpenters, his staging was so effective that audiences waited expectantly—sometimes as long as twenty minutes—before the first tremor behind the curtains of his cabinet indicated that he was out.

"Why do you take so long?" a fellow member of the Society of American Magicians once asked. "I'm sure with your know-how you could do it far faster."

"If I got out too quickly," Houdini replied, "the audience would reason that escape was easy. Every second that ticks by during my struggle builds up the climax. When they are sure I am licked, that the box will have to be smashed open to give me air, then—and only then—do I appear.

"Visualize it yourself. A man is enclosed in a sealed container. A few minutes later he is out, still neatly pressed with his hair slicked back and none the worse for wear. What's the response? Polite applause at most. Now, the same man, the same box. Minutes drag by. What is everyone thinking? Has something gone wrong? Is the man sick? Has he fainted? More time passes. The tension becomes almost unbearable. Suddenly the man, who obviously has had to fight his way to freedom, emerges. His shirt is wrinkled. His trousers are torn. His face is red. Perspiration drips from every pore. The pent-up mass emotion explodes into an ovation.

"Mind you," Houdini added, "unlike my imitators I don't bribe police officials or set up fake challenges. I get out with my specialized knowledge and muscle power."

Other escape artists were anathema to Houdini. Arthur Gans, a Baltimore magician, was warmly welcomed to Houdini's dressing room between shows at the Auditorium Theater. Gans turned to introduce his companion, "And this is our Maryland escape king." Houdini's cordiality disappeared. "I recognize no other escape kings," he said icily and stalked away.

After fighting his way up from dime museums and traveling circuses to show business eminence, Houdini used his knowledge of the techniques of deception to expose charlatans who bilked the public by pretending to communicate with the dead. From coast to coast, on stages and lecture platforms, Houdini demonstrated how messages were written on slates, not by spirit hands but by the substitution of a message-bearing surface for a blank one. He displayed lengths of luminous, compressible cheesecloth, which mediums manipulated in dark rooms to produce the streaks of light that appeared to be ghosts from another world.

Spiritualism was only one of Houdini's targets. Fortune-tellers, he charged, were cheats. Astrology had no scientific basis. Palm readers were quacks. Fakirs were frauds. Trances were not necessary for underwater survival in an airtight coffin. He proved the point by duplicating Fakir Rahman Bey's "living burial" in the swimming pool of a New York hotel.

Newspaper editorials praised Houdini as a public benefactor. Sir Arthur Conan Doyle, a champion of the spiritualistic cause, disagreed. Even though Houdini attacked spiritualists, Doyle believed that the man's own marvelous feats could be explained only in one way—Houdini himself was a medium.

J. Hewat McKenzie, president of the British College of Psychic Science, endorsed this view. He had been on the stage as a member of the committee from the audience when Houdini escaped from a padlocked metal can. Houdini didn't use trickery, McKenzie declared, he dematerialized his body and oozed out. McKenzie had felt "a great loss of energy" when this occurred "such as is usually experienced by sitters in a materializing séance." He called Houdini's demonstration "one of nature's profoundest miracles."

It is no simple matter to present a stage feat so effectively that men such as Doyle and McKenzie will accept it as beyond human accomplishment. But Houdini's capacity for work was prodigious. He seldom slept more than five hours a night. He was constantly working on new feats for the future and the early morning hours were devoted to reading, research, and notes for books and articles he hoped to write when there was time.

Two of his most fantastic ideas were never staged. He visualized himself escaping from handcuffs as he dropped by parachute from the top of New York's Woolworth Building, then the world's tallest skyscraper. He intended one day to be nailed in a box which would be swept over Niagara Falls and smashed to splinters in the whirlpool below. Then moments later, after the spectators had been convinced that he was dead, he would reappear mysteriously on the shore to acknowledge their applause.

Houdini's collection of memorabilia and literature relating to conjuring and magic was unmatched. He owned notable collections dealing with theater, spiritualism, witchcraft, and crime. He gathered autographs of the men who signed the Declaration of Independence, documents concerning Cagliostro, David Garrick's personal diary, and letters signed by such diverse celebrities as Edmund Kean, Robert Ingersoll, and Jenny Lind. Two of his prize possessions were an autographed Martin Luther Bible and Edgar Allan Poe's portable writing desk. He had the instincts of a pack rat. He preserved a heel from the last shoes worn by Robert Heller. The Philadelphia undertaker from whom he obtained it swore that it was authentic. The heels of the British magician's burial shoes were removed in the funeral establishment because Heller was too tall to fit in his casket.

Houdini bought the complete stock of a lithographer who specialized in theatrical posters when the firm went out of business. As the truck drove up to his house, his wife asked: "Now that you've got them, what are you going to do with them?" By then his home was a cross between a museum and a warehouse, filled with books, playbills, crated stage illusions that had once been performed by Dr. Lynn, Harry Kellar, Karl Germain, and Hermalin, as well as hundreds of locks, manacles, chains, keys, and escape devices. Still, when the first electric chair ever used at Auburn prison came up for auction, he couldn't resist the temptation to buy it. The chair had been on exhibit in a dime museum where he had performed as a young man.

Houdini's stage magic was as spectacular as his escapes. Earlier magicians had produced canaries and doves. He conjured up a live eagle! Herrmann the Great, everyone's idea of what a mystifier should look like, with his black moustache, trim goatee, and slightly satanic manner, startled audiences before the turn of the century by whisking his wife from view as she sat in a suspended chair. Houdini fired a pistol and a 10,000-pound elephant disappeared!

Houdini's professional career spanned the rise and fall of big-time vaudeville. When motion pictures began to displace the two-a-day as America's favorite form of entertainment, he performed his feats before the cameras. He was the first screen hero to vanquish a robot villain. The nation thrilled as he scaled tall buildings, leaped from plane to plane and broke from his bonds moments before a stream of acid reached his body. There were shrieks and cheers as Houdini hung from the edge of a cliff by his fingernails and swam through turbulent waters at the very brink of Niagara Falls to rescue a terrified heroine.

Many legends have arisen about Houdini, his career, and his fabulous feats. Some he plucked from thin air and circulated himself. Others evolved in the imaginations of those who wrote about him. Fortunately, Houdini was a prolific letter writer, author, diarist, note taker, and keeper of documents. Much of his vast storehouse of magical lore, thousands of the newspaper articles about him, hundreds of his challenge handbills, lithographs, and photographs have been preserved. From these records on file around the world and from the memories of those who knew him the story of the incredible showman who made "the impossible possible" can be told.

EHRIE

Mayer Samuel Weiss, the son of a rabbi in Keszthely, a city on Balaton Lake in western Hungary, came to Budapest from Grosskaniza, determined to make his livelihood as a lawyer. When the authorities ruled that he lacked the necessary academic credits, he became a teacher of religion. Samuel was never to continue his studies of civil law; instead, he read rabbinical commentaries on Judaic tradition and devoted himself to the Torah.

He married a sister of Rosa Czillag, a popular opera singer. In 1863, when Samuel was thirty-four, their first son Armin (Herman) was born—and his wife died. A year later, a young friend came to him for help. He wished to marry pretty twenty-two-year-old Cecilia Steiner, but was too shy to propose. He asked Samuel, who knew the Steiners, to present his case.

Cecilia was moved by Samuel's words. But as he spoke, Samuel realized with dismay that he was speaking for himself. That night the enormity of what he had done appalled him. He poured out his feelings in a long and passionate letter. He was thirteen years Cecilia's senior. He was a widower with a son. His income was small and not likely to increase substantially. He had nothing to offer but his love. It was ridiculous to hope that she would consider him as a husband.

Cecilia replied that it had been obvious Samuel was speaking on his own behalf. She encouraged him to approach her family. The Steiners knew and liked Samuel; their daughter loved him. A pompous uncle protested the liaison, but his objections were brushed aside. The wedding took place May 27, 1864. Their first son died. The second, Nathan, was born four years after they had taken their vows; William was to follow two years later.

The birth of the child the world was to know as Houdini is recorded in precise detail in the 1872–74 volume of the Pesti Izraelita Hitkozseg register. The names are given in the

original Hungarian spellings. Erik Weisz, the legitimate male
child of Samuel and Caecilia (Steiner), was born in the house
of his parents at Rakos arok-Gasse No. 1, on March 24, 1874.
The attending midwife was Anna Fleischmann; the godmother
was Miksa Dick. Seven days later I. L. Schill performed the
circumcision.

Shortly after this Samuel left Budapest. It is said that a
nobleman slandered him and his religion. A duel was fought
and his opponent was killed. To escape arrest and the ven-
geance of the dead man's family, Samuel fled to London and
there embarked for the United States to seek refuge with
Hungarian friends who had settled in Appleton, Wisconsin.

Cecilia, her mother, and the four children may have been
there before Samuel arrived; if not, they joined him soon after.
There was no synagogue in Appleton. When one was formed
in the spring of 1874, Samuel became its rabbi at a salary of
$750 a year.

Emigration from Hungary broke the pattern of Samuel's
life. He was never again to feel that he was the master of his
own destiny. Life in the post-Civil War Midwest was discon-
certing. He could speak German, Hungarian, and Hebrew
but the American idiom confused him. After several torturous
English lessons from a woodcutter who lived nearby, he gave
up the project.

Cecilia claimed that Ehrich never cried as an infant. If the
child pouted, she would pick him up and the sound of her
heartbeat would drive away the threatened tears. She worried
because he slept so little. No matter when she bent over his
crib, day or night, his blue-gray eyes were always open.

Ehrich was five when his father questioned him about some
spikes he brought into the house. Had someone given them
to him? No, the boy replied, he had taken them from along
the banks of the river where a bridge was being built. That,
the usually reserved Samuel thundered, was stealing. No one
should steal—especially not the son of a rabbi. He took Ehrich
back to the construction site, made him replace his plunder,
and confess his guilt to the foreman. The object lesson was
more effective than a thousand pious sermons.

Samuel wore his graying hair long in the old-country fashion. A moustache, beard, and spectacles added to the austerity
of his appearance. His congregation was impressed by his

Talmudic studies, but thought his teachings were out of keeping with the times. They replaced him with a younger, more progressive-minded, leader.

The Weisses, uprooted again, this time by the loss of Samuel's income, went to Milwaukee. "Such hardships became our lot," Houdini wrote, "that the less said on the matter the better." They moved frequently—perhaps just a step ahead of the rent collector. Between 1883 and 1887 they had at least five addresses in Milwaukee.

Cecilia, short, merry-eyed, with an infinite capacity for understanding, seldom complained. Her love for her family filled the sparsely furnished rooms in which they lived. English eluded her as it had Samuel; the household language was German. She was a good cook and adept with needle and thread. She altered the clothes of the older boys to fit the younger.

Perhaps to give Ehrich the security of American citizenship, she told him that he, like his younger brother, Theo, had been born in Appleton. The date, she said, was April 6, 1874. That became his "adopted" birthday. Poor Theo. He was born on February 29, 1876, and his birthday would come once every four years. Later two more children, Leopold and Cari Gladys, were to complicate the family's struggle for survival.

Ehrich and his brothers contributed to the scanty family income. He sold the first issue of the new Milwaukee *Journal* when he was eight; he also worked as a bootblack. Once as he brushed the shoes of a well-dressed citizen he looked up and recognized the man as the governor of Wisconsin.

His happiest childhood memory was of what he called his "professional debut." This came when he was nine. He had practiced acrobatics on a makeshift trapeze rigged to a tree. When a young friend, Jack Hoeffler, staged a five-cent circus on a nearby lot, the featured performer was Ehrich, "The Prince of the Air." Years later, Hoeffler, who went on to become a successful Midwestern theater operator, recalled that the young gymnast had worn long red stockings to simulate the tights worn by circus aerialists.

Houdini embellished the story. He vividly described his extraordinary feat of picking up needles with his eyelids as he hung upside down and insisted that he had also escaped when tied with a length of rope. He told the tale so convincingly he almost believed it himself.

Ehrich and Theo sold newspapers during a snowstorm in 1883, then hitched a ride home on a horse-drawn sleigh. When Theo reached in his overcoat pocket to give his mother the money they had earned, his hand came out empty. The coins must have fallen out somewhere along the way. Cecilia's eyes misted, but there was no reproach, although the family needed every penny. Ehrich took Theo aside. He still had a nickel—and an idea. They trudged to a flower shop. Ehrich bought a flower. He held it up to people sloshing by. Someone gave him a dime for it. He bought two flowers. Now both boys had something to sell. In a few hours, by reinvesting their profits and appealing pathetically to passersby, they more than made up for the lost newspaper money.

Rabbi Weiss took Ehrich to see a touring magician, whose feature trick was the talk of Milwaukee. Dr. Lynn, "Late of Egyptian Hall, London," advertised that he "Cut up a Man at Every Performance." The plump, gray-moustached wizard sharpened a butcher knife on the blade of a scimitar, then slashed away at his victim who was tied in place in a cabinet. Off came a leg, an arm, and after it had been covered with a black cloth, the man's head. When the audience's shock had subsided, Lynn tossed the pieces inside the cabinet and drew the curtain. Seconds later the man stepped out—whole again. The boy who marveled at Dr. Lynn's bloodless surgery had no thought then of becoming a magician himself.

On Ehrich's twelfth birthday, Samuel Weiss, distraught by his inability to provide for his family, made the boy vow that he would take care of Cecilia as long as she lived. The promise preyed on Ehrich's mind. He decided to run away from home and find a regular job which would enable him to shoulder a larger share of his father's responsibilities.

He left before dawn the next day with a shoeshine kit under his arm, following a detachment of the United States Cavalry. He reasoned that polished boots were as vital to horsemen as well-groomed mounts. By the time the unit reached the armory in Delavan, Wisconsin, Ehrich was disillusioned. The soldiers had been generous on the road, but once at the barracks, most of them shined their own shoes.

Al Flitcroft, a Delavan boy, was eager to see how the military men lived. He slipped into the armory one morning. The cavalry was away on maneuvers, the building was empty. He was about to leave when a mound of burlap bags caught his attention. The heap stirred. Ehrich sat up and yawned. He regaled the newcomer with the story of his adventures with the army, then admitted he hadn't eaten in days.

Al took Ehrich to the Flitcroft farm. His mother fed the runaway and patched his trousers while he took his first bath since Milwaukee. Mrs. Flitcroft assured Ehrich he could stay with them until he found a job, but there was no work for a twelve-year-old in Delavan. Ehrich went to Beloit; a few days later he returned. Mrs. Flitcroft asked if he had received her letter. Where, Ehrich wanted to know, had she sent it? In care of General Delivery at the Beloit Post Office, she replied. The next morning Ehrich was off again. When he came back, he had the letter—the first he had ever received. He had traveled fifty miles to get it.

Only a single postcard remains from Ehrich's runaway days. A part of the Houdini-McManus-Young Collection in the Library of Congress, it is addressed to:

Mrs. C. Weiss
517 6th Street
Milwaukee, Wisc.

Dear Ma,
 I am going to Galvaston [*sic*], Texas and will be home in about a year. My best regards to all. Did you get my picture? If you didn't, write Mead Bros., Wood Stock, Ill.
Your truant son,
Ehrich Weiss

There is an added note: "This postal card mailed by myself [Houdini] when I ran away from home to earn some money. I was on my way to Texas? got into wrong freight car and went to Kansas City, Mo. This card was mailed in a place called Withersmil [*sic*], I remember being in Hanibal [*sic*], Mo." The postmark on the card reads "Hanibal [*sic*] & St. Joseph R.R. 1886."

If his son could search for a better income, so could Samuel. He went to New York with the conviction that its larger Jewish population could support another small religious school. Ehrich, who had worked his way east, found him in

Mrs. Leffler's boardinghouse at 244 East 79th Street. Soon,
between the two, enough money was saved to bring the family
from Wisconsin. A proud Ehrich met them at Grand Central
Station and escorted them to a flat he had found on East 75th
Street. "We lived there, I mean starved there, several years,"
he wrote later. Then the Weisses moved to 305 East 69th
Street. This was to be home for many years to come.

Poverty continued to plague Samuel in New York. One cold
December morning Ehrich heard him pacing the floor, mum-
bling, "The Lord will provide. The Lord will provide." Ehrich
didn't wait for divine intervention. He was working as a uniformed messenger for a department store. He lettered a card
and pinned it to his hat:

> Christmas is coming
> Turkeys are fat
> Please drop a quarter
> In the Messenger Boy's hat.

His verse produced smiles and a generous flow of currency.
Before Ehrich entered the Weiss flat that evening, he hid coins
up his sleeves, under his lapels, in his hair, and behind his
ears. When his mother opened the door, he assumed a dramatic stance.

"Shake me," he commanded, "I'm magic."

Cecilia grasped his shoulders and gave him a healthy shake.
Silver pieces spun from his body in all directions. She laughed
and shook him again; more coins clattered to the floor. Mother
and son, now almost helpless with laughter, sank down and
gathered up the money. There was almost enough to pay the
overdue rent.

The story that Ehrich learned his first trick from a sideshow
magician is pure legend. Theo's employer, a photographer,
taught him a simple coin trick. Theo, in turn, showed it to
Ehrich. In Ehrich's hands the vanishing and reappearing quarter was a startling feat. During the months he worked as a
photographer's helper and an electric driller, his interest in
sleight of hand grew. And he began to read books on conjuring.

Confidence, he read, is one of a magician's greatest assets.
Confidence, he found, also was a great plus in everyday life.
Ehrich, at fourteen, was temporarily unemployed. Early one

November morning he saw a line of job seekers outside the firm of H. Richters' Sons at 502 Broadway. Realizing that he would not have a chance if he took his proper place at the end, Ehrich walked briskly to the door, took down the "Assistant Necktie Cutter Wanted" sign, thanked the applicants for waiting, and told them the position had been filled. The bluff worked. The other boys drifted away. He walked in with the placard in his hand and got the job.

On weekends, Ehrich ran with the Allerton Club and later with the Pastime Athletic Club track team. The Pastime exercise field, at 67th Street and the East River, was only a few blocks from his home. Cecilia made him a pair of red silk trunks. He took several first prizes in junior events. He also became a proficient diver and strong swimmer. To keep himself in top physical condition he began a series of daily limbering-up exercises which he was to continue the rest of his life. His father had condemned tobacco and alcohol from a moralistic point of view. The Pastime coach stressed their debilitating effects on an athlete. Ehrich resolved never to smoke or drink.

He attended a meeting of the Edwin Forrest Amateur Dramatic Association on Columbia Street. His first words before an audience were delivered there—under pressure. Everyone present had to take an active part. When he had said that he could neither act nor quote from memory, he was given an open volume of poetry and told to read. He began:

> Under a spreading chestnut tree
> The village smithy stands . . .

During the two and a half years Ehrich worked at Richters' tie factory his skill with magic increased. Using playing cards and small objects, he gave shows in the neighborhood. Jacob Hyman, a fellow employee who was also interested in conjuring, became a close friend. During lunch breaks and after-hours they exchanged tricks and confidences.

What had been a keen interest in magic became almost an obsession after Ehrich read a secondhand copy of the *Memoirs of Robert-Houdin*. Ehrich's previous books had dealt with the methods of magic; this was the autobiography of France's greatest performer. It told how Jean Eugène Robert-Houdin gave up the family clockmaking profession to open a small theater in Paris, how his entertaining presentations and ingenious devices made him a national favorite. There were exciting accounts of Robert-Houdin's performance for the French emperor, and his journey to England where he appeared before Queen Victoria. The saga of the magician's mission to Algeria was as thrilling as a dime novel.

He was sent by the French government to demonstrate that his brand of wizardry was more powerful than that of a fanatical religious sect, the Marabouts. Robert-Houdin produced cannonballs from an empty top hat, made a strong Arab so weak he couldn't lift a small chest, caught a marked bullet in the center of an apple impaled on a knife, and conjured away a young Moor under the cover of a giant cone. The assembled chieftains proclaimed the Frenchman's wonders far greater than those of the Marabouts who were advising them. Until the magician's arrival, a revolt was imminent. Robert-Houdin had made a revolution disappear!

"From the moment I began to study the art he became my guide and my hero," Ehrich was to write. "I asked nothing more of life than to become in my profession like Robert-Houdin." He mentioned his ambition to his friend Jacob Hyman. And Hyman said it was easy to be "like Robert-Houdin"; all Ehrich had to do was add an "i" to his name.

It has been suggested that Ehrich took a new first name because Harry Kellar was then the most prominent American magician. Theo, his brother, had a more logical explanation. He was called Ehrich by his parents, but the boys used a more familiar contraction, Ehrie—Erie—Harry—the change was almost inevitable. So Ehrich Weiss, the son of an impoverished, immigrant rabbi, became Harry Houdini.

Then with little more than his driving ambition, a letter of reference from H. Richters' Sons, tiemakers, saying that he had been "an Honest and Industrious young man," and a well-worn copy of Robert-Houdin's memoirs as his talisman, Harry Houdini, at seventeen, set out on a new career.

THE SMALL TIME

The dominant magicians when Harry Houdini made his first rounds of the New York theatrical agents in 1891 were Herrmann the Great, a Paris-born prestidigitator of rare skill and charm, and Harry Kellar, the American illusionist, who was as shrewd a businessman as a showman.

Alexander Herrmann lived in a mansion at Whitestone, Long Island. He had his own yacht, *Fra Diavolo*, a private railway car, and a stable of thoroughbred horses. His income was reported to have approached $90,000 a year. Kellar lived comfortably, but less ostentatiously than his rival; his profits were banked or invested. He had had successful tours in Asia, Africa, South America, and Australia, a record-breaking five-month run at the Comedy Theater in New York, and spectacular grosses across the nation.

Houdini had never seen either perform. His first partner was Jacob Hyman, his friend from the tie factory. Together they framed an act, "The Brothers Houdini," and auditioned for the few agents who would give them a showing. The results were disappointing. Reports came in that the boys were inexperienced, lacking in finesse and timing, and showed little potential. After four frustrating months, Hyman gave up, took the name Jack Hyman, and began practicing songs and dances with his brother Joe. Houdini's brother Theo, who had on occasion filled in for Jack in "The Brothers Houdini" act, took his place.

Samuel Weiss was distressed that two of his sons should waste their time with show business. Why couldn't they, he lamented to his wife, aspire to something more substantial like Leopold, who planned to be a doctor, or Nathan and William, who had the makings of sound merchants. Cecilia, diplomatically, listened to Samuel's views but still encouraged the young magicians. She made satin stage costumes—jackets and short pants—and was a tolerant audience of one whenever they wished to try out a new trick.

17

Samuel, at the age of sixty-three, was confined to his bed. He again insisted, as he had in Milwaukee, that Harry swear on the Torah that he would always provide for Cecilia. The repeated vow wasn't necessary, for the bond between mother and son had grown even stronger. Samuel died on October 5, 1892. Cecilia mourned at his bier: "Weiss, Weiss, you have left me with your children." Harry tried to console her. "When you have had heaven twenty-eight years," she said in German, "you too would weep."

"The Brothers Houdini" increased their efforts to get engagements. They performed at neighborhood socials, lodge meetings, and Manhattan beerhalls. When an opening act didn't arrive at the Imperial Music Hall, a harried booker called them in.

There were few people in the audience for the first show. Harry touched his magic wand to the buttonhole of his jacket. A flower appeared. He reached in the flame of a candle and produced a red silk handkerchief. He began his card tricks. They were not as effective on a big stage as they had been in more intimate surroundings. Then Houdini announced his feature mystery "Metamorphosis."

Theo's hands were bound behind his back. He was put in a sack, the mouth of the sack was tied, and the sack, containing Theo, was placed inside a large wooden box, which in turn was locked and doubly secured with rope. Harry then pulled a cabinet—a frame covered with cloth—around the box.

"When I clap my hands three times—behold a miracle!"

He darted into the cabinet. The audience waited expectantly. There were no handclaps—and no miracles. Instead, after what seemed an interminable stage wait, the theater curtains swung closed and the orchestra struck up the music for the second act of the bill.

Inside the cabinet, a baffled Houdini had discovered that his brother was still a prisoner in the box. He worked feverishly untying the outer ropes, opening the two padlocks. He threw up the lid. A red-faced Theo, free of the sack, gasped that he had left the device which opened the box from the inside in his dressing room. The act was canceled. Thereafter, it was Harry who was tied and locked in the box and Theo who made the "Behold a miracle!" announcement.

John Nevil Maskelyne, founder of the British conjuring dynasty, had introduced the escape from a roped-and-locked box in 1865. Robert-Houdin's successors, at the theater in Paris which bore his name, added to the mystery. A man, dressed as an East Indian, penetrated a sack and trunk. Then, after the spectators had satisfied themselves that the trunk was still locked, made his way back inside. Another French magician, Bernard Marius Cazeneuve, offered an extra twist of his own when he came to the United States in 1876. His wife was roped to a chair, and a large trunk, locked and sealed, was placed beside it. Both wife and trunk were hidden from view by the curtains of a large cabinet. After three minutes, the curtains were opened, the chair was empty. The trunk was unsealed and unlocked. A second, smaller trunk was taken from the first. Inside this was a tied bag. When the bag was opened, madame popped into view.

"The Brothers Houdini" variation featured an incredibly fast change between the performer in their box and the one outside it. "Metamorphosis" was an apt title.

Since the fiasco at the Imperial had obliterated their chances for other theater dates in New York in the near future, "The Brothers Houdini" left town to tour dime museums in the Midwest. Dime museums were the lowest rung on the ladder of theatrical entertainment. Their salaries were small, but they gave an act the opportunity to gain polish and experience. There were seldom fewer than six shows a day and sometimes, on weekends and holidays, as many as twenty. The first proprietors of American museums had relied on exhibitions of natural wonders and works of art to attract the public. Later showmen, among them P. T. Barnum, added live attractions, freaks and entertainers, to lure the curious. By the 1890's magicians, sword swallowers, fire-eaters, and contortionists were as much a part of the scene as midgets, giants, and Siamese twins.

Harry struck up a conversation with a bearded stranger who had stayed to see several shows in Milwaukee. Dr. Josef Gregorowich, who introduced himself as a spiritual healer and hypnotist, invited Harry to one of his séances in a private home. The German stood by the bedside of a sick woman. He held an empty glass aloft and called for darkness. Someone extinguished the lights. He pleaded for health-giving aid from the other world. When the gaslights were ignited, the glass was filled with "spirit" medicine.

Houdini was so intrigued that his new friend offered to show him even more fantastic wonders. He jotted down the man's address. "I thought surely a man who lived so close to the police station must be honest," Houdini wrote later.

At Gregorowich's suggestion, Houdini inspected an upright wooden post, which had been nailed to the floor in the bedroom. A metal ring was bolted at the center of the post. The German sat on a stool in front of the column. Harry tied Gregorowich's hands behind his back with surgical bandage, knotted it a dozen times, then bound the ends of the strip to the metal ring in the post. He tied the medium's neck at the back in similar fashion, and nailed the ends of the cloth to the top of the post. He used two more strips of bandage to secure the medium's ankles to the legs of the stool. Finally each knot was sewn with needle and thread and wound with adhesive tape. An ordinary spoon was placed in a coffee cup on the medium's lap, far from the reach of his tied hands or mouth. There was a curtained entryway between the sitting room and the bedchamber.

"Step into the parlor, close the curtain, and ask any questions that come to your mind. The spirits will answer with one clang for yes, two for no." Houdini complied. As soon as he proposed a question, the spoon, behind the drape, banged out an answer on the cup.

"Open the curtains."

The man was tied exactly as he had been when the drapes were shut. Houdini was stunned. He knew how wrists could be bound for a quick release; he had used the trick himself in his box feat. But Gregorowich could not have used that technique to free his hands.

Later Harry found Gregorowich's secret in an old book by John W. Truesdell. It was devilishly ingenious; little wonder he had been fooled. He had been looking for a cleverly camouflaged release, where none was needed. By sliding his seated body back and to the left of the post and straining to bring his tied hands forward, the performer could reach the spoon. *The Bottom Facts Concerning the Science of Spiritualism* explained that a series of knots, tied one on the other, plus the diameter of the ring to which the ends of the strip were tied, allowed just enough leeway for one hand to produce "manifestations."

"The Brothers Houdini" were in Chicago at the time of the 1893 World's Fair. The greatest of its marvels to Harry was performed on the midway by a Hindu conjurer. The East Indian swallowed a dozen needles and a piece of cotton, then brought out the needles—threaded. Earlier Hindu performers had used beads and horsehair for the trick. The sharp-pointed needles added an element of intriguing danger. Houdini traded secrets with the swarthy sorcerer and came away with a feat which he was to expand into one of his outstanding stage mysteries.

New York theater agents were still wary of "The Brothers Houdini," but they did play a week at Miner's Bowery in New York over the Fourth of July when more popular acts were entertaining at the seashore. In 1894 their dime museum bookings in Manhattan ranged from the Harlem Museum at 115th Street and Third Avenue to Worth's midtown showplace, where they were held over for a three-week run. At Worth's they broke in a new feature. Harry was padlocked in an empty beer barrel. He was out in twenty seconds.

Dinner with his fellow attractions was always interesting. Unthan, "The Legless Wonder," handled knife and fork with ease, though balanced precariously by Houdini's side. Big Alice, the fat lady, thoughtfully moved to one end of the table so that Emma Shaller, "The Ossified Girl," had space to sit as comfortably as an ossified young lady can sit. At Old Moore's Museum, Colonel Goshen, the giant, had Harry on edge. Goshen towered so high that the escapologist half expected to see his face looking down in the cabinet as Theo made the quick switch with him in the box trick. "In those days," Houdini said, "I did not have enough sense to put a cover on my cabinet."

Late in May came engagements at Coney Island; first at the Vachress Casino, then at Sea Beach Palace. In June, Harry met and fell in love with a tiny brunet from Brooklyn, Wilhelmina Beatrice Rahner. There are three stories of their whirlwind courtship. Bess said she was in the front row when Houdini gave a school show in Brooklyn. He accidentally knocked a glass from his table and spotted her dress. Her mother was furious. She threatened to have the apologetic magician arrested. Bess managed to whisper to Harry that she thought he was wonderful. Mrs. Rahner, sensing greater trouble in the offing, halted her tirade and stalked away with her eighteen-year-old daughter firmly in tow.

Harry said he first saw Bess on a streetcar. He was on his way to give a five-dollar show at a private party. He dropped his magic wand and his equipment in the car and a pretty little girl in a white dress helped him pick it up. To his surprise she was at the birthday party. It was there, according to Harry, that the spilling incident occurred. Wherever it happened, both agreed that he later came to her house to get her measurements so that his mother could make a new frock to replace the one the liquid from his wine-and-water trick had ruined.

In Bess' version, when Houdini brought the completed dress to Brooklyn, she slipped past her mother's usually watchful eye and went with him to Coney Island. In the evening, when she confessed she was afraid to go home and face Mrs. Rahner's ire, Harry proposed to her. He bought a ring and before midnight they were married.

Harry remembered the proposal, but not at Coney Island. Bess, he said, came to Cecilia for a final fitting. She wore the new gown when he took her back to Brooklyn. A bridal party was leaving City Hall as they passed. Bess remarked that Houdini looked like a bridegroom. Impulsively, he suggested: "Let's go in and get married."

Theo offered the likeliest story. Bess, he said, was half of "The Floral Sisters," a new song-and-dance act. He dated her first, then introduced her to Harry. It was instant love. Two weeks later they did a vanishing act and came back as man and wife. Everyone agreed on how the parents reacted. Mrs. Rahner flew into a rage and wouldn't speak to Houdini. She couldn't understand how her Catholic daughter could marry the son of a rabbi. But Cecilia was pleased, and welcomed the couple to her flat on East 69th Street with open arms. Following the civil ceremony on June 22, 1894, Harry and Bess, to please their parents, repeated their marriage vows in separate ceremonies before a priest and a rabbi. "I'm the most married person I know," Bess said, "three times—and to the same man."

Soon Bess replaced Theo in the Houdini act. She weighed ninety-four pounds and could change places with Harry in the box with a speed that Houdini's tall, hefty younger brother admitted was beyond his power. Theo went on the road billed as "Professor Houdini," with a girl as his partner and the barrel escape as his feature. In October, Harry and Bess, working as "The Houdinis," were held over for a second week at Barton's Theater in Newport News, Virginia.

Three months later they were booked for Tony Pastor's Theater in New York. Pastor's intimate showhouse in the Tammany Building on East 14th Street was a prime spot for a new act to be seen. Yet if Harry thought this was to be his entry into the big time, he was to be disappointed. There was no mention of a return engagement. Tony scrawled his opinion on a sheet of theater stationery dated February 4, 1895: "The Houdinis act as performed here I found satisfactory and interesting." The single sentence was enough to chill a sensitive performer's heart.

In the spring Harry signed with the Welsh Brothers Circus in Lancaster, Pennsylvania. For twenty-six weeks the Houdinis toured under canvas. Harry manipulated playing cards, produced an egg from a red felt bag, changed the color of silk handkerchiefs by pushing them through a paper tube, yanked two knotted pieces of braid through his neck, and shot a borrowed watch to the center of a target. He also worked a Punch-and-Judy routine. Bess sang and danced. Together they presented a second-sight number. Harry, as he walked through the audience, cued the blindfolded Bess with code words so that she could identify the various objects spectators took from their pockets or handbags. "Metamorphosis," always their most applauded feat, closed the act.

An old Japanese gentleman, a member of the San Kitchy Akimoto balancing troupe, was so bored that he sometimes dozed off as he supported one of the younger acrobats on a swaying pole. Between performances he taught Harry how to swallow an ivory ball, show his mouth empty, then bring the ball back. Houdini practiced the regurgitation stunt with a small peeled potato on the end of a string. If the string didn't permit the student swallower to retrieve the potato while he was developing the muscles in his throat, there was no danger. The potato would slide down into his stomach where it could be digested. A few weeks of practice and Harry could handle solid ivory balls almost as well as his instructor. Later the resourceful Houdini was to use the regurgitation technique to baffle committeemen who searched him for concealed tools during his handcuff act.

Handcuffs were seldom used by magicians when Harry acquired his first pair. Samri Baldwin, "The White Mahatma," had escaped from manacles during a séance sequence in New Orleans as early as 1871, conjuring supply houses carried trick shackles which could be opened without a key, but no performer had come to the fore with a feature escape act.

Houdini discovered that the various cuffs he accumulated were easier to open than people thought. Bits of steel and wire would spring the locks as readily as keys and one key could open any cuff of the same design. He perfected a routine for a handcuff escape act and offered it to the circus for a few additional dollars each week. The Welsh Brothers weren't interested.

When Houdini wasn't busy performing or practicing his new tricks he earned extra money selling toothpaste, soap, and other necessities to his fellow artists. At the end of the season, even with sending half of his weekly twenty-dollar salary home to his mother, he had saved enough to buy a small interest in a touring burlesque show through his cousin Henry Newman, an advance man who traveled ahead of the production, booking theaters and publicizing the attraction.

Burlesque then was a family entertainment. Striptease was far in the future. The only really eyebrow-lifting number in "The American Gaiety Girls" was presented by the buxom May Morgan. The 140-pound champion athlete took on all comers of her weight—male or female—during the catch-as-catch-can wrestling exhibition she offered as a finale.

Harry used his escape skill to promote interest in the show. An article in the Gloucester, Massachusetts, *Times* of November 22, 1895, told how he amazed the local police by releasing himself from their official handcuffs. Similar stories appeared in other towns along the route.

When "The American Gaiety Girls" played the Boston Palace in March 1896, the *Post* critic reported that a highlight of the evening was "the sensational illusion, or box trick, performed by the Houdinis. The act created a furor and mystified all present."

Something new had been added to "Metamorphosis." Now Houdini wore a spectator's coat, instead of his own, as his hands were tied. He emerged from bag and box in his shirtsleeves. When the box was unfastened, Bess' hands were tied as Harry's had been—and she was in the borrowed jacket. "The

American Gaiety Girls" closed abruptly in Woonsocket, Rhode
Island. There had been no hint of the impending disaster. The
general manager of the show was arrested for misappropriating
the company's funds.

That summer the Houdinis made their first appearance outside
the continental boundaries of the United States. With Edward
J. Dooley, who billed himself as "Marco the Magician," they
sailed for the Canadian Maritime Provinces. Dooley, until
then a part-time professional, was an admirer of Alexander
Herrmann. He had saved for years to build a show patterned
after the production of his idol. Dooley announced he was on
his farewell tour, that the strenuous feats he had once done
would be performed by his successors-to-be, "his daughter and
his son-in-law" Bessie and Harry. The first part of his statement was prophetic. Business was disastrous; the Marco tours
opened and closed in Nova Scotia. The amiable Mr. Dooley
returned to Connecticut and his regular job as a church organ-
ist and choirmaster.

Harry, determined to stay in Halifax and make a success on
his own, staged his first open-air publicity stunt there. It was
a brilliant idea. He advertised that he would make an escape
after being tied to the back of a wild horse. But the horse was
wilder than Harry expected. Once he had been roped in place,
the frisky stallion, disturbed by Houdini's contortions, took off
at breakneck speed. Miles away from town the horse stopped
from exhaustion and Houdini released himself. But there was
no one around to see him do it.

Nova Scotians that season were in no mood to attend magic
shows. The Houdinis moved on to St. John, the largest city
of New Brunswick. Here Harry had another brain wave. A
local doctor had taken him along on a call to an insane asylum. Harry watched through the small barred window of a
padded cell as an inmate rolled and tossed, desperately trying
to free himself from a straitjacket. The doctor commented
that only a madman would attempt a release from a straitjacket. It was the most effective device ever invented to re-
train the murderously insane.

That night Houdini's few hours of sleep were filled with
dreams of madmen, padded cells, and endless struggles. In the
morning he told Bess he was sure he could get out of the
canvas-and-leather punishment suit. His friend, the doctor,

provided the requested straitjacket. After a week of study and exertion, he was ready to make a test before an audience.

Volunteers strapped Houdini, then placed him inside his cabinet. Bess closed the drapes. Time dragged by with only an occasional thumping noise behind the curtain to hold the audience's attention. Finally Harry pushed the drapes aside and stepped forward, tired but triumphant, ready to accept the spectators' accolade.

There were neither torrents of applause nor roof-shaking cheers. The audience had lost interest while he was covered from view. So he had escaped! An assistant concealed in the cabinet could have unstrapped him. Houdini, the magician, had solved the technique of release, but Houdini, the show-man, had not learned how to make the feat exciting.

Not only was the Canadian tour a dismal failure, Houdini was violently seasick on the ship back to Boston. Perhaps his father had been right. Show business was too risky a venture. Somehow he scraped up enough bookings to get them through the winter. In the spring Harry wrote the Welsh Brothers suggesting another season with the circus. The reply was cordial, but said the acts had already been signed. Perhaps next year? By August, Houdini was so discouraged that he wrote Harry Kellar and Herrmann the Great. He offered the services of his wife and himself as assistants for the fall. Kellar replied that his staff had been engaged. He closed with best wishes for Houdini's success. Alexander Herrmann didn't answer.

Weary of the week-to-week struggle for bookings, depressed by the frequent layoffs, in the winter of 1897 the Houdinis joined Dr. Hill's "California Concert Company," a Midwestern medicine show. The regular salary—twenty-five dollars a week —gave them temporary security. Earlier traveling medicine shows had featured Indians in war paint and ceremonial regalia who vouched for the curative effects of the pitchman's product "made from a secret tribal formula." Dr. Hill used music and vaudevillians to attract his street corner audiences. With his flowing beard and long brown hair, he resembled a biblical prophet. His sales pitch was enlivened by topical comments, literary quotations, humorous asides, and flowery oratory. When he held a bottle of his patent medicine aloft and lauded its healing powers, even the most skeptical listener felt an urge to reach for his money and buy the marvelous potion.

Hill's closing words, after the last possible sale had been made, urged all present to go to the local opera house that night and see the sensational, unparalleled presentation of his far-famed concert company.

The evening show was a hodgepodge of singers, dancers, knock-about comedians, and the melodrama "Ten Nights in a Bar Room." The Houdinis presented their magic and escapes, Bess sang, and together they doubled as actors in the play.

The troupe was in Kansas when Dr. Hill learned that a professional spirit medium had been drawing large audiences in the territory. He offered Houdini top billing if he would add a Sunday spirit séance to the show. The appeal to Harry's vanity was too strong to resist. He had attended several séances in New York. At one the "spirit" of his father had spoken in flawless English—the language he had never mastered on earth. At another, "ghosts" walked so heavily on the floor that the boards creaked. He had been baffled by Gregorowich's manifestations in Milwaukee, but the book which explained the man's method also revealed the techniques of other mediums.

Houdini was convinced that every spiritualist he had ever seen had been a fraud. Their tricks were simple compared to the difficult sleight of hand he had mastered with playing cards and the physical contortions he used in his escape work. Eager to see his name at the top of a handbill, Harry assured Dr. Hill he could match any medium in the business.

MEDICINE SHOW MEDIUM

Modern spiritualism, which began in 1848 when two mischievous children, the Fox sisters, rapped out answers to questions in their father's Hydesville, New York, farmhouse, had gained wide acceptance by the turn of the century. Senators, judges, and professors said they believed that communication was possible with the dead. In England, distinguished converts swore that Daniel Dunglas Home, who never exhibited his wonders in public, had been lifted in dark rooms by unseen forces until his head brushed the ceiling. Viscount Adare, Lord Lindsay, and Captain Charles Wynne vouched that Home floated out one window of a London flat and entered through another in the adjoining room. No one had been in the first chamber at the start of the flight; the three men had been sitting without lights in the second. Home said he had floated horizontally across the face of the building, and they accepted his word. Other witnesses, in other dark rooms, reported that flowers flew like scented birds in Home's presence.

True believers flocked to professional mediums eager to communicate with their lost loved ones. A highly developed psychic could produce raps or conjure up words on freshly cleaned slates. Not infrequently ethereal hands, faces, and full-length forms materialized in the dark.

Mediums who needed more than faith to satisfy their followers could refer to the helpful catalogue issued by H. J. Burlingame through his Chicago firm, Ralph E. Sylvestre & Co. Slate-writing secrets and table-lifting methods were listed at a dollar each. A telescopic rod, small enough to be concealed in a pocket, yet long enough, when extended, to lift a guitar several feet away or cause a luminous form to float over the sitters' heads, was available for four dollars. A complete kit with rope-escape techniques, message-reading routines, and assorted dark room phenomena was more expensive. Yet twenty-five dollars was a small price for an enterprising psychic to pay. Many could earn back the investment at a single séance.

Houdini prepared for his appearance as a medium—a role his father would have abhorred—with characteristic thoroughness. He visited cemeteries, copied names and dates from tombstones. He listened to gossips talk about current crimes and past scandals, read old newspaper files and made copious notes. Bess tied him in the privacy of their boardinghouse room so that he could practice "manifestation" feats.

"Houdini the Great will give Sunday night a Spiritual Séance in the Open Light" read the California Concert Company handbill announcing his January 9, 1898, performance in Galena, Kansas. Audiences had seen Houdini escape from handcuffs, leg fetters, and chains during the week. Now, if conditions were favorable, he would cause tables and musical instruments "playing sweetest music" to float and spirit faces and hands to appear. These remarkable feats would be produced "by that strange power" which had enabled him to break away from challenge restraints.

The Opera House was full. The believers were out in force and those who had heard about spiritualists, but had never seen one, were there to find out for themselves what all the talk was about. The show started with the Invincible Resar Trio playing lively music, switching instruments frequently. La Petite Alleene, a "child prodigy," sang and danced. Not until Dr. Hill introduced Houdini did the thrill of excitement tingle through the audience.

A committee of businessmen tied Houdini to a chair and enclosed him in his cloth-covered frame cabinet. He was, the chairman asserted, firmly bound. The words were scarcely out of his mouth before a bell rang behind the curtains. A tambourine jangled, shot high in the air and crashed to the floor. Now the sounds of a mandolin filled the hushed hall. The instrument soared above the cabinet, then dropped from view. The curtains were opened. Houdini, breathing heavily, was slumped in his chair. Not a knot had been loosened, the chairman reported. Once more the curtains were closed. The bell began ringing again, the whole structure vibrated, swayed. Suddenly Houdini—free of the ropes—came through the curtains and walked to the footlights.

When the applause died down, Houdini talked about the spirit world. He said he could feel strange presences on the stage. He trembled. His eyes closed, then opened. Messages, he gasped, were coming through. He named names, gave dates, told family secrets, sent tremors down the spines of those for whom he had communications from the departed.

Building to a climax, he spoke dramatically: "Now what do I see? What is this coming before me? Why, it is a man— a black man." He paused, stared at something the audience could not see. "He's lame—and his throat is cut from ear to ear. . . . Who is this man?" Harry was almost screaming now, "Why—I know him. He is Efram . . . EFRAM ALEXAN- DER!"

That did it. Negroes in the gallery panicked. They fled from their seats, rushed down the backstairs and out into the good, clean Kansas night air, away from the mystic who had con- jured up a man whose recent murder had horrified the town. Dr. Hill was in a merry mood as he totaled the receipts for the night. Henceforth Sunday séances would be staged in every town.

In Garnett, Kansas, Harry delivered a spirit message to a woman who had recently lost her first son. She shouldn't grieve, he said. Her boy was calling to her. He was happy and had glad tidings. Soon she would be blessed with another son to take his place. The woman, who was pregnant, was embar- rassed. Her husband was furious. He stormed backstage, gripped Houdini by his shirt front with one hand, doubled up the other to hit him. Harry didn't flinch. He talked fast. He blurted out an incident in the man's past, which made him release his hold and drop his fist. Harry's preliminary research had saved him from a beating which, he later admitted, "I richly deserved."

An audience which came to see a medium, Houdini learned, was far easier to satisfy than one which expected to be baffled by a magician. Spiritualists accepted messages from the dead. They were convinced mediums could communicate with the departed. Even the skeptics were confounded by the accuracy of his revelations. The ruse of getting the information before- hand was so simple that otherwise rational onlookers refused to consider the obvious explanation.

The cast of the concert company changed frequently during the months the Houdinis traveled with Dr. Hill. For a time Joe and Myra Keaton were on the bill, offering Irish songs and sentimental comedy. Their young son, Joseph, appealed to Harry. "He's a real buster," Houdini proclaimed. The name stuck. Years later silent movie fans were captivated by the frozen-face antics of Buster Keaton.

The Sunday night séances enlarged Houdini's repertoire. He had used his hands and feet adroitly in his escapes. Now he practiced until he could pick up a piece of chalk between his toes and write with it on a slate placed beneath a table. He had seen armless entertainers in dime museums write, shave, and play musical instruments but he had never tried to develop these skills himself.

He mastered several table levitation techniques. One of the best, even then well known among professional psychics, was later a favorite of the famous Italian medium, Eusapia Palladino. Pressing firmly on the top of a table, Harry forced it to tip and balance on its left legs. Putting his right foot under the closest right table leg and clamping down with his right hand on the corner above it, he could make the table "float" by lifting his right foot. In the dark, with three spectators holding their fingertips lightly on the tabletop, the levitation had an uncanny effect. Afterward the participants would swear that the table soared up by astral power alone—and it rose higher with each retelling.

After Houdini left the Hill troupe he was booked with his magic and escape act in St. Joseph, Missouri. Several townspeople asked him to expose a spiritualist who had been victimizing their friends. The medium, who had excellent pipelines of information, heard about the scheme and arranged to meet Houdini. He was frank. Of course he used tricks. He was a showman, as Houdini was a showman. The public wanted séances so he gave them. Contrary to what most people thought, he made little money. He was almost broke. If he could give just one more uninterrupted séance to raise traveling money, he would pack his slates and tambourines and move on to another town.

Harry attended the meeting with no intention of revealing the man's methods. He had the medium's promise that he would leave the city. He decided to help make the last ghostly fling one to remember.

"While I had the table walking, someone threw a rock on it," Houdini said. "I am satisfied that somebody brought the rock along to help out the medium if he got in trouble. They [his supporters] were not taking any chances of his being unable to give a sign at the right time."

When bookings for their magic act became almost impossible to get, Harry and Bess traveled as mediums. Sometimes Houdini varied his routine and used Bess as the voice of the spirits. He noted in *Mahatma,* the magic magazine, in June 1898, "I have even trained my right ear to move up and down and thus give my assistant the tip." They were in Canada when a spectator named Mary Murphy asked where her long-lost brother John could be found. Bess called out an address on East 72d Street in New York. The next day the woman returned with the astonishing news that she had telegraphed New York and found her brother. Harry was amazed. How, he wanted to know, had Bess known the man would be there? Bess replied she hadn't. The name Murphy reminded her of Mrs. Murphy's confectionery shop a few blocks from their home on East 69th Street. This was the address she had given.

Another evening, in another town, Harry recognized a woman patron he had seen on the street scolding her son because he was reckless with his bicycle. The spirits had a message for her. Houdini described the youngster speeding down a hill. The youngster lost control of his bike as he turned a corner. Houdini's face contorted. He saw the boy, moments afterward, with his arm hanging limply by his side. For a second time a patron returned with confirmation of a prediction. The following day the boy had an accident and fractured his arm. Even with occasional, talk-provoking, lucky hits such as these, the Houdinis, as mediums, made scarcely enough to live.

Harry had certain scruples, unlike some other performers— Zan Zic, for instance. Zan Zic was a stage illusionist who decided to cash in on the 1893 World's Fair in Chicago by opening a spirit parlor in that city. Undoubtedly his most celebrated gull was an elderly German who complained that his eyesight was failing. Zan Zic sold the gentleman a pail of "spirit" mud, which—probably to Zan Zic's own amazement— did seem to help the man's vision. Perhaps the magician's powers of suggestion were a factor. Whatever the cause, the customers was convinced that Zan Zic could work miracles. Could Zan Zic reproduce the form of his long-dead wife? Since price was no object, Zan Zic was ready to oblige. He found a girl who closely resembled the faded portrait of his client's bride and, using his knowledge of stage illusions, produced her during a séance. The old gentleman jumped from his chair, threw his arms around her and kissed her. He had to be pulled away before Zan Zic could cause the "spirit" to dematerialize. There was no containing the victim now. He insisted he be allowed to spend an hour with his "bride" as he had on his wedding night. Zan Zic fitted up one of his rooms as a bridal chamber. Again the "spirit" appeared. The touch of her all-too-human flesh was too much for the elderly man and he died of heart failure. Zan Zic's assistants took the body from the house and left it in the street. One of the German's servants had been waiting to drive him home. He called the police.

Houdini had no intention of becoming involved in such chicanery. He looked on his message-reading and manifestation act as just another phase of show business. But Houdini, the medium, was no easier to keep working profitably than Houdini, the magician. "Things became so bad," he wrote, "that I contemplated quitting the show business . . . to work at one of my trades (really being proficient in several) and open a school of magic."

No single document is more revealing about the struggling entertainer at the age of twenty-four than his sixteen-page booklet *Magic Made Easy*. A few simple tricks and puzzles are explained, but it is largely a catalogue of secrets for sale. These range from the "Jumping Card, price ten cents" to "Metamorphosis Substitution, price on application." It is obvious Houdini was seriously considering giving up his life on the road, otherwise he never would have tried to sell the secret of his feature trick or his "Handcuff Act."

That he had no moral qualms about posing as a medium is shown by the statement: "I give Syscromantic [*sic*] and Clairvoyantic [*sic*] Readings, telling you the Past, Present and Future. . . . Do you believe in Spiritualism? If not, why not? If you want to give Manifestations and Slate Tests I can give you full instructions and make you a full fledged medium."

A list of books offered for sale or exchange indicates that Houdini was a collector even then and was familiar with the classics of conjuring: Hoffmann's *Modern Magic* and *More Magic,* Sachs' *Sleight of Hand,* and Hopkins' *Magic Stage Illusions and Scientific Diversions.*

Even if few readers sent for the advertised marvels, this booklet and another with the same title but a smaller format were good investments. They were sold after his performances in dime museums and the circus. The previous year, 1897, Harry had written to the Welsh Brothers too late to get a return engagement. This year he was in time. Harry and Bess began their second season under canvas in April. The handcuff tricks, which the Welsh Brothers had once rejected, now were an important part of the act.

When the circus returned to winter quarters in Lancaster, Pennsylvania, in October, the Houdinis were given an enthusiastic letter of endorsement: "We can cheerfully recommend Harry and Beatrice Houdini with their unique and mysterious act called 'Metamorphosis' as being the strongest drawing card of its class in America. Their act is totally unlike others and always creates a profound impression. . . . We will be pleased to play them at any time. The Houdinis are truly great people."

In New York, Harry was more depressed than ever before. He had been a performer for seven years. It was just as difficult now to get a theater date as it had been when he started. Seasons with a circus or a medicine show far from satisfied his ambition. Vaudeville was his goal, but variety agents thought of him as "Dime Museum Harry." His patience was almost exhausted. As he paced the floor restlessly, he told Bess he would set an absolute deadline. One more year. If he didn't make good as a magician by then, he'd get a steady job in some conventional business.

BREAKTHROUGH

On January 5, 1899, a story about a dime museum performer made the front page of the Chicago *Journal*. A reporter had been at police headquarters when Houdini boasted he could release himself from their official manacles. The law enforcement officers quickly and efficiently applied their restraints. Almost as quickly and just as efficiently Harry extricated himself.

A week later Police Sergeant Waldron locked his own personal handcuffs around Houdini's wrists at Kohl and Middleton's Clark Street Museum. This time one of the cuffs withstood the escape artist's vigorous and prolonged assault. When Waldron finally admitted he had dropped a slug in the lock Harry was furious.

It had never occurred to Houdini that anyone would deliberately fix the mechanism of a lock to defeat him. He profited from the embarrassing experience. In the future he would always specify that all challenge manacles must be "regulation" and in proper working order.

Near Houdini's platform in the Clark Street Museum was an act that intrigued him greatly. Madam Thardo, an attractive brunet, bared her arm and taunted a rattlesnake until it struck her, then the "poison-defier" calmly disengaged its fangs from her flesh. William LeRoy was another fascinating performer to watch. He gripped nails between his teeth and drove them through heavy planks. Pausing only to prove that the nails actually penetrated the boards, "The Human Claw Hammer" used his teeth to yank them out.

Mexican Billy Wells told Houdini that he had never had a headache. This was remarkable because spectators swung sledges to break rocks resting on his cranium, and there was only a blanket between his skull and the impact.

In St. Paul, Minnesota, Houdini had the good fortune to be seen by Martin Beck, the booker for the fast-growing Orpheum vaudeville circuit. Beck doubted that the handcuffs

Harry used were legitimate. He "purchased a few pairs and sent them on stage," Houdini later wrote. Harry escaped not only from the challenge manacles but also, with Beck's help, from the small time.

Martin Beck, a short pudgy man, had come to America with a German singing group. Realizing that his appearance and restricted vocal range would limit his earnings as a performer, he became an agent. Few men in the business could match his ability to size up an attraction. He was the first person in a position of theatrical importance to recognize Houdini's potential.

If the brash young escapologist could make good his boast that no regulation police restraint could hold him, Beck thought the theatrical exploitation possibilities were limitless. He booked an April showing date at the Orpheum Theater in Omaha for sixty dollars a week—the highest salary Houdini had ever received.

The feats of magic, which opened Houdini's museum routine, were eliminated at Beck's insistence. Emphasis was put on Harry's ability to release himself from apparently impregnable bonds.

When the curtain rose there were six chairs, a table loaded with manacles, a trunk to one side at the back, and a cabinet in the center of the stage. The cabinet was made of a pipe framework, with drapes on four sides and at the top. Houdini began the act with a brief speech. He said he would try to escape from the most difficult restraints ever created. He invited a committee to the stage, promising not to embarrass the volunteers. If anyone had manacles for a challenge, now was the time for him to come forward.

The committeemen were requested to examine the cabinet, to see for themselves that there was nothing concealed within it. Harry picked up a pair of handcuffs from the table. These were regulation police irons, he assured the audience, that were used to hold dangerous criminals. A committeeman examined the cuffs, then locked them on Houdini's wrists. The spectator was told to put the key in his pocket and not to let it out of his possession. As Harry entered the cabinet, fast music built up excitement. In thirty seconds Houdini emerged, with the cuffs still locked, but not on his wrists. He tossed them to the committee. Next, several pairs of handcuffs and leg irons were shown and inspected, and as Houdini identified each by name and history the irons were applied. This escape took longer than the first and created more suspense.

The challenge manacles were tested to make sure they were in working order and locked in place. Harry, with showmanly stress and strain, tugged at them and looked doubtful as he went into the cabinet. Music, which started slowly, then mounted to a frenzy, stopped abruptly when he pulled the drapes of his enclosure aside and walked forward—free!

The act moved to an applause-producing finish with the rapid substitution mystery "Metamorphosis," during which Harry escaped from a wrist tie, knotted bag, and locked-and-roped trunk in three seconds, and his wife, Bess, was found tied in his place.

Challenges at every performance added drama to the turn. He hired men who were given handcuffs from his collection and told to sit in the audience. If no legitimate challengers appeared, they were to come forward immediately.

Houdini proudly proclaimed himself to be the originator of the challenge handcuff act. Joe Godfrey, Louis Paul, and Zamora used their own manacles. The challenge element lifted the handcuff act from the dime museum and the small-time level to big-time vaudeville. The challenge performer, by necessity, had to be familiar with every type of iron, and to know how to open handcuffs without his methods being detected. Houdini spent endless offstage hours working with locksmiths, learning the secrets of their trade. He read every book he could find on the subject. He visited museums and police collections to study ancient and modern restraints. Duplicate keys could open any manacle, even better were picks made of twisted wire or bent steel. They were smaller, easier to conceal. Houdini's skill as a magician and his ability to palm, misdirect attention, and secrete his picks in unlikely places were invaluable assets.

In Omaha he slipped free from five pairs of regulation handcuffs and a set of official leg irons supplied by the police. Impressed by the enthusiastic report from the Orpheum Theater manager, Martin Beck signed Houdini for the Orpheum tour.

By the time Houdini reached California his weekly paycheck had soared to ninety dollars. There was, he thought, no stopping him now. The years of struggle and hardship were about to pay off handsomely. Then, after his successful week at the San Francisco Orpheum, the *Examiner* ran a half-page feature exposing the secrets of his handcuff releases. There was nothing marvelous about Houdini's work, the story reported. All anyone needed to open the most formidable manacle was an extra key or a specially made bit of metal to force the locks. The article, however, did not have the intended effect. Rather than lessening the handcuff act's appeal, the article strengthened it. People were talking about Houdini. Was the exposure true—or did he have a mysterious power? To capitalize on the controversy, a quick repeat date was arranged.

To disprove the *Examiner*'s revelation, Houdini announced that he would pit his skill against every restraint the San Francisco Police Department could muster. A less confident, less capable performer would have avoided the Bay City under the circumstances. Harry welcomed the confrontation. He had visited the police during his first engagement, had looked on as the officers displayed their collection of securing devices and had filed away the necessary release data in his mind. He had almost a photographic memory where manacles were concerned. He once claimed he could cut a blank to fit a lock after a mere glance at the key.

On his previous visit Houdini had entertained the police with card tricks. He returned not as an unknown challenger, but as a personable young man whose cleverness the officers appreciated. Still, they were determined to defeat him at his own game. A reporter from the *Examiner* was there to cover the story.

Houdini was stripped to the skin in the quarters of the detective force on July 13, 1899. Dr. R. H. Hartley, the police surgeon, searched his body for concealed keys and opening devices as thoroughly as if he were probing for a clue to an unsolved murder. He examined mouth, ears, and nostrils, ran his fingers through the escapologist's hair. Then Houdini's hands were shackled behind his back. His ankles were locked in irons. Ten pairs of prison handcuffs linked the fetters. Detectives carried Harry to a closet, which had been searched beforehand, and closed the door. Ten minutes later the door opened. Houdini stepped out. The manacles were still locked, one within the other, but not around his body. He let them clatter to the floor.

The ordeal was not over. He had claimed he could escape

from *any* official restraint. A thick belt used to subdue maniacal prisoners fastened his arms to his sides. Over this a straitjacket was strapped and padlocked. Once more he was lifted and taken to the closet. Again the nude performer released himself. The *Examiner* ran a second half-page feature, complete with pictures, retracting their "exposure" and lauding his talents.

Houdini's Orpheum salary jumped to $125 a week—an amount beyond his most extravagant dreams. Cecilia was bewildered by the sizable sums he mailed her from the west. His increased income opened the way for the most intensive personal promotional campaign in the history of vaudeville. He bought space in the theatrical weeklies on the sound theory that bookers must be sold before the public. He advertised in *Mahatma,* the magic magazine. If he was to be "like Robert-Houdin," the profession must be informed about his progress. He bought hundreds of copies of the newspapers which ran stories about him and mailed them across the country.

Modesty was never one of his handicaps. Harry shouted his success in large print in broadsides and advertisements:

"Who created the biggest Sensation in California since the Discovery of Gold in 1849? WHY! HARRY HOUDINI! The ONLY recognized and Undisputed King of Handcuffs and Monarch of Leg Shackles."

Smaller type told of his triumph at San Francisco Police Headquarters and quoted in full the official certification of his releases, signed by twenty-one witnesses. The "Naked Test," Houdini's first big publicity breakthrough, was repeated for police officials wherever he played. Booked for a single week in St. Louis, he stayed three. One week at Colonel Hopkins' theater in Memphis was extended to two. He was held over at the Hopkins' House in Nashville.

Martin Beck used the accumulated publicity and box-office reports to sell the escape king to the Keith circuit, which booked the leading vaudeville theaters in the east—as a headliner!

Before Houdini opened for B. F. Keith, the strongest mystery attraction in American vaudeville was Ching Ling Foo. The tall Oriental's conjuring appealed to the eye as it baffled the mind. Ching blew clouds of smoke from his mouth, then spurted out strips of colored ribbons and a slender barber pole fifteen feet long. From empty foulards he produced dishes of cakes and nuts, and for a climax lifted a cloth to disclose a ninety-five-pound porcelain bowl filled to the brim with water.

Houdini followed the "Court Conjuror to the Empress of China" at Keith's Theater in Boston in January 1900. He was held over a second week, then a third. The straitjacket escape, which had been a failure in the Canadian Maritime Provinces, was now a strong added feature. At the end of his run the Boston *Transcript* concluded: "He is certainly a wonderful trickster and more talked about than Ching Ling Foo, the Chinese magician who preceded him."

Still, Houdini had his problems. His act at the New York Theater in Manhattan had gone smoothly until the last minute. Houdini emerged from his cabinet, free of the sack and trunk. He acknowledged the applause, pulled the curtains aside, and rapidly untied and unwound the rope which secured the trunk. He knelt by the locks and reached in his pocket for the keys. They were not there.

Smiling, he hurried to the wings and called to a stagehand. The keys were in his fifth-floor dressing room. Thump, thump, thump came noises from inside the trunk. The audience began to laugh. The man who had been sent for the keys reported he couldn't find them. Another member of the stage crew was dispatched to the dressing room. Bess, his wife, was terrified in the darkness of the trunk. She shouted: "Let me out! Let me out!" William McCormack, the stage manager, appeared with a fire ax. He heaved it and brought it down. A muffled scream came from the trunk. At this point the keys were found. Harry unfastened the locks, lifted the top of the trunk. Bess, inside, was motionless. She had fainted. Houdini lifted her out and carried her offstage as the curtains closed.

When Bess revived she was in no mood for explanations. From that day hence she personally saw to it that a duplicate set of keys was in the stage manager's hands before the act began. The story of the unexpected drama in a February 4, 1900, newspaper filled the New York theater for the rest of the week. Those who expected an encore were disappointed.

After the Keith tour ended in mid-February, Houdini performed in Toronto, then returned to the Midwest for repeat dates in the theaters where his drawing power had been established.

In Kansas City, while making his first Orpheum tour, Houdini had escaped from manacles at the Central Police Station; now he was ready to introduce his second great publicity feat in that town. He was stripped nude and searched, his wrists and legs were fastened by five pairs of irons and he was taken to a cell. The three-bond lock— "guaranteed by the makers to be burglar-proof"—on the cell door was closed with the key of J. C. Snavely, the jailer.

"Never-the-less HOUDINI succeeded in making his escape out of all the irons. ALSO FROM THE CELL, in less than eight minutes. There was no possible chance of confederacy," attested the official document "signed and sealed" April 11, 1900, by the Chief of Police, John Hayes; the Inspector of Detectives, John Halpin; and Turnkey Snavely.

"The Undisputed King of Handcuffs" and "Monarch of Leg Shackles" added a new title after his name—"Champion Jail Breaker"!

Later that month Houdini played Hurtig and Seamon's Music Hall in New York. He had saved his money. His scrapbooks were filled with newspaper stories, official letters from law enforcement officials verifying his escapes, and theater advertisements and playbills with his name at the top.

Cecilia couldn't have been happier. Now, certainly, her son would be able to spend more time at home with her. Harry shook his head. He said he was about to take the biggest gamble of his life. There was only one drawback. It would be months, maybe years, before he would see her again.

AN OCEAN AWAY

Houdini sailed for England on May 30, 1900. Aboard ship, he was soon aware of an adversary he was never to conquer —the turbulent sea. The dull throb of the *Kensington*'s engines stirred memories of his agony, four years before, on the ship back from Nova Scotia. As the liner steamed past the Statue of Liberty and out of the New York Harbor, many of the passengers flocked to the rail for a last look at the shore and their first glimpse of the seemingly endless expanse of the Atlantic Ocean. Harry, churning inside, made his way through the narrow passageways to his cramped cabin.

When rough weather sent the ship buffeting against the waves, he writhed and squirmed. Bess valiantly tried to ease his pains with crushed ice and lemon juice. As the storm gained in intensity she forced him into a life preserver and tied him to the berth, fearful that he might carry out his threat to end his agony by hurling himself overboard.

Houdini never overcame his susceptibility to seasickness. The mere sight of a ship standing beside a dock could provoke uncomfortable feelings if he knew he would be traveling on her.

The decision to go to England was not a sudden whim. London was the center of British show business and a gateway to the theaters of Europe. American vaudeville performers were popular abroad—if they had something unusual to offer. T. Nelson Downs, the Iowa-born "King of Koins," sold his manipulation act to the Palace Theatre in London just by mailing some reviews of his performances in major American cities together with a lithograph showing him plucking silver coins from the air.

Downs opened in the spring of 1899 as a supporting act. He caught on, became a headliner, and for more than five months enjoyed remarkable success at the Palace. He went on to top bills in other British cities and was booked on the

Continent "at the salary of an ambassador." Downs and Houdini were old friends. They first met at the Chicago fair. If Downs could catch on abroad, Harry reasoned, so could he. Though his barrage of clippings produced no reply from England, he was confident he could sell the British in person. He sailed without a single booking abroad.

The first London theatrical agents Houdini visited were noncommittal. They leafed through his scrapbooks, read his reviews and the testimonials from American police officials, but said: "Let us know where you are performing and we'll come to see you." Harry met a young man, new to the business, Harry Day, who had no long list of imposing attractions to match those of his competitors. Charmed by Houdini's confidence and accomplishments, Day arranged an audition at the Alhambra.

C. Dundas Slater, the theater manager, agreed the challenge aspect of the handcuff presentation was new. He thought the trunk substitution finale would be as effective in England as it had been in America. Challenge acts, however, sometimes lost their appeal overnight. Annie Abbott, "The Georgia Magnet," drew crowds until a newspaper revealed that her ability to withstand the efforts of five men to lift her was based on a simple principle of leverage. "The Bullet-Proof Man" faded into oblivion when his secret was disclosed to be not personal invulnerability, but a concealed chest protector filled with pulverized glass.

Only a week earlier P. H. Cirnoc, an escape artist, had auditioned for the Oxford Music Hall and been found wanting in showmanship and popular appeal.

Slater was dubious about Houdini's claim that he could escape from anyone's restraints. Cirnoc had used his own manacles. Slater casually suggested that the young American test his skill at Scotland Yard. Harry, who had been eager for just such an opportunity, agreed immediately. At the Yard, Superintendent Melville instructed Houdini to put his arms around a sturdy pillar. He locked a pair of British manacles on Harry's wrists to hold him in place, then he ushered Slater to the door. They would return, Melville said, when the young man had exhausted himself. Before the doorknob turned, a shout and a clatter prompted Melville to look back. The Scotland Yard cuffs were on the floor. Houdini, with a broad smile, was standing to one side of the post—free.

Less than two weeks after his arrival on British soil, Houdini was signed for a July opening at the Alhambra. In the United States he had added the current makes of British handcuffs to his collection. There were only a few, "seven or eight at the utmost." The most popular, "English Regulation," was the easiest to open he had ever seen. But there was always the possibility that restraints from the Continent or antique irons would be offered as a challenge. He searched through the Sunday markets and the curiosity shops, made friends with London locksmiths, and took apart the manacles he found to study their construction.

A special press performance, prior to Houdini's opening, produced favorable notes in the British papers. Opening night a spectator ran down the aisle and mounted the stage. Houdini, he shouted, was an imposter. Not only was he not an American, he had never set foot in the United States. The attacker identified himself: "Cirnoc—The Original King of Handcuffs."

Chauncey Depew, the distinguished American lawyer, politician, and orator, by chance was in the stalls. He stood, gave his name, and stated he had seen Houdini perform in the United States. As the audience applauded this unexpected defense from their side of the footlights, Houdini whispered to Bess: "Get the Bean Giants." He displayed the outsize manacles, invented by an American, Captain Edward Bean, and defied Cirnoc to escape from them. His taunter backed away. Cirnoc said he would like to see Houdini try the unfamiliar irons. Harry permitted Cirnoc to fasten the cuffs on his wrists, then entered the cabinet. After a short, tense wait, he jumped out; his hands free.

Now Houdini fixed the irons on the rival escape king, and to dramatize his complete disdain for Cirnoc's ability, told Bess to give him the key. But the cuffs were so large that Cirnoc, struggle though he might, was unable to reach the keyhole with the key. After several minutes of twisting and turning, he conceded defeat and allowed Harry to free him. There was a roar of approval from the crowd and even Cirnoc unbent enough before leaving the stage to give Harry a limp handshake. Houdini had been quite safe in permitting Cirnoc to have the key. Anyone wearing the cuffs could reach the keyhole only by means of an extension rod attached to the key. Houdini himself had to invent such a device in order to win the five hundred dollars offered by Captain Bean to anyone who could escape from the massive manacles.

During the weeks Houdini was held over at the Alhambra no manacles were offered that he could not open. One Saturday evening a British detective produced a pair of shackles which he said had been specially made to test Houdini's powers. He offered to bet £50 ($250) that Harry could not master them. An American in the audience waved his wallet and shouted: "I accept the wager." The embarrassed detective admitted he didn't have £50 with him. Houdini took the irons, tested them to make sure they were in working order, then returned the key and extended his wrists. *The Music Hall*, a British vaudeville publication, reported: "Houdini released himself from the new cuffs in ridiculously easy fashion." The Alhambra engagement was extended until the end of August.

Along with the laudatory London reviews, Houdini preserved a sour one printed in New York. Alan Dale, the New York *American* critic, was in London on holiday. He was surprised to receive a sheet of Houdini's testimonials from America along with his theater program. Dale wrote: "I preferred Houdini's literature to his turn. He certainly opened a number of handcuffs, but this was spoiled for me because he generally retired into a cabinet to do so. His *pièce de résistance* was the usual trick of being tied up and fastened in a trunk, which when opened, was found to contain somebody else. But the 'Letters of Verification' seemed to go with the audience. It isn't every variety turn who can get a Kansas City detective to utter a 'This is to verify,' nor secure the testimony of a superintendent of an insane ward in San Francisco in his favor."

The agents who ignored Houdini on his arrival now besieged his British manager, Harry Day, with offers. He accepted a September booking at the Central Theater in Dresden. "Cuffs here are not regulation," Houdini wrote W. D. LeRoy, a Boston magic dealer. "I have to work locks and I've spent all my days in locksmiths learning how to make locks. It is essential in this country. I've challenged the magicians here to do the naked test. As cuffs are 1,000 times harder here than in America, I hardly think I'll get imitators, as keys are out of the question. And they don't use American cuffs. They say they are too weak. . . . I came nearly [sic] losing my right hand on account of thumb screw locks used here."

Opening night excitement at the Central Theater was heightened when an opposition theater advertised that it had engaged a man to expose Houdini's handcuff act. The exposer was to be Cirnoc again. As Harry and Bess waited in the wings, the top-hatted theater manager in evening clothes, Gustav Kammsetzer, approached.

Kammsetzer was jittery. Speaking in broken English, he told Houdini that he would stay in the wings to listen for applause. He hoped the audience would be pleased. But, the impresario added, if they responded with whistles—the German equivalent of Bronx cheers—Houdini's engagement would be ended after a single performance. This statement would chill a performer at any time but it was especially tactless of Kammsetzer to make it just as Houdini was about to go on stage.

"You can well imagine my feelings," Houdini wrote. "This manager had brought me to the continent with a contract which enabled him to close me right after my first performance if I was not a success, and I was not aware of that fact until just before going on. I was in no mood to do very much talking. . . . I had never addressed an audience in German before. I must have said some of the most awful things to make them believe I was good."

If Harry had never spoken German on the stage, he was used to it at home. It was the household language of his parents. Among the challenges opening night were leg irons and manacles from the Mathilda Gasse Prison. Heavy locks, some weighing as much as forty pounds, fastened the bonds. Never had Houdini worked to such an enthusiastic response. His opening handcuff release brought the spectators to their feet. "When that audience rose in a solid mass . . . I knew I was going to stay my full engagement," he said. "And above all the din and noise and shouts and screams of the public, I heard Herr Direktor Kammsetzer's voice shouting like a madman. He ran to the middle of the stage and applauded. He took off his hat and he cheered. In fact, I have no fear of saying that I recorded with him the greatest triumph of any artiste he had ever engaged."

There was no such wild ovation at the opposition theater. Cirnoc failed to live up to his advertising and was canceled.

Houdini broke all records for paid admissions at the Central Theater. The manager, who suggested that his star might have to return to the United States if he provoked whistles, attempted to persuade the Wintergarten in Berlin to postpone Houdini's opening there, though billboards and newspaper advertisements had been heralding his appearance in the German capital for weeks. The answer was an emphatic No.

In Berlin, Harry topped his Dresden success. Before the month was over the Wintergarten management paid Roanacher's in Vienna a sum equal to Houdini's salary for a month for the privilege of extending his profit-making run. While the public cheered him on, envious local handcuff performers plotted his defeat. Anonymous letters were sent to the theater management and to the police, claiming, among other things, that Houdini did not live up to his advertising and that he was a Hungarian, rather than an American, citizen. Some detractors also appeared in person—with equally little effect.

E. Hilmar, a German magician, boasted, when he came up on the Wintergarten stage, that he could "do things no American could do." Houdini snapped a pair of German cuffs on his detractor's wrists. Hilmar struggled. Finally, in tears, he gave up and begged Harry to release him.

Almost overnight imitators sprang up, attempting to cash in on Houdini's popularity. One, who called himself Hermann, was booked by a circus in Berlin while Houdini was still at the Wintergarten. Harry, who did not believe in sitting back and waiting for his rivals to gather up the courage to challenge him, made a point of attending one of Hermann's shows. And when Hermann called for a committee from the audience, Houdini rushed to the ring. A quick glance was enough to tell him that Hermann was not using police handcuffs.

Harry shouted that he would give the German five thousand marks if he could free himself from a pair of Houdini cuffs;

five thousand more if Harry himself couldn't escape from the irons the German was about to use, and another five thousand if Hermann could duplicate the naked release he had made at the police headquarters in Berlin.

Hermann snapped back that Houdini was attempting to deceive the audience. Why, his challenger was not even an American as he claimed to be, he was "a low-life Hungarian."

Harry whipped out his American citizenship papers and his passport. "This brands one of us a liar!" The excited spectators yelled, "Bravo Houdini!" But the newspapers, Harry wrote, sided with Hermann "because he is a *native* and I am a foreigner."

With so many handcuff acts being booked in Germany to satisfy the demand created by Houdini's spectacular success, Harry cabled his brother in New York: "Come over the apples are ripe." Theo arranged passage on the first available ship, the *Deutschland,* bound for Hamburg. He arrived at the dock with a week's supply of cold cuts, bread, pickles, and cheese, no one having told him that food was served on board. Not that he was to need any food, either his own or the *Deutschland*'s. Once at sea, Theo discovered that he, like Houdini, was a poor sailor. For three days he suffered in his cabin. Finally, on the fourth, he was carried up to the deck and wrapped in a blanket in a deck chair. There, in the chill November air, he regained his equilibrium and his appetite.

Harry met Theo at the Friedrichstrasse railway station in Berlin. A duplicate escape act was crated, ready to go in a nearby storage room. Trunk, cabinet, handcuffs, straitjacket, and orchestrations. Theo worked his first theater as "Harden," then he added another "e" and became Hardeen for the rest of his professional life.

During Houdini's two months at the Wintergarten he visited the police, escaped naked from their restraints, and added another official document to his collection. He prized it highly. It was signed by Von Windheim, the highest law enforcement official in Germany.

Harry Day had negotiated a return engagement at the Alhambra. Now with only ten days to fill before crossing the Channel, Houdini opened in Magdeburg at the Circus Variete.

Manager Jacobson, jubilant with the sellout business, offered the Alhambra the equivalent of the escape star's salary for two weeks if they would defer the London opening. C. Dundas Slater politely acknowledged the request and just as politely refused it.

Twelve men paced back and forth in front of the London theater that December, wearing posters, sandwich-board style, announcing that Houdini was back on the Alhambra bill. An improvement had been made in the staging of his handcuff releases on the Continent. Now rather than dart into the large "Metamorphosis" cabinet, Houdini used a second much smaller one, about three feet square and four feet high. This disproved the theory proposed by some spectators that an assistant with an assortment of keys was hidden in the larger enclosure to help him. For many escapes, he did not even bother to close the front curtains of the small cabinet. After his hands were fastened behind his back, he knelt directly facing the audience, using the enclosure only to screen side and rear views of his release. Now the audience could see his facial expressions, arm movements, and body twists—all of which added greatly to the excitement of the presentation. If a challenge restraint was more difficult than usual, the front curtains of the small enclosure could be closed. Even then his movements could be vividly imagined as the cloth sides bulged and swayed. The larger cabinet was always ready should it be needed for an outsize challenge contrivance.

Two sailors from H.M.S. *Powerful* challenged Houdini with a set of ship's irons and a broom handle. They had Houdini sit on the stage and bring his knees to his chin. His hands were pulled around his legs and handcuffed, then the broomstick was inserted under his knees and over his arms. In this contorted position it was impossible for Houdini to move. The seamen lifted him and deposited him in the large cabinet. Harry was free in less time than it took the men to fasten him.

Late in December, Harry went with a writer from the *Black & White Budget* to a shop that sold manacles, to prove he could do offstage what most people had seen him accomplish only behind the footlights. The clerk displayed two pairs of gleaming, new cuffs. Houdini asked if it was possible to escape from them. The clerk smiled tolerantly and offered to demonstrate the effectiveness of his merchandise. Harry extended his wrists. Both pairs were locked on. The salesman smiled and dropped the keys in his coat pocket. Houdini shook his head, turned his back, and walked to the other end of the shop. Suddenly he swung around, hands free, cuffs open. The clerk was in a tizzy until Harry identified himself.

After his two-month run at the Alhambra, Houdini played his first engagement in the English provinces, a week at the Palace in Bradford. On Friday, February 8, 1901, the overflow crowd paid ten shillings each for standing room and chairs were even set up on the sides of the stage itself.

Back in Germany, Houdini played the Crystal Palast in Leipzig and the Apollo in Düsseldorf. A review in the Düsseldorf *Burger-Zeitung* startled the not-easy-to-startle Houdini. The writer flatly stated there was only one explanation for the remarkable escapes—occult power. "Positively thought I was supernatural and could dematerialize," the amused escapologist noted when he pasted the clipping in a scrapbook. Ridiculous as it might seem, the explanation was to be a recurring one.

In London, Harry had been attracted by an elaborate dress on display in a shopwindow. It had been intended for Queen Victoria, but she died before the gown was finished. An intriguing idea hit him. Why shouldn't the mother of Houdini wear a dress designed for a British queen? He asked the price. Thirty pounds—or $150. That, he decided, was a small amount to pay for the expression of surprise and pleasure such a magnificent present would produce on Cecilia's face. With Bess' help, the dress was altered to approximately his mother's size.

As advance bookings accumulated, Houdini realized it would be a long time before he could return to New York. Another happy thought came. He would bring his mother to Europe. He wrote Cecilia that night. His mother's response reached him in Frankfurt on the Main. She had received his letter—and the money—and had arranged to sail for Hamburg.

Less than eleven months after she had waved good-bye to her son and his wife in New York, Cecilia was in Germany.

Harry and Bess met her at the dock and took her to their Hamburg hotel. That night the Hansa Theater was sold out, but Harry arranged for an extra chair to be installed in a box for her. After the Saturday closing performance, they took a train to Budapest. There in the Palm Gardens of the Royal Hotel, Cecilia, wearing the gown designed for the Queen of England, presided over a family reunion. The grandiose gesture was typical of Houdini. As a youngster, he had solemnly promised his father to watch over her; now he fulfilled the vow in superlative fashion. Cecilia sat in a thronelike chair with her son standing by her side and accepted compliments and greetings from relatives she hadn't seen in twenty-seven years. Then back across Europe they traveled for his opening in Essen an der Ruhr.

Booked originally for ten days at the Colosseum, Houdini first was held over five more, then extended to the end of May. The Krupp armament firm bought out the entire house one night so their employees could see Houdini frustrated by the complicated handcuffs made especially for the occasion by workers in the plant. Harry, with little trouble but enough dramatics to make the incident exciting, got out. This feat caused so much comment he had to repeat it for the public at large the following night.

Cecilia Weiss sailed for New York before her son's exciting closing night in Germany. The *Essener Volkszeitung* caught the mood: "Never in the history of the Colosseum Theater have so many persons been contained within its walls as on this memorable night. Not alone was the house sold out, but hundreds were turned away. Contrary to fire and police regulations, the aisles were packed and even the scenery had been removed and chairs were placed on the stage to accommodate the public. Not even the fearful heat could keep away this sweltering mass of humanity and prevent it from giving Houdini an ovation."

The huge audience ignored the announced program of variety. They had come to see Houdini and almost immediately began shouting for him to appear. There was a hasty conference backstage. The show was rearranged and Houdini came on stage to tumultuous applause. He began the evening with the magic he had once performed in dime museums, the California Concert Company, and the Welsh

Brothers Circus. He manipulated playing cards. An egg appeared and disappeared in a red felt bag. This was his night. He would do what he pleased.

The drama built up with his release feats. Men from the audience strapped him in a straitjacket and carried him to the large cabinet. He was out in four minutes. For the special challenge of the evening, representatives of the firm of Pussman & Feeth manacled him with police irons. Then they locked on the firm's especially constructed handcuffs and leg fetters. An iron collar was closed and padlocked around his neck, chains extended from it to bind his legs and arms. The force with which these were applied and padlocked pulled him into a squatting posture. He could neither walk nor move without toppling over. The challengers, satisfied with their work, carried him over to the cabinet. The orchestra played —first softly, then with increasing volume and spirit.

The challengers checked their pocket watches. One minute —two—three. The music changed its pattern. Five minutes— six. The volunteers on the stage, surrounding the cabinet, were wondering whether they had succeeded in defeating the escapologist. Ten minutes. The challengers were sure that any second now the American would give up. Eleven minutes. The curtains of the enclosure swept aside. A bedraggled, but smiling, Houdini was free. The house vibrated with cheers. A giant laurel wreath was brought to the stage, followed by baskets of flowers.

Herr Direktor Schultz quieted the audience. He had a presentation for the most successful entertainer in the annals of the Colosseum. An aide appeared at his side with a massive silver trophy. It was a thirty-five-inch-high, forty-pound urn, inlaid with three- and five-mark pieces, carrying a face value of six hundred marks. The silver lid was surmounted by a symbolic American eagle with spread wings. Deeply moved, Harry made a short speech which brought his fans to their feet as the curtain fell.

Twelve months after he had crossed the Atlantic without a contract, Houdini was the strongest vaudeville attraction in Europe. His challenge escapes had brought new excitement to variety theaters. His bold onslaught against the contenders for the crown of escape king had drawn venom from rivals, acclaim from the public. At twenty-seven, he had a solid bank account, more offers for bookings than he, or his brother Hardeen, could fill, and a new goal. He would make Houdini a more important name in show business history than that of Robert-Houdin, his boyhood idol.

THE DETRACTORS

In a desperate effort to save the Corty-Althoff circus from bankruptcy, Direktor Pierre Althoff offered Houdini—by now Germany's number one vaudeville attraction—more money than he was making in theaters. Houdini was to replace the circus's principal attraction: a world-famous trained stallion display. Tragically, all but three of the horses had become infected by disease and were destroyed by health authorities in Gelsenkirchen.

Houdini joined the circus in June 1901 in Dortmund and immediately gained publicity by escaping from manacles that had been worn by an especially sadistic murderer named Glowisky when he was beheaded just three days previously. This escape made good newspaper copy, but Harry was less pleased with the next story he inspired.

There had been a sudden increase in business in the small hotel where Houdini stayed. The hotelkeeper mentioned he needed access to a locked room. The longtime tenant was away from the city and had carried his key with him. Harry volunteered to put his expertise to work on the problem. He examined the lock, purchased a blank key, and filed it to fit. A newspaperman happened to be in the shop when Houdini bought the blank. The reporter returned to his office and wrote an amusing story. The great escape artist's secret was really quite simple. He "buys up" every available key when he arrives in a new town. "Ever since that time," Houdini wrote, "I shun hardware stores as I would a pest-house."

Althoff cleared more than 100,000 marks' profit with his new star in less than three weeks. The circus moved on to Bochum, Osnabrück, and Cologne with receipts spiraling to new highs.

Houdini's frequent letters from abroad kept his name in print in American theatrical publications and *Mahatma,* the magic magazine. He suggested in a note to Walter Peterkin, the editor of *Mahatma,* that he would like to write a regular column of European news: "I do not want anyone to know who it is from, you understand. You can put it in as from Our Own Correspondent. I always hear all the news and scandal."

The first column appeared in September 1901, attributed to "N. Osey." Herr Osey, it seemed, was a German magician with news sources throughout the Continent and the British Isles. While a few readers may have noticed that N. Osey without the period was "Nosey," the fact that Houdini was the writer has never been disclosed in print before now.

His name almost invariably was mentioned in the dispatches but informed readers were led astray by such paragraphs as:

"A handcuff mystifier appeared lately at the Empire Theater, So. Shield, England, calling himself Theo. Hardeen, who does a Houdini act. He is on the Moss and Thornton tour. He says he is an American and although I have seen almost all the conjurors in America, this man's face is not familiar to me, neither is his name. Perhaps some of the readers are acquainted with him. He is doing well."

Houdini was never critical of himself when he wrote as Herr Osey, but his comments on other wonder-workers sometimes sizzled:

"Despite the fact that he [Francis King] has an original act, when Downs came to Germany he copied the act. When the clever Houdini came to Germany he tried at handcuffs and when Thurston opened at the Wintergarten, Mr. King was right there in Berlin, at the Metropole Theater, doing Thurston's act.

"A. Toskana, who calls himself the Gentleman Magician, has let loose with a few bombastic ads, to the effect that he catches fifty coins several times and that he uses both hands. He does not say whether the coins are tied in a bag or not . . . from reports he is a bad imitation of Downs."

German straitjackets were more difficult to manipulate than similar restraints in the United States and Canada, as Houdini learned during his engagement at the Mellini Theater in Hanover in September. Challenged by Count Von Schwerin, the police commissioner, he struggled for an hour and twenty-nine minutes before he pulled the strapped, leather-and-canvas pacifier over his head and away from his bruised, chafed body.

As a younger man, Hermann Mellini, the owner of the Mellini Theater, had been a successful magician himself. He purchased the theater and a handsome home from the profits of his *Grosse Magish-Physikalische Vorstellung*. Houdini had a thousand questions to ask about performers he had heard of but never seen. He studied Mellini's scrapbooks and was intrigued by the advertising material—souvenir photographs, charming miniature pieces of sheet music for the "Mellini Polka," and illustrated heralds and showbills. To celebrate Houdini's record-breaking performances at the theater, Mellini staged a gala night in his honor and gave him a silver wreath and five hundred marks more than his contract specified.

Galenzie, the French agent, was at the station to meet Harry and Bess when their train arrived in Paris. That very day the owner of the Folies-Bergère, where Houdini was to open, had been committed to an insane asylum and his wife had sold the theater. The contract was no longer valid. However, the Isola Brothers were anxious for Houdini to appear at the Olympia Theater. It would, Galenzie said, take several days to work out the details.

In this, the city where Robert-Houdin, with his original presentations and clever staging, had given the ancient art of magic a new appeal, Houdini had an obligation to fulfill. He must visit the Théâtre Robert-Houdin on the Boulevard des Italiens to pay homage to the master. Where once the art of illusion reigned supreme, Houdini, to his dismay, found moving pictures getting top play. But as Harry watched the screen, he grudgingly admitted the flickering images were accomplishing marvels no living performer could duplicate.

Georges Méliès, a noted magician, was the current proprietor of the Théâtre Robert-Houdin. The movies were written by him, directed by him, and produced by him—and he played the principal roles himself. Méliès was to be honored years later as the first man to make a film with a plot and as the inventor of techniques of trick photography that are still used today. During his career he turned out an amazing number of short subjects—almost four thousand.

Méliès introduced Harry to Folleto (Joseph Ferraris), the theater's legal adviser, who told him that the widow of Robert-Houdin's son Emile was still alive. Houdini sent her a letter by a messenger, who had instructions to deliver it only to the lady herself and wait for a reply. The letter said:

> With all the respect due you in the world, and as a great admirer of the justly celebrated and famous conjuror Robert-Houdin, I, as a representative of American Magicians, do hereby kindly ask your consent to permit me as a representative of American Magicians to place a wreath on the tomb of Robert-Houdin, also to grant me a few moments, so that I may have the pleasure of thanking you in person for your extreme kindness.
>
> Thanking you in advance for your awaited for letter, I do hereby sign myself your most obedient servant.
>
> *Harry Houdini*

The messenger made a speedy return. The lady told him not to wait. There would be no reply. Harry asked Folleto to intercede with Madame Robert-Houdin. Folleto reported that Emile's widow had been ill for some time and did not wish to be disturbed.

Rankling from what he considered a rude rebuff, Houdini nonetheless was determined to visit Robert-Houdin's grave. He took the train to Blois, where the great magician was buried. There he learned that his idol's daughter Rosalie lived nearby with her husband Henri, who had honored his father-in-law by adopting his name, becoming Henri Lemaitre-Robert-Houdin. Henri greeted the unexpected visitor cordially. Rosalie, a sculptress, was busy in her studio and was not to be interrupted. The genial Henri, however, took pleasure in showing his guest several clocks which had been made by Robert-Houdin and memorabilia from the magician's library. He hinted that even if Emile's widow had refused to see the American or grant him formal permission to visit the grave of his illustrious predecessor, no one in Blois would stop him from completing his mission.

For thirty minutes Houdini stood hat in hand by the shaft which bore the sculptured profile of Robert-Houdin made by Dantan the Younger. Then he went to a florist and ordered a wreath with the words "Honor and Respect to Robert-Houdin from the Magicians of America." He returned to the cemetery and placed the wreath on the tomb as a photographer recorded the event. He spent four hours reliving the day in his mind on the train back to Paris.

Houdini opened at the Olympia Théâtre as a headliner. When the French police refused to allow him to attempt his naked test in their jails or to try their restraints, he was dropped to second billing. In France handcuffs were rarities. Gendarmes used chains and locks to bind their prisoners. The public was not familiar with modern manacles and fewer challengers came forth than in other countries. To fill the required time Houdini opened his act by making a pack of playing cards vanish at his fingertips. Then, showing his hand empty, back and front, he plucked them one at a time from the air. The feat, new to most Parisian theatergoers, was heartily applauded. Even the French magicians were surprised to discover that the American handcuff king also was an accomplished manipulator. Houdini was held over another four weeks.

One of Houdini's most diverting advertising stunts was staged in Paris. He hired seven men to sit side by side in the most prominent sidewalk cafés facing the traffic. They were similar in appearance and wore identical headpieces. Periodically they would look down and remove their hats. Emblazoned on seven bald pates were seven huge letters spelling out "HOUDINI."

The Swiss magician Melot Hermann was added to the Olympia bill during Houdini's second month. Hermann performed with handkerchiefs, flags, and flowers. There was no conflict. Throughout his career Houdini often worked on the same show with other magicians. His escape feats, as the public saw it, were something more than magic.

Houdini closed at the Olympia early in February and went to Cologne where a libel suit he had filed against a German policeman was about to be tried. Werner Graff had branded him a fraud in an article in the *Rheinische Zeitung* of July 25, 1901. Graff had written that the American falsely claimed he could escape from police restraints of any sort. Houdini, asserting that he had never failed to break free, said Graff owed him an apology. He demanded an immediate retraction. Graff refused. The story was printed in newspapers in other German cities.

Only a man with Houdini's unmatched confidence and thorough knowledge of escape methods would have dared to carry out his next move. He engaged Herr Rechtsantwalt Dr. Schreiber, Cologne's most prominent trial lawyer, and instructed him to institute an immediate suit for libel. Harry realized that this would be an expensive and time-consuming procedure but, as he saw it, his honor and his future were at stake.

The trial began in the Cologne *Schoffengerich* in February 1902. The policeman challenged the escape artist to free himself from a chain which was to be fastened with regulation locks. This restraint, Graff said, Houdini had never tried. It would settle Houdini's boasts once and for all. The judge gave his approval for the test. There was only one hitch. He ruled that the escape must be made in full view.

Houdini, in bringing the case to court, had not anticipated this. Hitherto he had kept his techniques secret. Now he had a choice of backing down in his legal battle or exposing his methods to public view. He said if the court was cleared, he would make the test for the judge and jury.

One of Graff's colleagues, a man named Lott, fastened the chain around Houdini's wrists as he had hundreds of times in the past when he moved prisoners from one jail to another. As the judge and jury watched, Houdini twisted his hands, brought the chain to his mouth, gripped one strand firmly, then began the arduous process of wrenching his left hand free. Once it was out he used it to force the chain forward as he released his right hand. Harry had arrived in Cologne a few days before the trial. When he learned that Graff would confront him with a transport chain, Houdini worked out the sequence of release and spent hours each day practicing the escape.

The verdict was announced February 26. Houdini had won. The court fined Graff and ordered him to make a public apology. There was no cause for immediate celebration, however; Graff's lawyer appealed the decision. At least Houdini could be thankful that a detailed explanation of his chain escape had not turned up in print.

During his engagement at Roanacher's Theater in Vienna in March, Harry made plans for a quick trip to the States. It had been ten months since Cecilia's visit and almost two years had passed since he had sailed from New York. He was eager to see his mother again and he wanted advice from Martin Beck, his American manager. Perhaps it was time to capitalize on the European successes with a Keith and Orpheum tour?

His April homecoming couldn't have been more hectic. He wrote W. D. LeRoy, the Boston magic dealer: "I was so busy that I really did not have time to sleep. I was home 10 days and slept one night, the rest of the time I was out, and slept in my motor car, while my brothers drove me about.

"I certainly saw all of my business attended to in that short time, why I rode 30 hours in a Pullman car traveling about with my manager, Martin Beck, so that I could see him, and he is also a busy man so we made our plans on the Pullman Palace cars. I went clear to Washington, where I met him, and went to Pittsburgh and back, never sleeping except when nature called a halt. I tell you I lived 4 months in those 10 days. But when I placed my foot on the steamer on my return trip, I'll bet you that I never left my stateroom until I struck Hamburg. And never in all my life have I ever suffered so much from sea sickness. I thought that we would never reach Germany."

Beck's advice to Houdini was to stay in Europe as long as he was in demand. Why waste time trying to get consecutive bookings in America at salaries to match his continental fees? So back Harry went on another tour with the Corty-Althoff Circus, this time through Holland.

The sight of the Dutch windmills along the countryside gave Houdini the inspiration for a radically different escape. He was tied to a wing of a windmill, primed to free himself as it turned in the air. Unfortunately, he miscalculated the supporting strength of the windmill's arm; as it turned, it snapped in half and he crashed to the ground. But Houdini's luck held. Not only did he escape with minor bruises, but the stunt, while an artistic failure, was a publicity coup. Word-of-mouth reports of his accident filled the Corty-Althoff arena seats.

A letter from a friend in June carried newspaper clippings heralding the appearance of an escape artist named Kleppini with the Circus Sidoli. Engelberto Kleppini claimed he had won a handcuff duel with Houdini in Holland, that he escaped from the American's cuffs, while Houdini was held by Kleppini's manacles. Harry exploded. Not only had he never been in a contest with Kleppini, he had never even met the man.

He went to Direktor Althoff's office at once and insisted that he be excused from his contract long enough to put Kleppini in his place. Althoff tried to calm him, but Harry was not to be placated. Either he would be given time to deal with the troublemaker or he would forget the show business dictum—the show must go on—and walk out of the circus then and there. Pierre Althoff granted him a five-day holiday.

Harry filled a satchel with his best handcuff-king-defeaters and took the first train to Germany. In Essen a barber rearranged his hair and fastened a false moustache above his upper lip, then he was off for nearby Dortmund. Engelberto Kleppini began his act in the Circus Sidoli by boasting of his triumph over the American, Houdini, in Holland. "Not true, not true!" shouted an old man, who leaped to his feet among the spectators. Kleppini snapped back: "How do you know?"

"I know," the elderly gentleman answered. Kleppini, warming to the battle, suggested a bet on the truth of the statement. The old man took on sudden youth. With a running jump he sprang from his place in the stands down into the circus ring. "You say I am not telling the truth," he shouted, ripping off his false moustache. "Well, look! I am Houdini!" Kleppini was taken completely by surprise.

Harry launched into a tirade against Kleppini's false advertising. He brandished a handful of German money. "I'll wager five thousand marks if this faker can escape from my handcuffs, another five thousand if I can't escape from his Chinese Pillory." (The Chinese Pillory, Houdini noted later, was not Chinese, but merely "a common set of hand and foot irons, on which you could hang your own locks.") Kleppini didn't accept the offer. Harry stalked away. The audience was thoroughly confused.

Herr Reutter, the Circus Sidoli business manager, approached Harry at his hotel the next day with an offer. The circus, he said, would sponsor a contest between the two handcuff kings. Houdini was not interested. "Would you put your cuffs on Kleppini if he challenged you?" Harry shot back: "You bet I would." Posters were printed. Dortmund was plastered with the announcement: "Houdini challenged and will appear at the Circus Caesar Sidoli this evening.

Kleppini will allow himself to be handcuffed and will immediately free himself."

Kleppini wanted to talk things over. He invited Houdini to visit him. Harry refused. Kleppini then came to Houdini's hotel. Harry ignored him. Herr Reutter returned. He wondered what sort of cuffs Houdini would use that evening. Harry opened his bag. In it were a dozen pairs of shackles. Kleppini could take his choice. Reutter picked up an odd-looking pair. He had never seen cuffs like these, he said. Harry, suspecting this was more than a social visit, explained they were French letter cuffs. They could be opened only by turning five cylinders to form a key word on each cuff.

"What letters or words open this cuff?" Reutter inquired.

Houdini played along. If Reutter promised not to pass on the information to Kleppini, he would show him. He spun the cylinders to spell *clefs,* the French word for keys. The cuff opened. The manager asked if he could show the cuffs to Herr Sidoli, the owner of the circus. He promised that Kleppini would not see them. Harry let him take them. It was four hours before the manacles were returned.

That evening, a huge crowd turned out for the confrontation of the two escape artists. Houdini, offering Kleppini his choice of the twelve handcuffs in his bag, hardly was surprised when the French letter cuffs were selected. He was startled, however, when Kleppini, cuffs in hands, rushed into the cabinet.

"Ladies and gentlemen," Houdini shouted. "Do not let him tell you that the cuffs have been locked. They are open. He will return and say he opened them."

Kleppini popped out from behind the curtains. "I will open these cuffs," he cried, waving them triumphantly. "I challenge Houdini to lock them on me. I'll show him that it's we Germans who lead the world."

It was apparent to Harry that his rival, during his quick dash to the cabinet, had double-checked the word *clefs* to make sure it opened the manacles. Kleppini insisted that the cuffs be locked on his wrists immediately. Harry had other ideas. A tussle started with the two men pushing and pulling each other around the circus ring. Finally Houdini snapped the cuffs shut and spun the cylinders, locking them.

Kleppini raised his manacled hands, turning in a circle so that everyone could see he was fastened tightly. Then, with a look of disdain toward Harry, he shouted: "After I open these handcuffs, I will allow Madame Kleppini to open them. She is very clever in this brand of work and she will open them in five seconds." He entered his cabinet.

"Ladies and gentlemen, you can all go home," Houdini retorted. "I do not look a cuff on a man merely to let him escape. If he tries this cuff until doomsday, he cannot open it. To prove this, though the regular closing time of the circus is ten thirty, I will allow him to remain here until two thirty."

Kleppini entered his enclosure at 9 p.m. After thirty minutes, during which nothing happened, he and his cabinet were moved aside. At nine thirty the feature ballet number went on. By eleven most of the spectators had returned home. The frustrated Kleppini still was in his cabinet at the side of the ring, no nearer to success than when he started. Herr Sidoli was furious. He instructed the roustabouts to remove Kleppini's cabinet. The harried handcuff expert, still shackled, ran out of the ring and into the manager's office while the roustabouts carried his cabinet away.

Houdini followed and stood guard at the door. Midnight came. Kleppini shouted for his wife to help him. Houdini stepped aside to let her in. Near 1 a.m. the manager ordered Kleppini to give up. In the presence of Sidoli, the manager, and a reporter, the exhausted Kleppini watched as Houdini spun the cylinders to release his hands. *Clefs* was not the key word now. Houdini had changed the combination during the tussle with Kleppini in the ring. The cuffs opened when the letters *F-R-A-U-D* fell into place. Kleppini, according to Houdini, by the next day was distributing handbills proclaiming he had trounced Houdini, the American, in his handcuff challenge and won five thousand marks.

After this Houdini paid little attention to Kleppini. He dismissed him as a serious competitor and regarded him as a handcuff clown. "He has a shirtfront jammed full of medals and a very large stage diamond star hanging on a red ribbon. Across his collar he has in golden letters—'The Champion of All Champions of Handcuff Kings.' The last time I saw him in Dortmund, Germany, he had four medals pinned behind his back.

"He has been closed in innumerable places, and one manager hires him simply to cause a lot of talk, pays him his salary, and then allows the audience to jeer at him. . . . He is either a crazy man or a handcuff man on the style of the once well-known Cherry Sisters, who were such wretchedly poor actresses they drew a large salary and large crowds simply to see how really bad they were."

VERDICT IN COLOGNE

The case of the American escapologist versus the German policeman was reviewed by Cologne's *Strafkammer*, the court of appeals, in July 1902. The defendant, Werner Graff, was better prepared than he had been at the first trial. He presented statements from thirty law enforcement officers to support his contention that Houdini could not justify his advertised claims. More important, the officer brought a specially made lock to the courtroom. It had been constructed by a master mechanic named Kroch. Once closed, Graff stated, the lock could never be opened.

The court decided Houdini could tackle this challenge in privacy. He was ushered into an adjacent chamber. Graff settled complacently for a long wait. But in just four minutes, Houdini was back before the judge—the unbeatable lock in his hand.

The *Strafkammer* upheld the decision of the lower court. But Graff still had another avenue of appeal, the *Oberlandesgericht*.

Houdini was playing the Palace Theater in Blackburn, England, when a cable from his German lawyer informed him of the *Oberlandesgericht* verdict.

The decision, dated October 24, 1902, ruled that Werner Graff had libeled Houdini as charged. He was fined thirty marks or six days in prison and ordered to pay the costs of the three trials. Further, the verdict was to be printed in Cologne newspapers at Graff's expense.

Harry was almost ecstatic. His honor had been vindicated. He worked overtime at his typewriter sending the news to his mother, his friends, his agents, and every publication he thought might use it. He ordered a new lithograph. "Apology in the name of King Wilhelm II, Kaiser of Germany," it proclaimed. Houdini, in evening dress with his wrists shackled, was shown before a German court. Helmeted police, all wear-

65

ing moustaches, stood guard. A bust of the kaiser looked down from a niche above the judges.

An open scroll gave Werner Graff the slap of anonymity. "The Imperial Police of Cologne slandered Harry Houdini. . . . The Police were ultimately compelled to publicly advertise 'An Honorary Apology' and pay all costs of the trials. By command of Kaiser Wilhelm II, Emperor of Germany."

Not the least of Houdini's talents lay in his ability to visualize himself in terms larger than life. In his mind he had bested not one policeman but the entire Imperial Police Force. This was the way he told the story to the world.

His return to England far exceeded his expectations. He had been uncertain how he would be received after his twenty-one-month absence. He doubted that he could equal his initial impact in the British Isles. Instead, he topped it. His jailbreaks in Bradford, Blackburn, and Halifax led to "rioting to buy tickets." He was flattered when the London police asked him not to reveal the time it took him to open their cells. "It made their cells look too easy," he wrote.

"If I don't come to America this summer," he said in a letter to W. D. LeRoy, the Boston magic dealer, "it will be at least three years before I will again land my small feet on the land of the free and the home of the dollars. I am booked up so far that it seems to me that I am booked for life . . . by the time I have my work all played, I think I can sit back and look at the world from my chair. . . . I talk German and French, as well as Hungarian or English, but you ought to hear my pronunciation, that is the whole secret of my success in foreign countries. It makes them all friendly with me ere I have performed a single trick."

Houdini's offer of a £25 forfeit ($125) if he failed to escape from regulation restraints brought a steady stream of challengers in every British city. The head of the School of Physical Culture came on the stage of the Blackburn Palace Theatre, October 24, 1902, with six pairs of irons and an assortment of chains and padlocks.

The locks had been tampered with, Houdini told the audience, and the irons had been wound with string. If the audience allowed him additional time to overcome these obstacles, he would accept the challenge.

Hodgson, the physical instructor, pinioned the magician's hands. He used more force than Harry thought was necessary. "This is not a challenge to break my arms," he shouted. Hodgson ignored the outburst. With Houdini in a kneeling position, he ran his chains through the links that held the escapist's hands behind his back, pulled them tight, and padlocked the ends to the irons that bound his ankles.

After fifteen minutes the cabinet that covered Houdini was lifted. Still trussed up, he had fallen on his side and seemed to be in a dead faint. He moved his lips weakly and asked to be put back on his knees. Hodgson refused. Theo, Houdini's brother, who was on the stage, brushed past the challenger and pulled Houdini upright.

Twenty minutes later, when the cabinet was lifted again, Harry had made no progress. He wearily asked if the irons could be unlocked for a minute or two to allow his blood to circulate. The pressure had numbed his body. "This is a contest, not a love match," Hodgson answered. Dr. Bradley, a member of the committee representing the audience, stepped over for a quick examination. Houdini's arms had turned blue, he reported. It was cruel, said Bradley, to keep him shackled any longer. Hodgson shrugged.

The cabinet was lowered again. This time it was apparent there was feverish action behind the drapes. In fifteen minutes Houdini extended a hand to show that it was free. The audience cheered. Eventually a leg was released, then the second hand. Finally Houdini came out. There were streaks of blood on his wrists and arms. His coat was torn. The wrought-up spectators shouted until they were hoarse. The escape had taken two hours.

Houdini said later that plugs had been jammed inside the keyholes of the locks. He had never been so brutally treated during a test. The Blackburn *Star* added: ". . . when Mr. Hodgson left the theatre, he ran to the police station for protection, fearing the wrath of the thoroughly enraged audience. He showed good judgement as he would have fared badly had he fallen into their hands."

Houdini smashed the house record he had established in February 1901 at Blackburn by more than £200 ($1,000). The following week in Halifax the crowds were so big that the Palace Theatre rented the Victoria Hall and ran extra matinees.

When provincial theater managers hesitated to pay Houdini's £100 salary ($500), he was so sure of his drawing
power that he played the dates for a percentage of the profit
from the ticket sale. Following a well-reported escape from
the jail in Leeds, demand for tickets to his performances was
so great that twice as many people were turned away as could
be admitted. As a result, Houdini's share of the profit was
double his regular salary. A week in Burnley was another
record-breaker, both at the box office and the local prison.
At the latter he opened six cells in five minutes. On December
15 he returned to Leeds. The business was even greater than
before. Extra matinees were played in a larger theater, the
Coliseum, and again he topped his previous income.

When he wasn't writing about actual triumphs, Houdini
concocted fables for the press. His "escape secret" was for sale.
A burglar heard the price and moaned: "I'm afraid we can't
come to terms. It would take me too long to steal the money."
Even the German government, another story said, was interested but hesitated to invest the required $50,000 until it
knew precisely what it was buying.

Harry romanced that he had made his first jailbreak in
Rhode Island while traveling with a circus. The sideshow attractions were arrested for breaking a Sunday blue law, and
Houdini was put in a cell with a fat lady, a legless man, a
giant, a bearded lady, a tattooed girl, and an India-rubber
man. The prisonkeeper went home for dinner. While the jail
was unguarded, Houdini reached through the cell bars and
opened the lock. When the jailer returned the cell was empty
and the show was on the road.

Houdini, who had built his reputation on accepting challenges, hurled a mighty defy of his own:

£1,000 CHALLENGE
OPEN TO THE WORLD

I, HARRY HOUDINI, known as the King of Handcuffs, at last becoming tired of so-called FAKE EX-
POSURES and MEDIOCRE MAGICIANS, who
claim to DO MY ACT because they possess a lot
of false keys and springs, DO HEREBY CHAL-
LENGE any person in the world to duplicate my
release from cuffs, irons and straitjackets, under test

conditions. That is to entirely strip, be thoroughly searched, mouth SEWED and sealed up, making it impossible to conceal keys, springs, or lock pickers, and in that state escape from all fetters that may be locked or laced on arms, legs or body.

Anyone accepting challenge who may, in searching me, find anything concealed on my person, even as small as a pinhead, I forfeit all money wagered, and I have the same rights regarding my opponent. Each competitor is allowed a physician and a mechanic, one to examine the human frame AS ONLY A PHYSICIAN CAN, and the mechanic who will examine all irons used, and if desirable each cuff or fetter can be broken open, so that it may be examined inside as well as out, and prevent faked irons from being used.

Committee shall be selected by mutual consent. No leaving the room to remove fastenings, but must be accomplished in the same room behind a newspaper, which is to be used as a curtain, and is to be examined BEFORE AND AFTER using. The place where test is to occur is not to be known by competitors, but must be decided on by committee, SO NO ONE can conceal anything anywhere. Committee is also to be SEARCHED so that they cannot assist the competitors. No less than 12 different styles of IRONS are to be used at one and the same time, also six different makes of Insane Belts, Restraint Maniac Muffs, Canvas and Leather Lace and Lock Straitjackets.

The challenge was never accepted. Even had a rival been tempted, he would think twice before having his "mouth SEWED."

It was unusual, outside of London, for a British theater to engage a variety act for more than a week. On the Continent month bookings were the rule. In January 1903 Houdini headlined at the Rembrandt Theater in Amsterdam. February he played a return engagement at the Mellini in Hanover. In March he made a hero's return to Cologne. There he was the man who had received a public apology from the Kaiser's police. This was on a percentage arrangement and earned him the highest fee he had received in Germany.

In Cologne he acquired his own "Kaiser"—Franz Kukol, who wore a Wilhelm II moustache and could speak several languages. He handled his tasks with the authority and precision of an Austrian ex-army officer, which he was. On March 2, 1903, he signed the document which swore him to eternal secrecy as to Houdini's methods and became a part of the act.

Houdini, the researcher, was busy in Cologne. In a German book he found a reference to Alexander Heimburger, who as Herr Alexander had been a famous magician. The volume, printed in 1896, said that Heimburger lived in Münster. Harry took an express train and arrived early the morning of March 17. At the police station he found Heimburger's name in the city directory and his address—16 Krumpentippen.

Though he arrived without an appointment he was warmly received by the eighty-three-year-old man. Heimburger was delighted that the young American knew so much about his early life. He talked happily about the great days when he had performed for President Polk in Washington and Emperor Dom Pedro II in Rio de Janeiro. He brought out his scrapbooks and diaries. Then he put on a pair of thick glasses so he could point out interesting programs and reviews. He was almost deaf. Harry had to shout to make himself heard. Robert-Houdin? He was not as inventive as most people thought, Heimburger said. A Parisian journalist had put his memoirs into publishable form. On the other hand, Herr Heimburger had written his own account of his life and travels. He presented Houdini with the two-volume set, *Ein Moderner Zauberer* ("A Modern Magician").

Heimburger reminisced about his tours in the United States. He had known Henry Clay and Daniel Webster. He had baffled Samuel Morse, the inventor of telegraphy. He had a bell, with no apparent motivating power, that rang in answer to questions. Morse thought he was using some new scientific principle. Actually, the bearded conjurer confessed, he had trained a canary so that it would hop and trip a lever. Of course the bird was well concealed.

He had been friendly with John Henry Anderson, the great Scottish magician, and Tobias Bamberg, whose feats were legendary in Holland. Few men, said Heimburger, were cleverer than Wiljalba Frikell. He must be approaching ninety. He lived a few minutes from Dresden, in Koetchenbroda.

Houdini wrote to Frikell from Cologne. He told of his

meeting with Heimburger and asked if he could make an appointment for a visit. The reply was puzzling. A brief note said Herr Frikell was on tour. This was ridiculous. Frikell hadn't performed in years. He decided to investigate the matter in person.

At four in the morning of April 8, Houdini arrived in the town. He found the retired magician's home easily. Villa Frikell was lettered on the front facade. He returned to the railway station to await a more reasonable hour to pay his respects.

He rang the bell at eight thirty. The door was opened by a lady who said Herr Frikell was not at home. Later he discovered she was the magician's wife. He went then to the local police. Yes, they knew Herr Frikell. He seldom if ever received visitors. He had an adopted daughter who lived nearby. Perhaps she would be able to help him. She told Houdini that Herr Frikell preferred to live a solitary life.

Persistent Harry hired a photographer, gave him instructions to take a picture when, or if, the veteran magician appeared.

"All morning the photographer lounged across the street and all morning I stood bareheaded before the door of Herr Frikell, pleading with his wife who leaned from the window overhead."

Houdini explained that he, as a young magician, wished to pay homage to a master. He hoped to write an authentic history of magic and tell of Frikell's contributions to the art. There were tears in Frau Frikell's eyes as she listened, but the front door remained closed.

Harry sent the old magician a stream of letters. Later, when Houdini was in Russia, one was acknowledged. It mentioned that Wiljalba Frikell enjoyed a brand of tea unobtainable in Germany. Houdini sent a package immediately. The tea had arrived safely another letter said and it carried the long-hoped-for invitation. The next time Houdini performed in Dresden, Herr Frikell would be at home if he called. Then Harry found an old engraving of Frikell as a young man, wearing a tarboosh and Turkish clothes. The recluse was delighted when this unexpected gift arrived. He had not known that this likeness was still in existence.

Saturday, October 8, 1903, Houdini returned to Koetchenbroda again. He rang the doorbell precisely at 2 p.m., the hour of his appointment. The door to the Villa Frikell, which had barred his way on his first visit, swung open.

Scarcely an hour earlier Wiljalba Frikell had put his scrapbooks on a table for easy reference. He squared the heap of programs and broadsides which had advertised his performances around the world, straightened the glass frame which held his decorations from kings and potentates. Then he clutched his chest and cried: "My heart! What is the matter with my heart? Oh—" He lay now lifeless surrounded by the souvenirs of his past.

Later Frau Frikell told Houdini that her husband had listened behind a shuttered window as he pleaded for admission on his first visit. Herr Frikell peeked out and mistook Houdini for his illegitimate son who had been threatening him through the mail. That was why the door had remained shut.

IMPERIAL RUSSIA

Moscow in 1903 was as gay as Paris or Berlin. The well-to-do flocked to theaters, cabarets, and restaurants. Entertainers from the Continent and America appeared in spectacular productions for the privileged classes. Czar Nicholas II seemed unaware that his subjects, long submissive to the imperial order, were even then plotting a rebellion.

The Moscow chief of police had extraordinary powers in the amusement area. He could change programs to suit his fancy. He had final approval of all theatrical advertising, and, Houdini noted, "should he take a dislike to you he can compel you to leave Moscow inside of twenty-four hours."

Harry was disturbed by the prisoners he saw herded through the streets, "carrying their black bread and a pot to cook their beloved *chey*, or what is known in English-speaking countries as common tea." Enemies of the state, condemned to exile in Siberia, were transported north in prison vans drawn by teams of horses. When one of the traveling jails stopped so that the horses could drink from a roadside trough, Houdini had an opportunity to study the contraption.

Escape was impossible through the sides, top, front, or bottom. The back offered possibilities. The entrance door was fastened by a single padlock. Above it was a small barred window. A week after his opening at the Establishment Yard, Houdini was ready to tackle the "escape-proof" portable prison.

He made his first contact with the police under unusual circumstances. The manager of the Yard cabaret told Houdini that his memorized patter was Polish, not Russian, and that he spoke with a heavy Yiddish accent. A new phonetic translation was hastily made. Harry practiced alone in a Moscow park, shouting the words as he would from a stage. Suddenly he was surrounded by plainclothesmen who carted him off to jail. Not until Bess arrived with the Yard manager, who explained that Houdini was not a maniac, was he released. Capitalizing on the situation, Harry entertained the officers with card tricks and persuaded Lebedoeff, the chief of the Russian secret police, to allow him to make an escape attempt from one of the traveling jails.

There were no reporters present May 11 when he was stripped and searched. Houdini claimed it was the most trying examination he had ever endured; far more thorough than that of the San Francisco police. Two iron bands, joined by a short metal bar, were padlocked around his wrists. A pair of fetters, linked by a chain, enclosed his ankles. He was locked inside the transport cell, then the wagon was turned in the prison courtyard so that the door faced away from Lebedoeff and his staff.

It took Houdini twenty-eight minutes to get free. The police were furious. They ran around the van to the door. It was still locked. Inside, on the metal floor, were his shackles. They seized Houdini again and once more searched him, more thoroughly, if possible, than before. They then turned on Franz Kukol, who had been kept at a distance from the van. They removed his clothes and searched him, too, to no avail.

Harry asked Lebedoeff to sign a document that would verify his escape. The chief of the Russian secret police refused: it was bad enough that the American had freed himself, Lebedoeff was not about to publicize the fact. Despite this, the news spread throughout the city. Houdini's month's booking was extended eight weeks. He wrote friends abroad: "I have been successful in escaping from the Siberian Transport Cell, and have made the biggest sensation that has ever been here."

In his book *The Secrets of Houdini*, J. C. Cannell, the British journalist, relates that Houdini pierced the "zinc" floor of the transport cell with a "cutter," that he folded back the metal, removed the wooden planking beneath it, and slipped out. This "explanation," which has been accepted and expanded by other writers, is as fanciful as many of Cannell's other "revelations." Houdini left no explanation for the feat among his private papers. It is likely that he stretched his arm through the barred window until he could reach the lock and opened it with a pick. The lithograph, which he had made to publicize the feat in other countries, shows the window smaller than it was and higher above the lock. A showman would not give a clue to his method in his advertising.

Three choruses, each with thirty girls, and ten acts were on the bill with Houdini at the Establishment Yard. Rival "summer gardens" also offered mammoth attractions. Orford's Elephants were featured at the Ermitage and Thompson's Elephants performed at the Aquarium.

One evening an army officer, a member of the committee from the audience, insisted on standing directly in front of Houdini on stage, blocking the spectators' view. Harry politely asked him to step to one side. The Russian declined to move. Houdini repeated his request more forcibly. The officer still didn't budge; he merely ordered the entertainer to proceed with his act. Harry appealed to the audience. If the man didn't step aside they would not see him make his escape. The capricious officer kept his ground.

Harry instructed Franz Kukol to push his "Metamorphosis" cabinet forward. If the front curtain was rung down it would fall only to the top of the cabinet. The audience by now was aroused, and the manager intervened. Entertainers, he told Houdini, ranked very low on the social scale in Russia. The military man was within his rights. Harry bristled. He informed the officer that in America he was no mere showman, he was considered a "millionaire." That was a magic word. The officer apologized to the self-proclaimed millionaire and to the audience. He walked to one side and the act went on.

The Russian was so impressed by the performance that, at his suggestion, Houdini was engaged for a private show at Kleinmichel Palace. There, on May 23, Houdini entertained Grand Duke Sergius and the Russian nobility for an hour and a half. A second-sight routine with Bess, that he had performed years before with the Welsh Brothers Circus, caused the most comment. The Grand Duchess was especially intrigued. Would it be possible for her to learn how to do it? In another room Harry taught her the rudiments of his system. When the Duchess returned to her guests she made an announcement. She, too, had the power to receive transmitted thoughts. With a handkerchief tied over her eyes, she gleefully called off a dozen objects as Houdini pointed to them. Before the evening was over the Grand Duke gave the "millionaire magician" a jeweled champagne ladle which had once been owned by Count Constantin Kleinmichel. Harry estimated it was worth a thousand rubles—five thousand dollars. But the present was almost incidental. What other magician could boast that the Grand Duchess of Imperial Russia had served as one of his assistants?

Houdini's principal detractor in Moscow was Robert Lenz, a German, who advertised he was the court magician to the Shah of Persia and dressed in exotic robes. Lenz belittled the newcomer's feats, claiming that he himself had performed the substitution mystery for thirty years and that his version of the feat was far more difficult. Mrs. Houdini, Lenz pointed out, was a mere slip of a girl, while his own wife was plump. Obviously, Lenz concluded, it was proportionately more difficult for his wife to change places with him inside the tied bag and locked trunk.

Houdini's handcuff escapes were ridiculously simple, Lenz said. He advertised a special performance during which he would reveal the American's secrets. Harry attended, ready to challenge him from the audience. It wasn't necessary. All Lenz exposed, Houdini wrote, was a lack of knowledge. "He did not even know what a handcuff key looked like and his entire exposure consisted in removing a rivet from all his manacles, which had been specially prepared for the purpose."

Following his run at the Establishment Yard, Houdini performed at the Ermitage and the Zoo cabarets. Frequently he spent his afternoons in the studio of T. Bolin, a Frenchman, who specialized in building illusions for the stage. Bolin's devices were the cleverest Houdini had ever seen and Bolin himself was a fund of information about the theater. The walls of his workroom were filled with framed portraits and playbills of the magicians he had seen. Bolin told Harry that Robert-Houdin, whom he had seen in Paris, was not as original as his books would have their readers believe.

During his browsing through antique shops Houdini found two engravings of Bosco, the great Italian cup-and-ball conjurer; several prints of the Viennese magician Ludwig Doebler; a photograph of Anna Eva Fay, the American stage medium; and numerous playbills, prints, and newspaper articles concerning the spirit cabinet séances of the American Davenport Brothers. All had been acclaimed in Moscow.

On the Fourth of July (actually June 21 in Russia, which

still adhered to the Julian calendar) Harry and Bess accepted an invitation to the traditional lawn party at the American consul's residence. The guests included a contingent of show people, among them Weston, who had a "loop-the-loop" act, Smith and Doretto, and four of "The Florida Girls." The grounds had been decorated with red, white, and blue buntings and American flags. Houdini had seen puzzled Russian faces during his performances; now he saw more as Muscovites passing along the road peeked over the wall and gaped at the strange celebration.

Houdini's debut as a professional safecracker was sponsored by Kirhoff Brothers, a Moscow locksmithing firm. They had been instructed to open an old safe as quickly as possible by the titled family which owned it. The combination had been lost for fourteen years. The brothers tried everything but dynamite, and it was ruled out only because a blast might damage the valuables inside. Harry worked for nine hours before he opened the door. Inside was a glittering array of jewels worth $210,000. Houdini received $750 for professional services rendered.

Another Russian strongbox presented an even greater challenge. Twelve miniature figurines—six police officers and as many criminals—were ranged about the keyhole. When the criminals were moved, their actions repositioned the officers. It took Houdini four days to discover the operational secret. Once the proper sequence was worked out, the policeman closest to the keyhole bent at the waist and inserted his sword in the opening. It appeared that this action unfastened the door. Actually, when the complicated mechanism was about to unlatch the lock, a concealed spring released a catch which brought about the sword byplay.

When offers came to play in other Russian cities at salaries too high to refuse, Houdini signed a two-month contract on the proviso that he could delay his opening in Holland. The day before he was to leave for St. Petersburg, word arrived that his Dutch contracts could not be postponed. In place of the longer tour he accepted a three-week engagement for the annual Nizhni Novgorod fair.

Most of each year the city (now Gorki) was covered by the Volga. Late in the summer the waters receded and the fabulous fair came to life. Merchants from Europe and Asia traveled for weeks to bring their choicest products and rarest delicacies to the August festival. Here, as in Moscow, the police were in control. No smoking was allowed on the streets. Women normally were barred from appearing in shows, and Harry had to obtain special permission for Bess to assist him in his act. "You see," he explained in a letter, "the soubrettes, chansonettes and other lady acts came to this town and made things so merry that the police had to put a stop to their money-getting pranks. The only women allowed are the chorus girls in the opera. They have to pay a sum equal to $100 to appear or have their names on the program. But the city is full of chorus girls (?). Talk about your 'talk-abouts'—the way they carry on here is a caution. I have seen the slums of Buda Pest, Paris, London and Berlin but this 'One Month in the Year City' takes the prize."

Gambling was forbidden, except at the racetrack. Harry thought a clever three-shell manipulator or a wheel operator could make a fortune. He met a card manipulator whose passport carried a restriction. He was not to play cards with strangers. There were other mystery performers among the fair's attractions. Les Tereses featured a hypnotic routine. Roberta offered a one-man version of the Davenport Brothers' cabinet séance. Houdini was amused by the billing of Herr Polinsk Piker—"The greatest eye deceiver that ever deceived an eye."

Houdini had hoped to put a wreath on Pinetti's grave in Russia. His researches had led him to believe that the Italian was a greater innovator of conjuring than his boyhood idol, Robert-Houdin. In the 1780's Giuseppe Pinetti introduced revolutionary techniques and devices in Germany, France, and England. Before Robert-Houdin was born, he exhibited a tree which blossomed and bore fruit. He featured a trapeze "automaton" similar to Robert-Houdin's and, with his wife, he presented the earliest known feats of second sight. Pinetti had spent his last years in Russia experimenting with ballooning. He was so famous that the Czar had been the godfather of one of his children.

After several letters from Moscow to magicians in Paris asking for the name of the town where Pinetti had been buried, Houdini received the information. By then it was too late. His September opening in Holland didn't allow him time for a pilgrimage to the grave.

Houdini's Russian salaries were the largest he had ever

made. The week in Moscow that included his performance for Grand Duke Sergius totaled $1,750. Yet he breathed more freely when his train passed the frontier. "After you leave Russia, you feel as if you had yourself come out of some sort of mild prison." He never returned to the Czar's dominion.

IMITATORS AND INNOVATIONS

A challenge escape act is difficult to stage. If the performer is too domineering, the audience roots for the challenger. There is no relationship between actual difficulty and applause, and sometimes the best-received feats are the simplest in execution. As an escapologist becomes more skillful with his releases, he must remember to act as if he is faced with problems that tax his powers to their utmost limits.

Less confident performers than Houdini avoided controversy on the stage. Harry welcomed it. Any unexpected spark of excitement was fanned by his dramatics until it burst into theatrical flame. He was quick to sense a rival by the way the man bound or shackled him. Laymen were unaware of the techniques an escapologist must use to gain slack; competitors knew, and, by attempting to guard against them, revealed themselves to Houdini.

The spectator who tied Houdini's hands behind his back at the People's Palace in Halifax was taking too long to do a job that the average volunteer completed in less than a minute. After six minutes Houdini said: "He must be a so-called imitation handcuff king." The man interrupted his knotting and told the audience that he knew nothing about escapes. He turned and tied a few more hard knots. Houdini entered his cabinet. The release took longer than usual, but he came out with his hands free.

The volunteer was not satisfied. He insisted on tying Houdini again. This was too much for Harry. He went to the footlights and asked if anyone knew the young man. No reply came from the audience, but a man walked out from behind the wings. "I know him," he said. "He is Pollard, the handcuff king from Bradford, who wrote that handcuff exposure in the *Strand* magazine."

Houdini raised his eyebrows. "Ladies and gentlemen. A few moments ago he led you to believe he knew nothing about handcuffs. . . . Now to show you how little he really understands . . . I pledge my word of honor to pay five hundred pounds to the poor of Halifax if he will allow me to handcuff him—and he releases himself."

He called offstage to the manager: "Mr. McNaughton, will you stand good for me?" McNaughton came on stage and agreed that he would. The audience cheered. Franz Kukol brought out a pair of manacles which Houdini held up for all to see. Pollard backed away. He shook his head violently and said he escaped only from British cuffs. Kukol took away the American Bean Giants and replaced them with British Regulation Cuffs.

"Mr. McNaughton, pay this young man five hundred pounds —when he gets out of these." Pollard's bluster had disintegrated. He left the stage as the audience jeered.

Houdini's allotted twenty minutes had stretched to an hour. No one complained, certainly not the manager of the theater. He knew the newspaper and word-of-mouth coverage of the incident would fill the house for the remainder of the week.

Harry was constantly adding newsworthy touches to his jail escapes. In Huddersfield, in late November 1903, he escaped nude from one cell and opened nine others. In January 1904, in Sheffield, he released himself from a "triple-locked" cell, put on his clothes, which had been locked in an adjacent compartment, and passed through an iron gate with a seven-lever lock. Two weeks later during his jailbreak in Liverpool he moved a prisoner from one cell to another, then locked him in so securely that the police had to ask Harry to open the cell before he left.

Houdini's first night at the London Hippodrome in late February was a press agent's dream. He was shackled with the manacles Count de Lorge had worn for fifteen years in the Bastille; two pairs of cuffs that had held Jack Sheppard, the famous highwayman; the irons archcriminal Charles Peace had been locked in when he jumped from a train near Sheffield, and four other restraints. The lot weighed 131 pounds. He was clear of them all in twenty-seven minutes.

The high point of Houdini's engagement at the Hippodrome was his dramatic escape on March 17 from the complex handcuffs with which the *Daily Illustrated Mirror* challenged him. The release, before a packed house of four thousand, took Houdini an hour and ten minutes.

Near the end of his extended engagement at the Hippodrome, Houdini was ordered to bed by his physician. His strenuous work night after night left him wet with perspiration. The chill spring air which struck him as he left the theater brought on a debilitating cold.

Confined to his hotel room, Harry sorted out the programs, photographs, clippings, and notes he had gathered during his travels. A journalist wrote about the interesting historical material he had seen as he interviewed the master escapologist. The afternoon the story was printed a note came from a retired magician, Henry Evanion. He said he had a number of early handbills which he thought Houdini might like to see. Harry sent an immediate reply, inviting Evanion to call at one o'clock the next afternoon.

There was no word from the magician the following day. Just after four o'clock Houdini's doctor said he was in good enough condition to take a brief walk. As Harry left the elevator, the hall porter informed him that an old man had been waiting for three hours in the lobby. His arrival had not been announced because of his unkempt appearance.

Harry approached the balding, bewhiskered Evanion, who sat in a nearby chair. The old gentleman arose, introduced himself, and fumbled to open a large package. Houdini, still weak from his bout with the grippe, scarcely heard the hesitant: "I have brought you, sir, only a few of my treasures." In the trembling fingers of his caller were rare bills and lithographs of Robert-Houdin, Philippe, Pinetti, Breslaw, and Anderson, which Houdini thought were unobtainable at any price.

"I remember only raising my hands before my eyes, as if I had been dazzled by a sudden shower of diamonds. . . . I felt as if the King of England stood before me and I must do him homage."

At home, Evanion said, he had an extensive collection. Ignoring his doctor's advice, Harry took a taxi early the next morning to 12 Methley Street on Kennington Park Road. There in the basement room where Evanion lived with his wife, he sat enthralled as he leafed through stacks of memorabilia and listened to Evanion's accounts of the magicians he had seen.

For more than fifty years Henry Evans Evanion had been a performer and collector of magic. Many of his finest heralds and handbills were bequeathed to him by James Savren, the first great collector of British magicana. Savren, a barber, periodically left his shop to assist such noted performers as Anderson, Herrmann, Doebler, and Cornillot. Later Savren performed with a repertoire made up of the best tricks of the mysterymakers for whom he had worked.

Evanion, then seventy-two, had spent his free time for many years searching in the British Museum for references to conjurers of other days. No longer able to perform, he sold bits of his collection to the museum and the few contemporary magicians who shared his interest.

The hours sped by. From time to time Evanion took a teapot from his stove and poured a fresh cup for the escape king. Houdini was so excited and overpowered by the fabulous collection that his hands shook. He spilled a few drops of tea on the precious papers. It was past three thirty the next morning that Houdini's doctor and his brother Theo found him in Evanion's apartment. They took him back to the hotel, but not until he had purchased a thick bundle of Evanion's material.

Houdini escaped from a box made by a staircase manufacturer during his week at the Brighton Hippodrome in May. The next day there was a formal presentation of the promised solid-silver handcuffs from the *Mirror*. The day before he sailed for a vacation in New York he visited Evanion again and came away with another armload of treasure.

Aboard the *Deutschland* he talked with Martin Beck, who had been in England scouting new acts for the Orpheum circuit. Beck visited the Houdinis in their second-class cabin. He couldn't understand why a man who was making as much money as Houdini would travel in anything but the best accommodation. Beck offered to pay the difference in price and move the Houdinis up to first class. Harry thanked him, but refused the offer. It was just as uncomfortable, he said, to be seasick in first class as in second.

The Society of American Magicians had been organized in 1902 by professional and amateur conjurers, who banded together to promote greater public interest in mystery attractions and to keep each other posted on the latest tricks at their monthly meetings. Houdini's application, mailed from England, had been accepted. His formal initiation, two nights after he arrived back in New York in 1904 was more a welcome home party than a ritual.

Francis Martinka locked handcuffs on Houdini's wrists during the ceremony in the backroom of Martinka's Sixth Avenue magic shop. He was free in twenty seconds. The cuffs were put on display in a glass case in the shop the next day. Doubters could verify for themselves that Houdini escaped from regulation irons as easily as some of his rivals slipped from gimmicked shackles.

During Harry's eleven-week American holiday he bought a home in the German section of Harlem. The brownstone at 278 West 113th Street was, he proclaimed, "The finest private house that any magician has ever had the great fortune to possess," forgetting perhaps Alexander Herrmann's Long Island estate, Robert-Houdin's château in St. Gervais, and Hermann Mellini's mansion in Hanover.

His mother was reluctant to leave the familiar surroundings on East 69th Street. But as always she wanted to please Harry. She was persuaded to quit the apartment where she and her beloved Samuel had struggled to bring up their large family.

She approached the $25,000 four-storied brownstone with awe: "What will you do with all the rooms?" When the crates Harry had been sending home from abroad were removed from storage, she had a partial answer. Hundreds upon hundreds of conjuring books, rare programs, pictures, and documents filled three of the twenty-six rooms. "Someday," he told Cecilia, "when I'm too old to perform, I'll spend my time writing about magic. And I won't have to search for source material. It will be here."

Houdini also purchased a family burial plot in the Machpelah Cemetery in Cypress Hills, Brooklyn, and supervised the moving of the remains of his maternal grandmother, his father, and his brother Herman to the site. He noted that Signor Antonio Blitz, a famous European magician who had come to the United States in 1834 and had performed for Abraham Lincoln during the Civil War, was buried a few hundred yards away in another graveyard.

He traveled to see old friends in Chicago, Milwaukee, and Appleton and talked with Martin Beck, theater managers, and theatrical reporters. But most of the vacation he spent with Bess and his mother. A delegation from the Society of American Magicians had been at the dock to greet him;

another was there, with Cecilia and other relatives, to see him off.

The powerful Moss Empire circuit in England sought a court order to stop Houdini from opening at the Zoo Hippodrome in Glasgow. The circuit claimed it had an exclusive agreement with the escape king; he had agreed not to play opposition theaters. The order was denied. For three weeks Houdini was the talk of Scotland. One of the first challenges he accepted was from the saddlers, Lockie, Graham & Co. It took their men fifteen minutes to buckle him in a newly designed strait-jacket. Houdini was behind the curtains of his cabinet fifty-five minutes, rolling and tossing, but he got out. The Glasgow *Times* of September 23, 1904, caught the pitch of excitement of his closing week:

> You might have walked on the heads of the surging, strug-
> gling, swaying mass of people almost from George's Cross
> to the Normal School. A stranger within the city gates
> might well have wondered what strange happenings were
> abroad to bring out such a curious congregation. And yet
> the explanation was simple. Houdini, the Handcuff King
> and Prison Breaker, was announced to have accepted a
> most unique challenge which he would try in front of the
> spectators in the Zoo.

Eight carpenters from the firm of J. & G. Findlay nailed the magician in a box they had made, then wound and tied it with heavy rope. The box was lifted to a raised platform to demonstrate that no help would be available from below the stage. Curtains were closed around the platform. For fifteen minutes the orchestra played and the huge audience waited. Nothing was happening on the stage. Yet if the spectators used their imaginations, they could visualize the struggle behind the curtain.

When Houdini pushed the drapes aside and stepped down from the platform to the stage, there was bedlam. Perspiration streaked his face. During his battle for freedom, he had lost both his shoes. He stood there in his stocking feet, smiling and accepting the ovation as the eight puzzled carpenters examined the box and admitted that the rope was still tied, and that the box had not been broken open.

There was pandemonium at the stage door when Houdini left the theater. He was lifted on brawny shoulders and paraded through the streets to his quarters on New City Road. Even then his admirers were reluctant to go. They carried him up a flight of stairs to his room. Harry had to open a window and talk to the people before the mob outside dispersed.

Months after this engagement, Houdini's marvels were still fresh in young Scottish minds. A curate explained to his religious class that he, as a curate, could pronounce absolution, but only God could forgive sins. As a parallel, he told of a man serving a prison term. He was innocent, but the chief jail official could not free him. Only one man in all England could do that. The clergyman paused. He asked if anyone could name the man. "Houdini," an alert youngster shouted.

Another handcuff performer, Carl Mysto, boasted he was far superior to Houdini. Harry was annoyed. Two years before, Mysto had written asking him to arrange an audition. He pulled the letter dated October 30, 1902, from his desk trunk and wrote at the top of it: "Carl Mysto at this time was working in pubs, doing magic and passing his hat. He was a tramp. I gave him a pair of pants and a few old shirts and half a dollar. He gave a trial show and did not make good. He was a common bum and a dirty one at that."

A Manchester theater manager was promoting Mysto. To build him as an attraction, the manager said that Houdini just got out of handcuffs, talked endlessly about his triumphs, then closed with the same old box trick. Mysto, on the other hand, talked little, gave an exciting show, and could be booked for ten pounds whereas Houdini demanded one hundred and fifty. Further, the manager asserted, Mysto performed a coffin escape that was beyond Houdini's powers.

Houdini, greatly upset, prepared a counterattack. He hired Reuben Shaw, the carpenter who had constructed Mysto's burial box, and for two pounds and ten shillings had him make an exact duplicate. Then, with Shaw on stage to vouch that he had built both coffins, Harry exposed Mysto's method.

Mysto was a cheat, Houdini shouted. The coffin was faked. He showed how short screws replaced long ones in one end. He pushed open the end to make his point. Houdini thundered that he could escape from the coffin even with the proper long screws holding the end. With all screws legitimately in place, he was shut up in the coffin where he proceeded to make good his claim.

The *Daily Mirror* of October 4, 1904, gave the story a big play. Houdini's reprisal brought the obscure Mysto a short-lived prominence. Almost overnight he was in demand by second-string theaters eager to cash in on his sudden notoriety. This in turn brought a rash of acts designed to expose the secrets of handcuff releases. Frank Hilbert, who had tried with little success to sell himself as an escape artist, became an exposer. Theaters that couldn't afford Houdini played Hilbert in opposition. Harry got out his old disguise kit.

He turned up during Hilbert's act in Cardiff wearing a gray beard and spectacles. A cane added realism to his "old man" impersonation. When Hilbert began his revelations, Harry shouted from the audience that Hilbert was a fraud, that he didn't know what he was talking about. The theater management took prompt action. Ushers seized the irate heckler and threw him out. Fuming, Houdini stormed to the police station and insisted he had been injured by the rough handling. An examination, however, proved that only his vanity had been wounded, and the police advised him not to file a complaint.

In April, Houdini and Hilbert were at opposition theaters in Newport. They applied to Chief Constable Sinclair for permission to test the cells of the police station jail. Sinclair offered his facilities to both men for the same time on the same day. Harry, his brother Theo, the manager of the Newport Lyceum, and several friends arrived at 4 p.m., the appointed hour. A crowd had gathered outside the station house eager to see the rivals meet face to face. Hilbert didn't appear.

After a brief wait for the missing Hilbert, the chief constable said Houdini could get to work. Harry stripped in one cell, left his clothes there, and was searched. He was locked in the adjoining cell. His clothes were locked in the original cell. The officials withdrew to another part of the building. In five minutes and thirty seconds Harry, fully dressed, rejoined the party. He informed the constable that on the way he had opened the massive iron gate which normally would block a prisoner's exit—even if he succeeded in fleeing from his cell.

By now the crowd outside the police station had grown in

size. Harry and his retinue drew cheers as they left. He
tipped his hat in acknowledgment and walked briskly to the
theater. The crowd followed him to the stage door and those
who could still find tickets to buy at the box office helped
pack the theater.

Despite the acts imitating his handcuff technique and those
who purported to reveal his methods, Harry continued to
break box-office records and to garner more free newspaper
space than any other performer in England. One of his most
ingenious ploys was to invite businesses to cast aspersions on
his trunk trick and challenge him to escape instead from their
own crates. This dare from Thomas & Edge, builders and
contractors, during his week at Woolwich was typical:

> Mr. Houdini.
> *Dear Sir*—Having witnessed your trunk trick, I am
> inclined to think it is NOT GENUINE and believe
> the box has been specially prepared for the trick. I
> should be glad if you would undertake to escape from
> a box made of one-inch deal in the form of a packing
> case securely put together and the LID NAILED
> DOWN BY ME and the box roped up on the stage.
> > *Yours truly,*
> > *H. D. Greenwood, manager*

Woolwich was peppered with thousands of HOUDINI
CHALLENGED handbills. These flamboyant throwaways
reproduced the letter and revealed Houdini's acceptance and
gave the time and place for the test. The last lines helped to
build up interest: "If unsuccessful, will forfeit fifty pounds to
the funds of the Cottage Hospital. (Signed) Harry Houdini."
Since the challenging businesses shared in the torrent of
publicity, there never was any shortage of baiters for the
act.

Harry's salary on the big circuits was $750 (£150) a
week. When he played an independent theater on percentage,
the figure frequently rose high above the $1,000 mark. On
February 18, 1905, Houdini jotted in his diary: "$2,150 clear
salary." This was his highest income to date for a single week.

Houdini's free time as usual was spent in searching for

data on early magicians and writing articles on his adventures for newspapers and magazines.

Whenever Harry performed near London he took the Sunday morning train in to visit with Evanion, the retired conjurer. Each trip he bought more of the old gentleman's marvelous collection of playbills and documents. Houdini was performing in Wigan when a letter from Mrs. Evanion informed him that her husband was near death in the Lambeth Infirmary. Houdini hurried to the hospital. Evanion could scarcely speak. His main worry was the welfare of his wife after he died. Harry assured him she would be provided for. Evanion's mind at rest, he said he had a surprise for his young friend. He had saved some of his treasures until the last possible moment. Now he gave Harry a magnificent array of Robert-Houdin's London playbills. Houdini called them "the central jewel in my collection."

When Evanion died, Houdini paid the funeral expenses and inserted a death notice in the papers. He was distressed that so few people came for the final rites. Not long afterward Mrs. Evanion died. Again Harry assumed responsibility for all the details.

While Houdini pioneered the straitjacket release as a challenge test, it was his brother, Theo Hardeen, who discovered its greatest dramatic potential. Two constables strapped Hardeen on the stage of the Swansea Empire in Wales. They put him into his cabinet and a committee from the audience surrounded the enclosure. One of the officers tried to peek between the curtains. Hardeen's assistant pulled him away. As time dragged by, the audience grew impatient. There was an occasional hoot or catcall. When, after fifteen minutes, Theo released himself, there was little applause. A constable expressed the thoughts of a large portion of the audience. He was not convinced, he said, that Hardeen could escape without outside help and he challenged Theo to repeat the test. Theo was in a quandary: No one believed that he had freed himself, yet if they strapped him up a second time that evening, sheer exhaustion would keep him a prisoner. He stepped to the footlights. If his challengers would return two nights later, he promised, he would escape without using the cabinet—*in full view of the audience*.

The theater was sold out when Hardeen was strapped into the formidable restraint for the second time. As his arms, encased in canvas, were tugged and secured, Theo said he would expect an apology from his detractors after he slipped free. The crowd cheered him on. Hardeen began his struggle, first kneeling, then rolling on the stage, twisting and turning as he, with sheer brute strength, forced his crossed arms over his head and worked on the buckles with his fingers through the canvas. The audience went wild. He squirmed, shrugged, and pushed the jacket over his head and off—to a mighty roar of mass approval.

The next day Theo mailed the newspaper accounts to his brother. Harry was impressed. What an idea! Why hadn't he thought of it? Of course this was the way to dramatize the straitjacket. His handcuff releases, box escapes, and the trunk illusion were done behind curtains. Let the spectators see the tremendous effort it took to get a jacket off. This could be more exciting than a wrestling match. Houdini tried the new presentation in March during his month at the Alhambra in Paris. The French police were still refusing to let him escape from their jails, so it was a welcome and successful new feature. In England it produced almost as much applause as his closing "Metamorphosis" substitution feat.

Houdini made a farewell speech after his last show in Leith, Scotland, on July 8. He was on his way back to America, he said. It had been five years since he had performed in his native land. The audience rose as one and gave him three rousing cheers. He changed to street clothes in his dressing room and made a final check of his packed equipment before it was loaded on the truck for the train to England and the transatlantic docks. His fans were massed by the stage door. Several men lifted him shoulder-high and jogged him through the town to the railway station. Others sang as the procession sped along—"And when ye go, will ye nae come back?"

Houdini was so moved by this demonstration that he "wept like a child."

AMERICA AGAIN

Robert Cunningham, who shortened his stage name, appropriately enough, to Cunning before he left his native Utah, was the most successful of the escapologists who played in American vaudeville during the five years that Houdini performed abroad. "I was born," he proclaimed, "in the wilds of the far west among the rocky mountains, where panthers sneak from rock to rock . . . where the coyote's howl echoes through the dark ravines, and where the rattlesnake's hiss is a common sound."

He claimed, with showman's license, that he had shown his feats in India, Tasmania, and New Zealand. At thirty, he was boasting: "Last year I met thirty-five hundred policemen and succeeded in removing the handcuffs placed on my wrists in every case." He billed himself as "The Jail Breaker" and used his own "jail," a portable steel cage, in his act.

Houdini and his brother Hardeen were in the audience on September 11, 1905, when Cunning appeared at Hyde and Behmen's Theater in Brooklyn. Hardeen was one of five men who brought manacles to the stage at Cunning's invitation. The fetters offered by the others were accepted. Cunning took one look at Theo's irons and refused to put them on. He used the Houdini line: "These cuffs are not regulation." Hardeen pulled a British fifty-pound banknote from his pocket and said it would go to charity if Cunning escaped from his cuffs. The theater manager came out from the wings. He offered to bet a hundred dollars of his own money that Cunning would succeed. Cunning shook his head and pushed the cuffs back in Hardeen's hands, thereby bringing on a wave of jeers and hoots from the audience. The fire curtain rumbled down. Someone took a punch at Hardeen. He struck back. For a moment it seemed that a free-for-all brawl would erupt. A policeman pushed his way through the melee, arrested Hardeen, and took him to the station house, where a disorderly conduct charge was entered against him. Houdini put up the bail money. The next day a judge heard the case. He dismissed it, commenting that it was obviously a publicity stunt.

Cunning sensed more trouble at Hurtig and Seamon's Music Hall on 125th Street in Harlem. He told his audience that one of his challengers was a rival's brother. The man insisted that his handcuffs be accepted. The audience shouted for Cunning to comply. Against his better judgment, the harassed Cunning agreed. He entered his "jail" with seven pairs of manacles locked on his wrists and arms. A cloth had been draped over the bars to form a cabinet. There was a long wait. Rowdy spectators yelled insults: "Drag him out" . . . "Come on, get it over with" . . . "Give him the hook."

When Cunning emerged, only one of his wrists was free. The challenger shouted: "I want my handcuffs back." Again there was bedlam. The asbestos curtain slammed down to the stage. The challenger tried to push through one side of the curtain. Stagehands shoved him back. He ran backstage. Four men grabbed him and hustled him out into the lobby. He waited until his irons were returned, then he shouted: "They're ruined. The teeth have been filed off." The manager of the theater had him arrested. When the case came up, the man was identified as William G. Weiss, of 278 West 113th Street. The charge was dismissed and Houdini's older brother went free.

Houdini's younger brother, Dr. Leopold Weiss, journeyed as far as New England plaguing handcuff performers with Harry's "defeater" cuffs. Houdini, who regarded himself as the originator of the challenge escape act, insisted that anyone else who tried it was a thief. If his imitators were so good, why shouldn't they escape from his manacles? He escaped from theirs!

To stir up excitement for his American opening, Harry devised a novel press stunt. The New York papers said that Houdini would compete with his pupil, Jacques Boudini (some spelled it Bondini), in an underocean escape contest. Each was wagering five hundred dollars on the outcome. The winner would take all. The tugboat *Fred B. Dalzell* chugged out into the Atlantic basin at 3 p.m. on September 20. The competitors were shackled hand and foot, tied to ropes, and dropped overboard.

For a minute and thirty seconds newsmen and photographers saw only the ripples of the ocean's waves. Then Houdini's head surfaced. He spat out a stream of water. "Is Boudini up yet?" "No," came a shout from the boat. Harry surged up, waved his hands to show they were free, then sank out of view. A minute later Houdini bobbed up again. He gasped for breath, looked around, then submerged again. Another minute. Harry reappeared. "Boudini up yet?" He laughed when he heard the answer and kicked a leg in the air to demonstrate one of his ankles was free. Down again. Another minute. Houdini, completely free of his bonds, swam to the side of the boat and was lifted aboard.

Boudini, "more dead than alive," was retrieved at the end of his safety rope. His manacles were still in place. After artificial respiration, he opened his eyes and mumbled: "I swallowed some water." The tug steamed back to the dock. Two of the reporters aboard thought the contest was simply a showcase for Houdini's skill. But that didn't matter. It was the sort of story that people liked to read.

Houdini opened at the Colonial Theater in Manhattan on October 2. The years of steady work in Europe had sharpened his showmanship, honed his timing. His dynamic manner won the audience completely. After two weeks at the Colonial and two more at the Orpheum in Brooklyn, he went on tour. Business was tremendous in Detroit, Cleveland, Rochester, and Buffalo, but it wasn't until he played Washington that he hit the publicity jackpot.

His escape from the United States Jail, January 6, 1906, had all the elements of a great press story. The cell in which Houdini was locked had held Charles J. Guiteau, the assassin of President Garfield. The naked escapologist shared it briefly with its regular tenant Walter Hamilton, a Negro who had been sentenced for smothering his wife. Houdini was out in two minutes and off on the wildest escapade ever carried out in the federal prison. He speedily opened all the cells on "Murderers' Row" and moved the convicts like pawns in a human chess game. The inmates, shocked by the sudden appearance of the nude cellbreaker, meekly followed his orders. Richard Chase, who was serving a ten-year term for manslaughter, asked hesitantly: "Have you come to let me out?" Then he stared at the stranger in the raw and gulped: "What are you doing without clothes?" He didn't resist when

Harry pulled him across the corridor and locked him where Clarence Hewlett, a burglar, had been. Hewlett he put in Chase's cell.

With the housing plan of the cell block completely changed, Houdini dressed and walked blithely to the office where Warden Harris, his staff, and the reporters waited. The whole operation had taken less than twenty-seven minutes. Two signed statements verified his feat—one by the warden, the other by Major Richard Sylvester, the prison superintendent.

Sylvester's document said in part: "The experiment was a valuable one in that the department has been instructed as to the adoption of further security which will protect any lock from being opened or interfered with." Houdini's suggestions effectively blocked any future rival who might try to duplicate his feat.

Harry's return to Boston was heralded with lithographs picturing his exploits in Germany, Holland, and Russia. Advance stories told how he had escaped from the *Mirror* handcuffs in London and the United States Jail in Washington. He had enjoyed a three-week run at Keith's before he sailed to England in 1900; now he stayed for seven. New features kept the theater packed. One night he was enclosed in a locked-and-strapped barrel. The iron-hooped barrel was pushed into a wooden cell. The cell's door was padlocked. In five minutes Houdini walked through the drapes of the covering canopy. Committeemen reported that the padlock on the cell door was still locked. It was opened. The barrel was pulled out. Harry emphasized that straps and locks were still in place. The top of the barrel was removed. Inside was Houdini's black-moustached Austrian assistant, Franz Kukol.

His packing-box releases produced amusing conjectures in the Boston papers. One woman thought that Bess, concealed in the top of the cabinet which covered the box, used a powerful magnet to remove the nails. Another spectator insisted that Houdini never left the box, but that he had a double who took the applause. This, despite the fact that the challenge boxes were always taken immediately to the lobby when the act was over so that anyone could examine them.

A challenge from the Wakefield Rattan Company resulted in Harry, wearing three pairs of handcuffs, being placed in an iron-bound wicker hamper. The top was fastened at five points with as many locks. Marked paper wafers were pasted on the keyholes. Then a steel chain was locked around the hamper and it was bound by rope. An hour and two minutes later Houdini was out. There was no evidence that any of the fastenings had been disturbed.

One night Houdini revived the needle-swallowing-and-threading trick he had learned at the Chicago World's Fair. Another, he escaped from a chair to which he had been tied with fifty feet of strong rope.

Houdini's most publicized Boston escape was made March 19 from the Tombs. He broke from Cell 60, entered Cell 77, where he dressed; then, instead of going to the superintendent's office he ran across the prison yard, climbed the Somerset Street wall, vaulted an iron railing, and hustled through the snow to his dressing room at the theater. He phoned the Tombs. The startled newsmen insisted that he come back to the prison so that photographs of the exploit could be made for the papers.

Between shows one night he went to Cambridge and performed in Harvard Union. He wriggled out of handcuffs, a straitjacket, and a roped chair. As he sped back to Keith's, the students were cutting the rope into tiny pieces and distributing them as souvenirs.

Houdini gave a lecture performance at the Boston Athletic Club, Sunday afternoon, March 25. He talked of his travels, displayed a lock which the governor of Tomsk, Russia, had given him. A concealed bell in its casing rang when it was opened. This was the inspiration for the Houdini Bell Lock Handcuffs, which set off an interior alarm when an escape was made from them.

He was critical of the people who believed that Hindus worked miracles. Anyone could do their feats—with practice. He pushed a long steel needle through his cheek without drawing blood to illustrate what he meant. There was no deception involved. Houdini had learned the feat during his dime museum days. His straitjacket escape brought the audience of 1,680 spectators up from their seats for a standing ovation.

He was given a head-to-toe examination after the show by Dr. J. E. Rourke, anatomist of the Massachusetts General Hospital. The doctor, who had examined Sandow, the strong man, and other physical prodigies, was eager to see how

Houdini's arduous work had affected his body. He pronounced Harry in excellent shape. He had only one qualification: Houdini's arms were too hard for the tissue to be healthy. Dr. Rourke said there was a distinct possibility that the escape king would eventually become muscle-bound.

Houdini's "birthday" matinee was a gala event. The theater manager sent up a giant pair of handcuffs made of flowers. Then he presented his record-shattering headliner a token of B. F. Keith's esteem—a thousand-dollar Tiffany pocket watch.

Despite his full schedule, Harry found time in Boston to publish a book. In *The Right Way to Do Wrong* he revealed methods of burglars, pickpockets, bunco men, and spirit mediums. He told how a clever British thief walked backward in the snow. Only footprints coming away from the scene of the crime were found. He explained how a woman embedded a diamond in a wad of chewing gum and stuck it under the counter of a jewel shop as she was shown a tray of gems. She was suspected of theft and searched. Later an accomplice scraped up the loot as he leaned against the counter.

After warning his readers how easily a burglar could force his way into their homes, Houdini gave this advice: "The best of all fastenings for the bedroom or other inner door is a simple wedge of wood pushed under the bottom of a door." With this in place an intruder is stopped, unless he cuts away a section of the door.

Harry even worked in a boost for his brother Leopold: "Dr. L. P. Weiss of New York discovered that he could detect a fake mummy from an original by placing it under his X-Ray machine."

Whitman Osgood, an enterprising promoter and newspaperman, aided Houdini in the writing and editing of the book; now he suggested that the escapologist tour with his own show. Why let the circuits take the major share of Houdini's profits?

"Mr. Whitman Osgood presents, for a Limited Tour of the United States, HOUDINI, The World's Handcuff King and ONLY Prison Breaker with Houdini's Own Company of Internationally Celebrated Entertainers and Startling Sensationalists," the new fliers proclaimed. The route included Hartford, Newark, and other eastern cities.

When the show played the Auditorium Theater in Baltimore, it opened with the Kita-Muras—"Oriental Ambidexterity." Marshall & King followed with their "Grotesque Terpsichorean Diversity." The Mysterious Zancigs offered "A Triumphant Demonstration of the Actuality of Telepathy." Miss Anna Chandler, "The Broadway Favorite in her Popular Musical Diversion," preceded the star—"The Mysteriarch Houdini, The Greatest Sensation of England and America in his Preliminary Science Baffling Substitutional Phenomenon. The Prison Cell and Barrel Transposition."

After the intermission the Japanese jugglers returned with a new routine, followed by a comedy act, Louise Carver and Eugenie Pollard. Houdini closed with his challenge escapes from handcuffs and leg irons.

In May, Houdini announced that his road show was closing for the summer, but would reopen in August. By the time August arrived, however, he had decided to return to vaudeville and was occupied by another project. Long annoyed because the *Sphinx*, an American magic monthly, had given minimal space to his activities, and eager to begin his long-delayed history of magic, he became the editor-publisher of his own periodical. The first issue of the *Conjurers' Monthly Magazine* was dated September 15, 1906. In its pages Houdini attacked Robert-Houdin, the French magician who had been his boyhood idol. When the widow of Emile Robert-Houdin refused to meet him in Paris and the magician's daughter was too busy to greet him in Blois, Houdini had been hurt. But Harry's new opinion of Robert-Houdin was not based entirely upon emotion. His recent research had undercut the Frenchman's reputation. Alexander Heimburger, asserting that the famous autobiography was in fact the product of a ghost-writer, contended that Robert-Houdin was not worthy of the title "The Father of Modern Magic." This view was shared by T. Bolin, in Moscow, and by Houdini himself, who discovered, while going through old programs purchased from Evanion, that many of the feats presented as innovations by Robert-Houdin had been performed by earlier magicians. Harry, who previously had wanted to be "like Robert-Houdin," now regretted that he had taken Houdini as a stage name. He lashed out against his ex-hero, declaring in the monthly that Robert-Houdin "was not original . . . only a little bit better than average entertainer."

Houdini also used the initial issue of the monthly as a platform to attack *The Old and the New Magic,* a new book by Henry Ridgely Evans. The volume undoubtedly angered Houdini because it quoted an explanation of the handcuff-release act from the British *Strand* magazine. In this review Houdini said Evans' work was "full of bad mistakes, misstatements and a great deal of worthless material."

Other features of the new monthly included the first installment of Houdini's own treatise, "Handcuff Secrets Exposed," revealing the methods of his "would-be imitators in various parts of the world." His brother Hardeen sent a column of news from London, while Harry, under his old pseudonym, "Herr N. Osey," covered activities on the Continent.

To show that he could take criticism as well as give it, he published a letter that had been sent to him at Keith's in Boston in April: "You are advertised as if you intended to expose some evil in astrology, clairvoyance, mediumship, etc. . . . Fake mediums are not any worse than a mechanical fake magician. I have seen you perform once, but what good are you to society?" The writer, A. F. Hill, had been prompted to write by Houdini's ads for his book *The Right Way to Do Wrong.*

Eight days before the publication date of his new magazine, Houdini suffered a more painful barb. The New York *Sun* ran a short account of his escape from the Yorkville police court jail. The officers there, the story said, watched Houdini through a peephole. They saw him take something from between the toes of his right foot and use it, as he reached his arm through bars to open the Yale lock on the cell door.

Someone mailed the clipping to Dr. A. M. Wilson, the editor of the *Sphinx,* in Kansas City. Wilson, who resented Harry's new competitive magazine, duly printed the story. To Wilson's way of thinking, Houdini was just an upstart who used the pages of his magazine to disparage his rivals and to destroy the reputation of the man from whom he had taken his name. Wilson, who had some talent himself for hurling invective, said that Houdini was "swelling out his chest like a pouter pigeon, protruding his abdomen like a cormorant and dropping calumny from his lips like the malodorous emanations from the glands of a Mustelidae mephitis."

The public did not share Wilson's opinion. Five times as many people saw Houdini in Pittsburgh in October 1906 at the Grand Theater as were attracted to Ethel Barrymore's performances at the Nixon Theater in Barrie's *Alice-Sit-by-the-Fire*. His offstage publicity kept his name in the news. In the course of a naked jailbreak at the Allegheny Central Police Station, Houdini switched a deserter from the 11th U.S. Infantry from one cell to another. The soldier gaped at the nude intruder and asked where he had left his clothes. Harry replied: "I pawned them."

At the Chase Theater in Washington, D.C., Houdini extended the scope of his stage challenges. He escaped from a giant paper bag and a zinc-lined Knabe piano case as well as the usual packing crates. After he left town Maurice Joyce, a physical culture teacher, drew a large audience at the Columbia Theater by advertising that he would reveal Houdini's methods. Joyce claimed that the wooden boxes had been faked to Houdini's specifications. Spokesmen for Saks & Company and S. Kann Sons & Company, the builders of the challenge containers, branded Joyce a liar. Joyce stated that the escape artist had used a specially made, double-sided paper bag. George F. Killian, whose firm issued the dare, answered that the bag had not been gimmicked in any way. It was made under his personal supervision from a single sheet of paper.

BRIDGE LEAPS AND
WATER CANS

A tempestuous week began November 26, 1906, at the Temple Theater in Detroit. Houdini refused Patrolman Alphonse Baker's challenge handcuffs. They were not in proper working order, having been rigged to defeat him, Harry said. The audience shouted for him to try them anyway.

As Harry walked, manacled, to his cabinet he spotted Harrison L. Davies in an upper box. "Is this your work?" the thirty-two-year-old showman shouted. Davies, a bookkeeper for the Art Glove Company and a part-time magician, shook his head. Houdini began a struggle which lasted an hour and thirty-five minutes. Long before he was free, Bess, in tears, left the stage. The Detroit *Journal* reported that her tears gave way to hysterics in the dressing room. As Houdini returned the cuffs to the police officer, he asked if they were his personal manacles. No, Baker replied, another Detroiter had asked him to take them to the stage.

Deputy Sheriff James V. Cunningham offered one hundred dollars to anyone who could make a successful break from the Wayne County Jail. Houdini inspected the cell block. When he saw that a single sliding bar locked every cell in the row, he knew escape was impossible without outside aid. He could pick a lock that could be reached through the bars, but when the control lever was at the end of the corridor he was helpless.

To save face he announced he would make a bridge leap. Tuesday morning Houdini and Franz Kukol, his assistant, went to the police storage barn and borrowed a coil of heavy rope. There he wrote a hasty will on the back of an envelope: "I give it all to Bess." Several officers added their names below his signature as witnesses. He passed the envelope to Kukol for safekeeping. Despite the winter weather, many Detroiters on their lunch hour came to the Belle Island Bridge to see the spectacle.

Harry stood by the railing, stripped off all his clothes except his trousers. He shivered in the raw November wind as two pairs of police handcuffs were locked on his wrists and one end of the safety rope was tied around his waist. He poised briefly for the photographers, then jumped into the cold water twenty-five feet below.

A mighty gasp went up from the crowd on the bridge and the shore as his body plummeted through the air and vanished beneath the surface of the river. There were cheers as he surfaced, waved the released bonds, and swam several yards to a waiting boat.

His wife hadn't known of the bridge jump until a happy but wet Houdini returned to their room at the Ste. Clair Hotel. Bess was furious. A bridge leap in warm weather was bad enough; on a bitterly cold day it was ridiculous. If he had no regard for himself, he might at least consider her. Her tirade over, she helped him undress and change to dry clothes. That afternoon at the Temple Theater the packed house, attracted by the stories of the underwater release, saw Houdini escape from a challenge packing case in nine minutes.

The date listed for the Belle Island Bridge leap in Houdini's souvenir books is December 2 and the temperature given is zero. It was made November 27. Though that day was cold, the mercury was well above the freezing mark. The compiler had perhaps taken the later date from the Sunday newspaper story which summed up Houdini's exploits for the week.

Houdini himself is responsible for the most frequently retold fable about this feat. The river, he said, was frozen over. A hole had been cut in the surface so that he could enter the water. After releasing his hands, he rose toward the surface but was unable to find the hole in the ice. Refusing to panic, however, he turned his head sideways to inhale air trapped between the ice and the water. Then he swam in ever-widening circles until he found the opening. Bess gave biographer Harold Kellock another fictional detail. She said she heard a newsboy shout that Houdini had died under the river moments before he walked into their hotel room.

And to make matters more confusing, Houdini in later

years occasionally changed the locale of his "under-ice escape" in articles and newspaper interviews. Sometimes he said it had taken place in Pittsburgh.

The night Houdini opened at the Temple Theater in Detroit, Russell Grose, a young Canadian handcuff artist, performed at a rival house, the Crystal Theater. Sid Eliot, the Detroit *Times* critic, wrote that Grose was "unquestionably better" than Houdini. He had been locked in the handcuffs that held Houdini an hour and thirty-five minutes and succeeded in releasing himself in seven minutes.

Houdini noted that as the Temple didn't advertise in the *Times*, that paper was always critical of its headliners.

The news that Grose would try for Deputy Sheriff Cunningham's hundred-dollar prize at the Wayne County Jail produced an uninvited spectator—Houdini. The policemen who searched Grose prior to his incarceration neglected to probe between the Canadian's toes. Harry reached down and pried them apart. There was nothing concealed.

Then Houdini pulled a lock from his pocket and said he would fasten it on the door to the enclosure which surrounded the cells. J. J. Nash, the manager of the Crystal Theater, objected. So did the police. This was Grose's stunt, not Houdini's. They told him to mind his own business.

Escape from the cell was impossible, Houdini insisted, unless the police helped Grose break out. He waved five hundred dollars in bills. The Canadian could have the money, Harry yelled, if Grose could pass through the door fastened with his lock. The officers ignored him. Grose was put in a cell at 11:35 a.m. Deputy Sheriff Cunningham threw the lever which locked the cell row. Harry attempted to put his padlock on the outer door. Cunningham stopped him. "I'm running this jail," he roared. He ordered Houdini to leave. "I take back my five-hundred-dollar offer," was Harry's parting comment.

A newspaper reported that Grose stayed behind bars an hour, then called for the police to release him. Houdini's own *Conjurers' Monthly* made two references to the exciting week in Detroit. One, a news item in small type, noted that Grose, who had been playing at the "Crystal Ten-Cent Theater," labored two hours before admitting defeat in the county jail and "he tried again the following morning and again failed."

The other, in larger type, reproduced a letter to Houdini from the manager of the Temple Theater. "This is to certify that you have during your engagement . . . broken all existing records of the theater for attendance . . . the record you have just broken was made by yourself on a previous engagement."

Louis Paul, a Midwestern escape artist, challenged Houdini with Tower and Lyons cuffs at the Majestic Theater in Chicago in December. Harry convinced the audience that the manacles were fixed. He in turn challenged Paul to escape from an "untampered-with" pair. Paul refused and was hooted offstage. A man who identified himself as a special detective from the Central Police Station offered irons which Houdini examined and approved. Harry turned so that the man could manacle his hands behind his back. He worked for an hour and a half before he released himself. The theater, which usually closed at ten thirty, stayed open that night until midnight. Once free, Houdini examined the cuffs again. The closer he looked, the madder he got. He showed the audience how an extra rivet had almost prevented his escape. "You changed cuffs!" he accused. Other members of the committee on stage seized the man and searched him. They produced a second, matching pair, from his pocket.

"For years there has not been such a sensation as Houdini," the Chicago *Daily News* reported. "His coming into the ranks of vaudeville brings a new light which is not likely to be extinguished by the army of imitators, of apes, of envious fakers." Richard Mansfield, the actor, was entranced by the feverish action. Madame Schumann-Heink admitted she had never seen anything in the opera to match his dramatics. Anna Held practically swooned as Harry, after almost an hour, mastered a challenge dry-goods box with grooved boards which had been glued together, then nailed. *"Oh, mon Dieu—quelle horreur. N'est-ce pas magnifique!"* she cried.

Amy Leslie, the critic, described the straitjacket release: "He battled with the canvas prison, tore at its leather and writhed, squirmed, crept and twisted like a tortured thing of muscles and emotion and no bones. Suddenly George Ade turned to me when I imagined I was most calm and said, 'Gee, you're having a worse time than Houdini.' "

The University of Pennsylvania football team was matched against Houdini on the stage of Keith's Chestnut Street

Theater in Philadelphia on January 4, 1907. The entire squad, in gridiron uniform, jogged down the aisle with a giant football and lifted it up behind the footlights. Then they manacled Houdini, bent him double to fit inside the opening of the ball. The pigskin was laced with a brass chain and padlocked. Harry was out in thirty-five minutes.

Back at Keith's in Boston for the last three weeks of the month, Houdini was bound to a ladder by five men who spent fifteen minutes chaining and locking him in place. Escape time: seven minutes. When he was rebooked in February, six riveters sealed him in a galvanized-iron boiler. The sealing-in process with blowtorches spurting flames was a show in itself. A full hour passed before Harry emerged, his face and hands and clothes covered with soot, his stiff collar gone, his hair wildly disheveled. Another night, employees of the Derby Desk Company pushed a six-foot-long rolltop desk on stage. They removed the upper storing compartments and blotter rack, put the handcuffed performer inside. The rolltop was locked at eight minutes past ten. Shortly before eleven Houdini added another victory to his list.

The coast-to-coast route in 1907 brought Houdini in proximity to a former friend who now claimed eminence as a handcuff artist. The San Francisco *Chronicle* reviewed the act: "Hail to Brindamour, who has the audacity to call himself the 'King of All the Handcuff Kings' at the Princess Theater with Houdini showing next door. . . . Brindamour is not as good an actor as Houdini. . . . the police force seems to have ignored him, so the spectacle of bluecoats climbing over the footlights with a pair of handcuffs from the city prison was denied."

When Houdini first met Brindamour (George W. Brown) in Woonsocket, Rhode Island, he was a professional photographer, dance teacher, and part-time conjurer. "He could no more pick a lock than the Czar of Russia will give the Russian newspapers the right of free press," Harry gibed. To prove the point, he brandished a clipping from the San Francisco *Examiner* of October 15, 1907. It told of Brindamour's last performance in Sacramento the night before. T. J. Coonky had fastened him in leg irons from the city jail.

An impatient audience gave catcalls and tattooed on the floor with their canes for thirty minutes. Then Brindamour appeared with the irons off. *They had been sawed open with a steel file!*

On the opening day of a two-week engagement at the Columbia Theater in St. Louis, the manager bluntly informed Houdini that his act wouldn't mean a thing at the box office. Receipts for the first week must have been far below par. Harry opened the second week, January 27, 1908, with the new blockbuster mystery he had been holding in reserve for just such an emergency.

A committee probed a large, airtight, galvanized-iron container. It was similar in shape to the milk cans dairies supply to farmers but capacious enough to hold a man. While the can was being filled with water, Houdini made an offstage change to a bathing suit. He announced, before he entered the can, that a man can live only a short time under water, "deprived of life-sustaining air." He would first demonstrate his ability to remain under water longer than a normal man. If the spectators wished to test how long, they could hold their breath; they should start the moment his head was submerged. He mounted the tapered top of the can, put his feet in the water, raised his hands over his head and slid inside the narrow opening. Water spilled over the sides. Extra bucketfuls were added to fill the can to the top.

As Harry faded from view, most onlookers held their breath. Within thirty seconds the majority was gasping for air. Still he remained submerged. After a minute passed, it was a rare athlete who still had control. Long after the final gasp on the other side of the footlights, Houdini still was submerged. His endurance feat alone produced mighty applause. But the most thrilling part was yet to come.

Houdini's wrists were handcuffed. Again he slid down under the water. Once more additional liquid was added to compensate for the overspill. Quickly the top of the can was jammed in place, then secured with six padlocks. A cabinet was pushed forward to cover the receptacle and the curtains were closed. The orchestra played: "Many brave hearts lie asleep in the deep. Sailor, beware; sailor, take care." Time ticked by. Thirty seconds. One minute. *Ninety* seconds. Eyes suddenly were diverted as Franz Kukol appeared with a fire ax in his hands. He walked quickly to the side of the cabinet, put his ear to the cloth, then gripped the ax more firmly. Two minutes. The tension was almost unbearable.

Two minutes and a half. Nervous women bit their lips. Men furrowed their brows. Three minutes. Something must have gone wrong. Any second the assistant would slash the curtains and cut into the can to give Houdini air. Kukol raised the ax to a striking position. At this moment the smiling, dripping-wet Houdini stepped out to accept a rafter-shaking ovation.

Jubilant with the success of his new feature, Harry had a shock awaiting him in Cleveland. When he saw the billboards outside the theater, he couldn't believe it. At the top was "Mr. Julius Steger." He read on. The actor would appear in a dramatic sketch, "The Fifth Commandment." His eyes dropped to the bottom of the bill. There his name appeared. It was larger than Steger's, but the week was ruined for him.

He had another jolt later in New York when he read the review of his act in the *American*. Alan Dale, the critic who had seen him at the Alhambra in London while on vacation abroad and who had panned him there, was after him again. Harry pasted the scathing review in a scrapbook along with his glowing notices, to read whenever he felt he was getting too self-satisfied or complacent:

The "famous" Houdini is a clever manipulator of handcuffs who appears to suffer in the very worst way from that terrible and baffling disease—the swollen head. Houdini devoted the greater part of his "turn" to talking about himself in a cheap and rather pitiful way. It was all as dull as ditch water. A good deal of his poor talk was "gallery play"—what a hard time he had of it in England, how they hated to see him earning money over there, how cruelly jealous they were of him in Blackburn, but that he'd go back there and get more money. If he doesn't do a better turn in Blackburn than he did here in Harlem, I don't fancy that he'll succeed in his design of "getting more money." This was all piffle and sad piffle.

Years ago I saw this really clever young man in London and was delighted with what I saw, but now it all seems spoiled. Even the particularly effective trick in which Houdini is apparently padlocked into a huge can of water, from which he successfully "emerges" in his cabinet, is marred by the offensive manners of the man.

Far from being "delighted" in London, Dale had written that he "preferred Houdini's literature to his turn." He also said the handcuff escapes were "spoiled for me" because they were made under the cover of a cabinet.

By now the Water Can was solidly established as the new climax of his act, but Houdini continued to accept special challenges to attract repeat audiences. There seemed no end to the unlikely restraints from which he freed himself—a government mail pouch, a transparent box put together by the Pittsburgh Plate Glass Company, even a man-size sausage skin. In April during Automobile Carnival Week in New York, he fought his way clear of an enmeshment of eight Weed "Tire Grip" chains, two rubber tires and various padlocks, handcuffs and leg irons. The chain firm was so pleased with the publicity that appeared in newspapers and magazines that it bought the back page ad on Houdini's souvenir program and arranged for their Philadelphia branch to issue a similar challenge when he returned to Keith's Chestnut Street Theater.

Harry's jump from the Market Street Bridge was witnessed by ten thousand, according to the Philadelphia *North American*. The front-page story, May 15, 1908, carried the head: HOUDINI SHACKLED, LEAPS INTO RIVER, ALMOST DROWNED. Mayor John Edgar Reyburn was caricatured on a bridge ready for a leap, bound by strips labeled: "Depleted Treasury," "Extravagant Financing," and "Exhausted Revenues." He was smiling confidently as he said: "Oh, everything'll be all right."

The "almost drowned" was explained in the article. There was an unusually long wait—a minute and nineteen seconds —before Houdini surfaced. Gustave Olson, one of Houdini's assistants, who had been with him on the seven previous bridge jumps, started to strip off his clothes and dive from his boat a moment before Houdini appeared. Harry showed no signs of any unusual strain. He swam a few quick strokes, rolled onto his back, flaunted the handcuffs and chains, then made for the rowboat.

"And how those excited thousands did cheer and the tugs

added their noise to the din. It was a spontaneous outburst
of relief," the Philadelphia paper's story ran. "After all, there
is nothing in life, paradoxically perhaps, which man so loves
to see as his fellow man risking his life in an encounter with
death."

During his two weeks at Keith's in Boston earlier in May,
Houdini had been busy promoting another book. His *Conjurers' Monthly* articles lambasting Robert-Houdin had been
expanded into a 319-page, cloth-bound diatribe. He took space
in the *Sunday Herald* to advertise the volume. Handbills of
the type that usually announced his challenge escapes were
distributed through the streets and in the theater lobby:

HOUDINI

Challenges the Reading Public

I want every Bostonian who has seen my performance
at Keith's Theater to read my new book, *The Unmasking
of Robert-Houdin*. First, because the truth about magic
was never told until this book was written. I have proved
to Boston that my stage challenges are genuine. I now
challenge the reading public to find one mis-representa-
tion in *The Unmasking of Robert-Houdin* or, in all the
literature of magic, one book that can compare with
mine.

In the paragraphs that followed, he told of the years he had
searched for data in Europe and his conviction that the French
conjurer "had so cleverly and unscrupulously robbed dead-
and-gone magicians of all credit for their inventions and
accomplishments." Houdini's biased attack boomeranged. He
succeeded in adding to Robert-Houdin's fame and made himself the target of sizzling rebuttals from conjuring scholars,
who listed his many errors of fact and reasoning. The book,
which he published himself, is valuable, however, for the many
historic handbills and illustrations which he reproduced to
"document" his conclusions.

Bess arrived late for Harry's jump from the Harvard Bridge
into the Charles River on May 1, 1908. She pushed her way
through the crowd and tried to go onto the pier. A patrolman
stopped her. She explained she was Houdini's wife. "Lady,"

the officer snapped, "that gag don't go. You're the ninth wife of his that has tried to pass here in ten minutes. It'll take you a marriage certificate to get through these lines."

When Houdini entertained at Harvard Union this time, he brought along his Water Can. As he stripped to a pair of blue trunks there was a roar of disapproval. Yale blue at Cambridge! "Wear Harvard crimson," came the shouts. Harry, the showman, calmly stripped off his shorts and amazed his all-male audience by escaping from the water-filled canister in the raw.

At the annual meeting of the Society of American Magicians in New York in June, Houdini was elected vice-president. A few weeks later he resigned from the organization. Most members thought he severed his relations with the society because the S.A.M. would not name his *Conjurers' Monthly Magazine* as its official organ. This was a contributing factor, but the immediate cause was a line in the *S.A.M. Yearbook*.

While he was in Dresden, Houdini had visited the grave of Bosco, the great Italian magician. No one had tended the grounds in years. He bought the plot and sent the deed with his compliments to the Society of American Magicians. The *S.A.M. Yearbook* noted a "member" had taken this action, but neglected to mention him by name.

Two years to the month after the *Conjurers' Monthly Magazine* first appeared, it ceased publication. The editor-publisher and his wife sailed for Germany on August 10, 1908. When Cecilia Weiss returned from the docks, she wound the grandfather clock in the living room of the house on West 113th Street. It remained mute while her son was at home. Now when she heard it chime and strike the hour, she knew that each minute that passed would hasten his return to her.

CHALLENGING CHALLENGES

The challenge handcuff routine was missing when Houdini opened at the Circus Busch in Berlin in September 1908. Nor was he ever to feature it again; the army of imitators around the world had destroyed its commercial value. Now his features were out-in-the-open straitjacket releases and the dramatic escape from the liquid-filled, padlocked Water Can. Between the two he could take a breather by bringing up swallowed needles on a long thread and still be assured of show-stopping applause.

Five Chinese sailors—Ng Yong, Ching Chun, Wang Yonn, Youn Chang, and Chang Youn—sent Harry his most unusual challenge at the Oxford Theatre in London in November. When the letter wasn't answered, they went to the *Star*. The newspaper reported that the challenge was in Chinese and a yard long. When translated, it defied the escape king to release himself from a *"Sanguaw."* This, it developed, was a torture device used to punish criminals in China. In its most vicious form the victims' feet were nailed to vertical shafts of wood while leather straps held their bodies motionless and a chain from an upper crossbar garroted their necks.

The day after the challenge was printed in English, Harry said he would accept it if his feet weren't nailed and two doctors were on stage to ensure that he was not strangled during his release attempt. He also specified he would have to inspect the device and that if he didn't succeed in escaping in full view, he must be given the opportunity to complete his struggle in a private room.

He went with a *Star* reporter to Limehouse to view the torture instrument. Apparently it met with his approval, for on the next night, Friday, November 20, the five Orientals, in western clothes but wearing pigtails, set up the *"Sanguaw"* on the Oxford stage. Attached to a solid base were two slanting posts which supported a crossbar considerably wider than the base. The structure resembled an inverted triangle. The seamen crossed Houdini's feet and strapped his ankles with a thick leather strap. Four chains extended in as many directions from this strap and were pulled taut and nailed at the far ends to the floor. Harry's neck was encircled by a tangle of rusty chains. The chains were tightened and the ends were nailed to the extremities of the upper crossbar. Finally his wrists were strapped together and the far ends of the chains attached to the strap were nailed to the tapering sides of the structure.

Five minutes of strenuous maneuvering succeeded only in yanking a nail, which held a chain to the upright, out of place. The nail was pounded back in the wood and the struggle began again. Bit by bit, he managed to ease his left foot out of his shoe. The shoe clattered to the stage. Next the right shoe fell. He uncrossed his ankles in the strap which wound them and pulled his left foot up and out. Now his right foot was free too. The strap and chains banged down on the floor. With an agile leap, he swung his body until he caught the top bar between his legs. He pulled himself up until he was astride the bar. Perched precariously, he got to work with his teeth on the buckles of the strap which enclosed his hands. When his hands slipped out, he used them to loosen his neck from the rusty chains and jumped down to the stage—just sixteen minutes after he had been trussed in place. He assured the *Star* reporter he would never accept a *"Sanguaw"* torture test again.

On November 11, Houdini accepted another challenge for an escape to be made in full view. He was strapped, laced, and roped to a "Crazy Crib" by three men who had worked as attendants in London insane asylums. He had seen his first "Crazy Crib" in 1896 in the same St. John, New Brunswick, institution where the struggles of an inmate with a straitjacket had inspired him to try the release on a stage. At that time he had also devised a method of escape when shackled to a bed with handcuffs and leg irons. In those days he thought a canopy was necessary to hide his struggles from the audience. Now his contortions provoked as much excitement as his out-in-the-open straitjacket feat.

Some two weeks later six suffragettes wrapped Houdini in sheets and bound him to a mattress with bandages. Once the girls were sure he was securely tied, one of them bent and kissed him. That was probably the only time the he-man challenge-defier blushed on any stage.

If Houdini had any doubts as to how he would be received in England with his new act, they were soon dispelled. Following his run at the Oxford Theatre, he broke box-office records again at the Euston Theatre in another part of London. He accepted a challenge from William Jordan & Sons on December 2 and escaped from one of their milk churns rather than his usual Water Can. Two nights later he took on a test with a safe.

Subsequent accounts of this escape have distorted it almost beyond recognition. It has been written that the safe was so heavy that braces had to be erected under the stage to support it and that it was large enough to hold three standing men. The release, one legend has it, took Houdini "forty-five minutes."

Actually, the safe was a small one. To quote J. R. Paul's letter to Houdini, it was: "A genuine old burglar-proof safe, weighing about eight cwt., which will easily hold a human being." As to the time Houdini required to get out, in the escapologist's own words, "I escaped in fourteen minutes."

Houdini jumped from the upper deck of a tugboat into the Mersey River, Liverpool, on December 7, weighted down with twenty-two pounds of chains and irons. He was up in forty-five seconds. The next week in Birmingham he dived from a houseboat, moored in the Edgbaston Reservoir, during a driving rainstorm and divested himself of his manacles in forty-two seconds.

In Scotland the Dundee police refused permission for Harry to jump from the parapet of Tay Bridge. Hundreds of spectators were lined along the West Protection Wall and the Esplanade. Rather than disappoint them, Harry boarded the pleasure steamer *Marchioness of Bute*, and, after being chained and manacled, dived from the ship's bridge. He was free and above water in thirty seconds.

During his engagement at the Alhambra in Paris in April 1909, still frustrated because the police would not allow him to make escape attempts from their jails, Houdini dispatched letters to the press and theater managers inviting them to gather at the Pont de l'Archevêché. Shortly before 3 p.m. a car drove up. Out stepped Harry, a French private detective, and several reporters. Houdini pulled off his coat, trousers, tie, shirt, shoes, and stockings. Clad now in a swimsuit, he extended his hands. The detective shackled them, locked a chain around his neck. His assistants erected a folding ladder and in seconds Harry was atop the wall of the Paris Morgue. He jumped up and down, yelled and waved his manacled arms. Soon thousands of puzzled Frenchmen were pointing out the madman on the morgue to their neighbors. Still and movie cameramen with the Houdini party set up their equipment and focused in. Excited watchers were calling for the police as Houdini leaped off the wall and plunged into the muddy waters of the Seine. Once the cameramen had recorded the escape, Harry swam ashore, slipped into an overcoat, took his place in the car, and was whisked away.

Returning to England, Houdini was seen in early June by Harry Rickards, the leading Australian vaudeville impresario, who was in London on a booking expedition. Rickards caught Houdini's show at the Chelsea Music Hall on an evening when three challenges were met. Overflow seats were sold on the stage and hundreds were turned away from the door. The upshot was that Rickards offered Harry what he said was the highest sum he had ever paid for an act for a season Down Under.

"I RECEIVE FULL SALARY WHILE ON BOARD THE STEAMER," Houdini typed in underlined capital letters. "So I get paid twelve weeks for resting and twelve for working. This is the only condition I would go all that distance." The opening was set for February of the following year. Houdini was booked too far ahead to accept an earlier contract.

Houdini's principal irritant in England this trip was John Clempert, a Russian-born showman, who had been a professional wrestler. Later he billed himself as "The Man They Cannot Hang." Dangling by his legs from a trapeze, Clempert would attach a rope to his neck, then release his leghold. After a breathtaking fifteen-foot drop, he hung by his neck in the air. At least he did until the night in Rochdale, England, when the sudden jar injured his spine.

"As I lay in bed I thought that I should not be able to wrestle again, and I began to think out a new act," Clempert wrote. "Having had experience in gaol breaking I hit upon the idea of the 'Great handcuff, chain, rope and trunk act,' and up to this very time I am making a huge success as the 'handcuff and Siberian Gaol Breaker,' and doing big business in the principal music halls and am acknowledged by public and press the masterpiece of the age."

"The masterpiece of the age" performed a riveted-in-a-boiler test, escaped from packing cases, and copied Houdini's bridge jumps. The July *Wizard* noted that Clempert, in addition to duplicating Houdini's act as closely as he could, was exposing the Water Can feat: "Clempert is 'the man they could not hang.' Perhaps this is a pity. . . ." Since theater entertainments could be copyrighted in Great Britain, Houdini entered suit against Clempert. When his rival swore he would mend his ways, Harry dropped the court action, and Clempert faded into the background.

The challenge escape Houdini introduced at the Oxford Theatre in London was now given a more dramatic production. New handbills read:

Dear Sir—If you will allow the undersigned Trained Nurses and Asylum Warders to roll you in soaking wet sheets, fasten you down with wet linen bandages and pour several buckets of water over your form after we have secured you down to a hospital bed, we will guarantee that you will not be able to affect your escape.

We warn you that the water will cause the sheets and bandages to shrink and hold you in absolute helpless condition, from which you will be only too pleased to have us release you.

The white-uniformed challengers from leading hospitals and the extra impact of the water-soaked bindings were trappings enough for a showman of Houdini's skill to lift this soggy stunt into the sensational category.

Too busy to return to New York for a summer holiday, Harry brought his mother and Bess' mother to England for a visit. Mrs. Rahner had finally warmed to her son-in-law during his last American tour. Better still, she and Mother Weiss, once they met, enjoyed each other's company.

Harry's prime spare-time project at the moment was readying a book explaining the handcuff act—not as he did it, he qualified, but as performed by his rivals. He had written the material during his first tour of Britain. Most of the text already had been printed in his *Conjurers' Monthly Magazine.*

Though the introduction to the series had promised chapters on sensational effects and jailbreaking, Houdini decided not to use them. It was enough for his copyists to get a few tips on the cuffs. Why enlarge their repertoires? The extra chapters were filed away. *Handcuff Secrets* was published in a somewhat different version in Germany as *Mein Training und meine Tricks.*

Many people thought Harry made considerable money from the various editions of his illustrated souvenir book which was sold in theater lobbies. He confessed: "I lost dozens of pounds on my American books as I sold them for less than they cost. Books sell only for a penny and I often give away thousands, when I come to a new town, to advertise myself." He estimated in August 1909 that he had sold "at least quarter of a million" since his arrival in England.

While the thirty-five-year-old "Elusive American" was performing at the Hansa Theater in Hamburg, Germany, in November, a news item, announcing that an aviator named Grade would show his skill in a French biplane, attracted his attention. Aviation was one of Houdini's current interests. In London a year before he told reporters that he had offered five thousand dollars for the use of a Wright brothers airplane. He planned to be handcuffed and flown over the West End. There he would parachute down, escaping from his manacles on the way, and land in Piccadilly Circus. A follow-up story reported that the project had been canceled due to technical difficulties.

Houdini hired a car to go to the racetrack "flying field." Enthralled, Houdini watched the machine soar aloft, circle the track, then come in for a perfect landing. He elbowed his way through the crowd and bombarded Grade with questions. How could he learn to fly? Where could he buy a plane? How much did one cost? Less than a week later he owned his own Voisin, price tag: five thousand dollars.

Houdini charmed German Army officials into granting him permission to use their Hufaren parade grounds in nearby Wandsbek as a temporary airport. They made only one stipulation: he must teach the officers the mechanics of flight. For the next two weeks he wriggled free from challenge restraints as usual at the Hansa each night. Before dawn each morning he was driven to the wooden shed which housed his plane.

Biting winter weather, high winds, and occasional snow kept the Voisin on the ground. Patiently the would-be aviator filled in the hours going through the motions of flying on the instructions of Brassac, the French mechanic he had hired to assist him. Later he fulfilled his pledge and passed on his newly learned technique to the cooperative German Army brass.

A Voisin plane, like his, had stayed in the air an hour and twenty-five minutes in Reims and was awarded a prize for the simplicity of its construction. Houdini's machine had been souped-up with the latest EN 60–80 horsepower English motor. He was impatient to get it off the ground.

Finally the weather cleared. A confident Houdini took his place behind the controls. Brassac spun the propeller. Smoothly the biplane lifted from the field; Harry settled back comfortably in his seat. He was in flight! His exultation was brief. "I smashed the machine. Broke Propeller all to hell," the fledgling airman scrawled in his diary that night. Houdini was unhurt. The damage to the plane was slight, but it took another two weeks to get the necessary replacements from France. Then Brassac got to work with his tools.

Houdini made his first successful flight on November 26, 1909, over the Hufaren parade grounds. A photographer was there to record the event for posterity. And to leave no doubt to even casual viewers of the pictures as to the identity of the aviator, Houdini's name appeared in large letters on the side panels of the machine.

During the rest of his engagement at the Hansa, which ended at the close of December, Houdini spent all his spare time with his flying machine.

UP OVER DOWN UNDER

When Houdini sailed January 7, 1910, from Marseilles to honor his long-standing contracts with Harry Rickards in Melbourne, aviation was still in its infancy. Wilbur and Orville Wright had made their first flight near Kitty Hawk, North Carolina, barely six years before. The flimsy planes of the time seldom stayed aloft for very long, and aviators were generally regarded—with some reason—as reckless daredevils. Records for speed, distance, and altitude were broken with regularity and fliers feverishly competed to be the first to make specific flights. As yet no one had conquered the air above the Australian continent.

Stored in the hold of the *Malwa* along with his theatrical paraphernalia were crates containing Houdini's Voisin airplane, an extra motor, and numerous spare parts. Brassac, the French mechanic who had taught him to fly, shared a cabin with Franz Kukol, his assistant.

This was Houdini's first trip through a part of the world that had always intrigued him. Magic had been performed in Egypt since the days of the pharaohs. When the ship stopped at Port Said for refueling, he was one of the first passengers down the gangplank. He saw six native magicians perform as he roamed the streets. "All worked exactly alike. Think there must be a school of magic, for all have the same tools, apparatus, patter and tricks. When you have seen one you have seen them all."

One gali-gali man came aboard. He, like the others, performed the cups and balls, changing the balls into baby chicks. He cut and restored a strip of cloth. When he asked for a cigarette, a passenger proffered his pack. The magician took one, put it between his lips, and said, "I will make it go far away." Houdini watched closely. Perhaps this was something new. The conjurer picked up his bag of tricks, spun on his heel and left the ship.

Away from the sea with dry land in view Harry enjoyed the *Malwa*'s passage through the Suez Canal. Then came the dreaded pitching and tossing as the vessel steamed through the Red Sea to Aden. Two nights from Ceylon, where he took Bess to see the sights in a rickshaw, he gave an eighty-minute show for the passengers during the ship's concert. He escaped from the ship's irons, conjured with playing cards and silks and performed the needle-threading feat. He mailed his share of the profits of the entertainment to London for a fund which was being raised "to build a home for poor old actors, Music Hall artists and worn-out magicians." The passage, as usual, was agonizing for Houdini; he was sick more than half of the twenty-nine days between France and Australia. He made it to the dining room only fourteen times, and then with great effort. He lost twenty-eight pounds during the voyage.

There was no problem getting his stage equipment through customs; the crated plane was another matter. "They charge you 35% duty or you can bring it in . . . in bond. The Wright machine that is here is under 800 pounds bond. My machine is not quite that much, but by the time I am ready to leave Australia, it will cost that much." Actually he brought the Voisin through with a mere 154 pound deposit.

Impresario Harry Rickards gave Houdini a Barnum-type buildup for his opening at the New Opera House in Melbourne. "The Talk of the Town in Train, Tram and Taxi," proclaimed the ads, "Absolutely the Greatest and most Sensational Act that has ever been engaged by any Manager."

Films of his underwater escapes in Philadelphia, Paris, and Berlin opened the act. Then Houdini, in evening dress, appeared ready for his nightly bouts with the straitjacket and the Water Can.

The movies of his bridge leaps elsewhere in the world naturally created a demand for a similar exhibition in Melbourne. On a brisk February 18, twenty thousand people lined Queen's Bridge and the banks of the Yarra River to see the greatest free show in town. When asked after the jump how he liked the flavor of the Yarra water, Houdini grimaced and answered: "The least toothsome I have ever tasted."

There was a chilling report that Harry's leap had dislodged a corpse from the muddy river. Some spectators thought it was Houdini when the body surfaced before he did.

Six days after the Queen's Bridge exploit the Voisin was uncrated and assembled at Digger's Rest, a field twenty miles from Melbourne. Brassac, the mechanic, said the engine wasn't functioning as it should.

Ralph C. Banks, the owner of the Melbourne Motor Garage, was already there experimenting with his imported Wright machine. As yet he hadn't gotten it in the air.

Some weird reasons were advanced to explain why Down Under fliers were having so much difficulty. A *Daily Telegraph* writer asserted that the air in Australia was "more rarefied" than in Europe. This produced a letter signed by Paul Chaleur. He maintained that barometric readings disproved this theory. The air pressure at sea level in Melbourne and Sydney was essentially the same as in Europe where many flights had been made.

He answered the critics who claimed that Australia's temperature was not suitable for aerial maneuvers. Successful air meets had been held in Nice, France; Heliopolis, Egypt; and Los Angeles, U.S.A. The thermometer rose higher in these cities than in Paris, which had an atmospheric pressure closely akin to that of Melbourne. The basic fault, Chaleur wrote, was that would-be Australian fliers lacked proper training and experience.

Brassac finally solved the engine problem and reported that the plane was ready to go. Again came the frenzied routine as in Hamburg. Strenuous performances at the theater, little sleep, and pre-dawn dashes to the airfield. But here the challenge was greater. With luck, Houdini could be the first man to fly over the Australian continent.

Melbourne aviation buffs were intrigued by the design of the Voisin. It looked like a giant box kite. A steering wheel controlled the rudder. The wheel was pushed forward to elevate the plane, pulled back to bring it down. The two propeller blades were aluminum, each four feet long. They were tiny in proportion to the machine, which weighed 11,400 pounds and measured 33 feet 6 inches from end to end. White balloon sheeting was used on the wings of the craft.

Those in a betting mood gave odds that the Wright plane would win the honors. Houdini was anxious to have a trial run. Brassac refused to permit it. "Too windy," was his excuse day after day.

Ralph Banks, the Melbourne sportsman, was less cautious. An envious Harry looked on as Banks took off. Seconds later the wind buffeted the plane, and Banks was forced to land.

On March 1, Banks rose twelve feet in the air. "There goes the record," Houdini moaned. Brassac didn't comment. Abruptly, the Wright nosed earthward and crashed. Damage to the plane was extensive, but Banks was scarcely scratched.

It was impossible for Houdini to sleep in Melbourne now. He sped for Digger's Rest after his last bow every night and bedded down in the three-hundred-dollar tent that sheltered his Voisin. Three weeks passed before Brassac was satisfied with the weather.

March 16, 1910, five o'clock. The first pale streak of dawn slashed the dark Australian sky as the Voisin was wheeled out to the wooden planks which formed a takeoff area. One end of a mooring rope was tied to the machine, the other was knotted to a dynamometer. There was a nip in the air. Harry wrapped a scarf around his neck as he kept pace with Brassac, who was checking the controls and the landing gear.

A still photographer set up his tripod and adjusted his camera. Houdini pulled on a pair of goggles and a cap, and he climbed to the seat behind the steering wheel. He waved to Bess; she waved back, crossing her fingers for luck. Brassac took a firm grip on the left propeller, and with a mighty pull, set it whirring. Then he started the right propeller. The flimsy machine began to vibrate and strain at the mooring rope. Brassac rushed to the dynamometer, watched the indicator hand move as the motor gained speed: 110, 120, 130, 140, 150, 160, 170 kilos—a lateral strain of 340 pounds. "Ready?" he shouted. Houdini nodded. The mooring line was cast off. The engine roared and the plane shot forward and up. It soared like a bulky paper kite, as a vagrant wind rocked it from side to side.

By now, from nowhere, people appeared on the field. They shouted as the Voisin headed for the top of a tall gumtree, but the machine skimmed over the uppermost branches. Houdini had moved the elevating control just in time. There were cheers as the craft circled the field at an estimated fifty miles an hour, then headed back to the plank runway for a perfect landing.

The crowd went wild. Houdini ripped off his goggles, waved his arms, jumped down. Brassac threw his arms around him.

Bess kissed him. His friendly rival, Ralph Banks, was there to shake his hand.

The first sustained flight in Australia had been made!

On Houdini's second attempt the biplane reached a height of one hundred feet. He kept it in the air for almost five minutes and covered an estimated seven miles.

Two mornings later he flew two and one-half minutes in a high wind as a Pathé cameraman cranked away to record the event for theater newsreels. Stories and photographs of Houdini's flights filled Australian newspapers and magazines. Cables sent the news abroad.

Harry set a new time record, March 21 at 7 a.m. Despite a dangerous crosscurrent of air he was aloft seven minutes and thirty-seven seconds, at an altitude of ninety to one hundred feet. Walter M. Meeks, owner of the yacht *Culwalla II*, was the official timekeeper, while a reporter from the *Argus* double-checked on his own stopwatch. Sixteen people, including Ralph Banks, signed the eyewitness report.

The Australian *Punch* editorialized:

Here is Houdini, who is an amateur, a beginner. He has taught himself to fly here amongst us, and he has shown us what his machine can do. He may be doing it for advertising or he may be doing it for love of adventure. The reason doesn't matter. . . . When his great machine was circling and whirring round like a gigantic bird, the great thought was "What of the future?"

We in Australia are remote from the great world centers, we are peculiarly exposed to attack, and we are deeply busy at present upon the solution of our defense problem. We are building ships and training men. Our ships are to fight on the seas, our men on the land. We are ignoring the air. Yet the battles of the future will go to whoever is strongest in the air.

In late March, Houdini, the man who had conquered the Australian air, opened in Rickards' Tivoli Theatre in Sydney, featuring: "Escaping Out of an Air-Tight Galvanized Iron Can, filled to the brim with water and locked with six padlocks. To Fail Means Death by Drowning . . . bring your own padlocks."

One night a committeeman, searching Houdini even more thoroughly than usual, found a key. He held it up so the audience could see it, then refused to part with it. After the show he learned it had nothing to do with Houdini's act. It was the key to the escape artist's dressing room.

An Air Week was advertised at Rosehill Race Track during Houdini's run in Sydney. Weather permitting, the ads said, Houdini would fly daily between 9 a.m. and 3 p.m. Admission to the track and grandstand was a shilling. Bess presided as hostess at teatime.

The papers said that Harry Rickards was paying Houdini £20,000 ($100,000) for ten five-minute flights. This sum was conjured from thin air by the Tivoli Theatre press agent.

Houdini had complete confidence in himself and his plane, the *Daily Telegraph* reported on April 20. Harry said the craft had "flown hundreds of times and had never been broken." Bess warned him to knock on wood; something might happen on his next flight. Two days later, one hundred feet above the racetrack, the Voisin was struck by a crosswind and fell rapidly, hitting the ground with a heavy thud. Had the earth been level the plane would have landed without damage, but the jagged surface caused one of the wheels to snap and break.

That night at the Tivoli, three asylum attendants tied Houdini with linen bandages, rolled him like a mummy in sheets, then strapped him to an iron frame hospital bed. Buckets of water were doused over the sheets to make his release more difficult.

He began his struggle by attempting to free his feet, kicking, turning, twisting. In the process he slipped his left hand from its bonds. More footwork distracted attention as he released his right hand. Now he squirmed his way bit by bit until his head reached the railing at the end of the bed. He called to Franz Kukol, who wiped the perspiration from his face with a handkerchief, then carefully tilted a glass of water so Houdini could drink it.

The brief rest period over, Harry started anew, rolling his legs from side to side, then kicking upward until his feet were free of the sheets. This brought cheers from the spectators. He had squirmed now into a sitting position. Vigorous twisting and rapid short pulls released his arms as well as his hands.

It seemed that he was almost completely free, but there were still bandages tied around his knees, thighs, and chest.

Finally, straining and maneuvering to stretch the cloth strips, he pulled his legs out, then his midsection, then he drew his head through the bandage around his chest. Free of the cloth strips tied to the bed, he was still wound in the wet sheets. He dropped from the bed to the floor. One of the men who challenged him to make the escape bent over to help him unwind the sheets. Harry waved him back. With a mighty effort he rolled across the stage and suddenly jumped to his feet completely free.

Only a man in excellent physical condition, with complete control of his muscles and a cool head, could have hoped to beat this challenge. It took thirty-seven minutes of sustained strain with only a brief pause for a sip of water. Since Houdini introduced this feat in London he had worked incessantly to improve it. Now it was as well constructed in plot as a tightly written play.

The next morning, apparently fresh and relaxed, Harry was back at the racetrack, working with Brassac on the broken landing gear of his plane.

Friday, April 29, the Sydney flying enthusiasts invited Houdini to a special meeting at the Town Hall. He arrived after his Tivoli performance and was greeted by a standing ovation. The group had shown the films of his flights earlier in the evening, now they presented him with a trophy. In the center of a wooden plaque was a winged bas-relief globe showing the continent. Engraved on the plate above were the words: "The Aerial League of Australia to H. Houdini for the First Aerial Flight in Australia, March 16, 1910."

"Even if history forgets Houdini, the Handcuff King," he wrote his friend Thomas Driver, a New Zealand magician, "it must write my name as the first man to fly here. Not that it will put any jam on my bread. . . . Pity I can't carry enough petrol to fly home with my good wife, as I can carry a passenger in the machine with ease."

Australia's aviator number one sailed for home May 11 on the *Manuka,* a 4,500-ton ship of the Canadian Pacific Line. A day earlier he had supervised the loading of his plane and props aboard "the miserable, wretched looking steamer." The sight of it alone had its effect: "I am certain that I will break all records for being seasick on this trip. I saw the steamer . . . and am sick already."

With the aerial triumph in Australia behind him, Houdini lost the urge to pilot a plane himself, but his interest in aviation continued. He had written, on his return to the United States: "Count me in on the big air prize offered by the New York *World* and the St. Louis *Post-Dispatch*," but he accepted vaudeville bookings which kept him out of the competition.

Harry was in Chicago for the International Air Meet at Grant Park in August 1911. He wrote Bess, who was ill in New York at the time: "At 3:15 four Wright machines left the ground and all remained up until it was dark. At one time I saw twelve machines in the air. I never before saw such wonderful sights. No accidents today. Twice I grew weak in the knees at near accidents. A Curtiss flyer, Beachy, dived 3,000 feet, but, as his machine did not break, he was saved.

"I saw Meustac in a biplane fly 80 miles an hour for two hours. Seven men were flying over 5,000 feet in the air. I spoke to Orville Wright and [Glenn Hammond] Curtiss. They all seemed to know me as an Australian flyer and want to know all about my country."

The Chicago air meet was a thrilling spectacle. Twenty-five planes were flown. Five machines crashed on the opening day, but none of the pilots was seriously injured. The tail of St. Croix Johnstone's plane was shattered, but the Chicagoan had his mechanics at work on it minutes after the crash. Lincoln Beachy, who once flew under the Suspension Bridge at Niagara Falls, was the star performer.

Two aviators fell into the lake, Monday, August 14, and a biplane burned to cinders when it struck a power cable. Tuesday, William Baker fell on the shores of the lake. St. Croix Johnstone, whose plane had been repaired, nosedived six hundred feet and was killed in Lake Michigan.

A benefit flying show, which raised fifteen thousand dollars, was staged for Johnstone's widow the day after the formal meet ended. One of the stars was Houdini. With hands and feet shackled, he jumped from a plane as it flew fifty feet above the lake, then released himself underwater and swam to the beach. If Wright and Curtiss hadn't been aware of Houdini's escape work when they met him, they were now.

THE IMPOSSIBLE POSSIBLE

When Houdini returned to England in August 1910, he learned that during his absence Empress, "The One and Only Lady Masterpiece," had played the smaller theaters with a near facsimile of his act. She escaped from handcuffs, a straitjacket, a padlocked water can, and she broke out of a packing case. There was another cause for alarm. British sellers of secrets were advertising steel pries and folding jacks which they claimed were the secret tools Houdini used to force open challenge boxes.

Houdini met the new threat by posting a £20 reward ($100) for anyone who could find a release instrument on his body. On the stage of the Hammersmith Palace in London, November 4, he wore the athletic suit and shoes which the challengers, employees of Moss & Company, provided. The firm's carpenters searched him before they nailed him in place. Still he escaped.

The following week at the Islington Empire, Houdini forced his way free from a full-length restraint made of heavy sacking and fastened with belts and straps. This "in-the-open" escape was so effective that he encouraged other manufacturers to challenge him with similar devices.

The workers at the plant of Andrew Howard, who made tarpaulins and sailcloth, issued a dare, November 23, during his week at the Olympia Theatre in Liverpool:

> We defy you to escape from a restraint that we will manufacture, used in the days of Sailing Vessels to restrain the MAD-WITH-GROG Sailors or Desperate Criminals on the High Seas. We refer to the greatly dreaded SEABAG, which has been abolished on account of the extreme torture to the prisoner.
>
> This we intend making from Strong Sail Cloth that has been treated with oil and tar to prevent slipping, and will envelope you from the neck down to and including

your feet; on the outside of this you will be encircled with stout heavy canvas straps held into place with adjustable leather straps and steel buckles.

If you accept this challenge we demand at least one day to manufacture the Seabag, and you must make the attempt to release yourself in full view of the audience. No cabinets, screens or scenery allowed.

Two nights later Houdini was enclosed in the bag. Its mouth was fastened by a strap around his neck. Other straps were buckled tightly around his shoulders, waist, and ankles. The release was as strenuous—and as exciting—as the straitjacket test. He kicked, squirmed, and pulled the sailcloth down from the strap around his neck. Then he inched the shoulder strap off and over his head. Meanwhile he slipped his shoes off and worked one foot through the strap that held his ankles. As the second foot was tugged free, he used his right hand to unbuckle the strap at his neck. Finally, with both hands out of the waist strap, he stripped the bag down past his knees and with his feet kicked it up in the air and away.

A challenge with all the appeal of an old-fashioned melodrama came during Houdini's week at Barnard's Palace in Chatham, in February 1911. It was issued by four petty officers at the local naval barracks:

We CHALLENGE you to stand in front of a loaded Government 8-cwt. Steel Gun, to which we will secure you, insert a fuse which will burn 20 minutes, and if you fail to release yourself within that time you will be blown to Kingdom Come.

The Chatham chief of police robbed Houdini of the danger element. He permitted the cannon to be loaded on the stage but refused to allow the officers to light the fuse.

As a packed house looked on, February 17, the navy men tied Houdini to the muzzle of the cannon. A rifle barrel was thrust under his arms while his hands were behind his back, then they brought his hands forward and lashed one wrist to the other across his chest. His feet were roped and knotted to an iron ring nailed in the stage floor.

Harry began his struggle by kicking off his shoes and

untying the knots with his bare toes. Then came the wriggling, twisting, and straining to release his body from the cannon. He had three minutes to spare when the last rope dropped.

James Vickery had been Houdini's first British-born assistant; now he hired James Collins. Both were to stay with him for the rest of his life. Collins signed his oath never to reveal Houdini's secrets at the Ardwick Empire in Manchester, December 3, 1910. He was an expert carpenter and metalworker. On stage, under Franz Kukol's direction, he was an efficient aid; offstage he was put to work on Harry's most pressing problem—the construction of a feature escape to take the place of the Water Can.

Jean Hugard was featuring the can in Australia; it had been done by Clempert and Empress in England. The Great Raymond, an American illusionist, had ordered one from Ornum, the London dealer, despite Houdini's protest that he had originated the escape. A magician in South Africa wrote that he would like to include it in his program. As Houdini had no intention of making the long sea voyage to Johannesburg for a few weeks' work, and as he was pleased that at least one performer had the courtesy to ask his permission to duplicate the feat, he granted the man exclusive South African rights.

Houdini was intrigued with the idea of an escape from a solid block of ice. As he visualized the presentation, he would wear a diving suit and a helmet. He would be lowered into a tank with a glass front. A quick-freeze chemical solution would be poured in, over and around his body. Once solid ice had been formed, the tank would be enclosed in a cloth-sided cabinet and he would free himself.

He found that a diving helmet would hold a ten-minute supply of air. No hitch there. Collins built a tank. For months he tried unsuccessfully to mix a solution which would freeze the water quickly enough for a stage presentation. Houdini caught a severe cold during the tests and abandoned the experiments.

Then he devised another release. He was sealed in an oilskin bag. The bag was enclosed in a rubber sack and he was lowered into the water-filled tank. A top was locked in place. Under the cover of a cabinet he freed himself, emerging through the curtains dry.

The effect was good, but not as dramatic as he had hoped it would be. Finally, in March Houdini perfected an escape made while he was padlocked upside down in the tank of water. Rather than patent the device—anyone had access to patent papers—he applied for protection by presenting it to the Lord Chamberlain in the form of a play. Only one spectator, who paid a guinea for a seat in the pit of the theater, was admitted to the special performance. The new "plot" was duly approved, registered, and licensed.

Harry crated the device and put it in his London storeroom. When the right time came he would have a blockbuster attraction to bolster his act. He named it "The Chinese Water Torture Cell."

Though his competitors had appropriated the Water Can and the packing-box escape, Houdini was still drawing capacity crowds. He was billed this tour as "The Impossible Possible"; no dare seemed beyond his capabilities. In May at the Finsbury Park Empire in London he featured a double escape. He was nailed and roped in a box which was lifted into a second larger container. This too was nailed and roped as securely as the first. It took him twelve minutes to penetrate both.

In Leeds, a local brewer filled his Water Can with beer. Padlocked inside, Harry, who didn't drink, was overcome by the alcohol. Had it not been for Franz Kukol, he might have drowned. He was only partially conscious when Kukol, disturbed by the quiet behind the curtain, dashed into the cabinet and hauled him out of the can. Afterward a stagehand joked: "Why run away from the beer, Mr. Houdini? It's what most of us run after." He was in no mood to laugh.

In London, he accepted a challenge to release himself from a "Rum Punch Hickory Barrel" at the Shepherd's Bush Empire. He made sure the barrel was empty before he was locked inside.

When Houdini returned to the United States in the fall of 1911, he found that challenge escapes still packed houses here just as they had in England. During Houdini's two weeks at Keith's in Boston in September, he accepted two new dares. The first was an escape from an eight-foot-long plank, to which he had been roped by four veteran sea captains. He released himself in full view of the audience. The second was one of the most improbable of his career.

A "sea monster"—a cross between an octopus and a whale —had been beached not far from Boston. The strange creature was trucked to the theater. The lieutenant governor of Massachusetts and a committee of businessmen had challenged Houdini to escape from it. Harry, shackled hand and foot, was forced through a slit into the monster. Its belly was laced with a heavy chain—the eyelets a mere three inches apart. More chains were wound around the carcass and fastened with locks. A large cabinet was moved forward and the drapes were closed.

Houdini took fifteen minutes to free himself. His principal hazard had been the fumes from the arsenic taxidermists had sloshed inside the creature to preserve it.

In early November, as Houdini had forced his way out of a challenge bag at the Temple Theater in Detroit, he had been injured internally. One of the round leather straps that encircled the bag had been buckled with such pressure that it burst a blood vessel in a kidney, though he did not realize it at the time. He bled for two weeks before he even considered going to a doctor. In Pittsburgh, a Mercy Hospital physician, Dr. Wholly, was shocked to learn that Harry was continuing his strenuous performances without a letup.

Houdini grudgingly canceled a few weeks' bookings and returned to New York for an enforced layoff. Bess and his mother tried to keep him in bed. The doctor said he must rest until the injury healed. Harry dictated answers to his mounting heap of correspondence, jotted down ideas for possible future escapes, leafed through the old documents and programs in his ever-growing collection, read many of the volumes he had put aside for future study.

He was back on the road in December. He escaped from a tank of beer at Keith's in Columbus, Ohio. Since his near-drowning in beer in England, Houdini had learned how to cope with the unfamiliar intoxicant. A coating of oil on his body prevented the alcohol from penetrating his skin. In early January 1912, at Keith's in Philadelphia, the Bergdoll Brewing Company sent eight gallons of lager to fill the Water Can. Later that month at Hammerstein's Victoria in New York, Harry invited Jacob Ruppert, the challenger, to deliver "eight to one hundred gallons" of Knickerbocker beer. The stage-hands always enjoyed the surplus.

Houdini received a dare at the Colonial Theater in Norfolk, Virginia, in March:

We wish to challenge you to allow us to bring to the theater a U.S. Government Navy deepsea diving suit, which is at present on board the U.S.S. *Severn,* tender to Submarine Flotilla.

You are to allow us to place you in apparatus, which consists of high pressure water proof heavy garment, which encases the entire body from neck down to and including the feet, we will then place the breast and neck plate of copper over your neck fastening it to the lower garment with bolts, then placing the brass and steel diver's helmet over your head and securing this down to complete the suit with the usual brass wing-bolts, and nuts in the usual manner.

We will finish up by handcuffing your hands behind your back and locking your feet together with ankle irons of the adjustable kind.

Houdini accepted this challenge immediately, and had no difficulty making the escape. During the tests with the quick-freeze ice escape in England he had learned how a diving suit could be divested in an emergency.

A new outside-the-theater publicity feat was perfected in the summer of 1912, while Harry was headlining at Hammerstein's Roof. He had scored with feature stories and photographs in the New York press of the Houdini-Boudini underocean handcuff contest years before. Now his handbills proclaimed that on Sunday, July 7, 1912, at 11 a.m., he would be nailed in a box and thrown into the river. He would attempt to release himself while the box was submerged.

The New York police, unlike those in other American cities, were uncooperative. They told Harry and the reporters and photographers who had assembled on Pier 6, East River, that the stunt was off. Houdini, not to be stopped, hired the tugboat *Catherine Moran* and escorted his party aboard a lighter towed by the tug. Off Governors Island, outside the jurisdiction of the New York City police, he was manacled and leg-ironed and put in a heavy packing case. His brother, Dr. Leopold Weiss, informed reporters that the box was twenty-four inches wide, thirty-six high, and thirty-four long. The lid was nailed in place, the box was roped, then encircled by steel bands. Two hundred pounds of iron were lashed to its sides. The box was shoved down an incline and overboard. It hit the river at 11:44 a.m. Eleven seconds later it lurched to one side, then righted itself, the top level with the water. Less than a minute afterward Houdini appeared fifteen feet away. He waved to the men on the lighter and swam to a rowboat. His two assistants and a longshoreman hauled him in.

The overboard box test caused so much talk that a huge, specially built tank, which held 5,500 gallons of water, was installed on the stage of Hammerstein's Roof. Nightly Harry repeated the escape. Fifteen days later he came up with another brilliant conversation-maker. He was roped to the highest point of the Heidelberg Building Tower at 42d and Broadway at noon. Thousands watched from the street as he worked himself free three hundred feet above their heads.

To Houdini the most memorable event of his two-month run at Hammerstein's was not one of his escapes, but the little drama he staged solely for his mother. He arranged to be paid his first week's salary in gold coins. Back home on West 113th Street, Harry told his mother to hold her apron outstretched between her hands. He asked if she remembered his promise to look after her. She smiled and nodded her head. With a dramatic gesture, Houdini produced the money and let the gold shower down.

He was, at the age of thirty-eight, the best-known mystery performer in the world. Even the Society of American Magicians finally recognized the fact. Unanimously in April 1912 they had elected him an honorary member. By early fall Houdini was on his way to England. In London, he picked up the glass-fronted Water Cell act he had registered with the Lord Chamberlain on his previous visit, then sailed for Bremen.

The Chinese Water Torture Cell was first shown publicly during his engagement in Germany with the Circus Busch. The heavy metal-lined mahogany tank with a plate-glass front could stand the most rigid examination. It was filled with water while he changed to a bathing suit. Then an upright metal "cage" was put in the tank. Houdini stretched out on the stage. His ankles were fastened in stocks. A massive frame held the stocks in place. He was hauled aloft, head down, then lowered into the cell. The top was quickly locked.

The audience could see him through the glass front—upside down in the water—confined by the barred "cage." A curtained cabinet was rolled forward to cover the device and the curtains were closed. Franz Kukol and Collins stood by ready for any emergency with fire axes as the band played "The Diver." For two minutes the audience was on tenterhooks. Then Houdini swept aside the curtains, stepped out free, water streaming from his body. He extended his arms, smiled, and accepted the applause of a thoroughly baffled public.

He wrote Will Goldston from Berlin on September 27: "The new stunt I am doing is a marvelous success, and is without doubt the greatest spectacular thing ever witnessed on the stage. Am sending you some billing, which will show what Busch thinks of your friend Houdini."

Not only Busch but also the audiences agreed that the Water Cell escape was the greatest escape he had ever made. Let his imitators have the challenge handcuff act and the Water Can. He had something now which wouldn't be duplicated in a hurry—or so he thought.

Two German impresarios saw the act several times in Berlin; they came up as part of the committee from the audience to inspect the apparatus and assist in the locking of his feet in the stocks. They noted the measurements and construction of the equipment. When Harry left Germany, they had a similar water tank made, hired an attractive girl, and billed her as "Miss Undina." Houdini, experienced in German law as a result of the Graff libel suit, acted immediately when he learned of "Miss Undina." First an injunction stopped the performances, then a court action terminated her upside-down career, and the imitators had to pay court costs.

Years before, Harry had set up his brother Theo as his rival. Now he was to play impresario again. The pirates in Germany had given him the inspiration. He tutored a girl to master the dramatics of his straitjacket and his Water Torture Cell, told Franz Kukol to arrange bookings for her in theaters on the Continent which would not conflict with those in which he intended to play again. The billings for the act featured

Houdini's name. In smaller letters was the explanation that his mysteries would be presented by "Miss Trixy." The new act did well in Germany and Russia.

THE STOPPED CLOCK

He writhed and sweated in a straitjacket, then cooled off upside down in a padlocked water tank, but he dreamed of a less strenuous life delighting audiences with amazing tricks that depended on mental agility. He filled page after page with his ideas for a supermagic show, with which he would surpass the masters of the past.

Although he was working harder than he ever had before, he still had time for sentiment. Houdini called Franz Kukol to his side in the middle of his performance at the Finsbury Park Empire, in London, March 2, 1913. Franz, he told the audience, was the best assistant he had ever had. For exactly ten years he had traveled with him around the world. He gave the Austrian a handsome gold pocket watch and chain. The watchcase had been engraved to mark the anniversary.

He also found time to help British magicians establish the Magicians Club. Nearly two years previously, on May 27, 1911, Houdini had presided at the group's organizational meeting in the Crown Room of the Holborn Restaurant. The club, said Will Goldston, should not be just a fraternal order, like the Society of American Magicians. Goldston contemplated a more formal league that would have its own permanent meeting rooms, a stage, workshop, and library. Such an elaborate scheme presented a fund-raising problem, but Harry offered to get the club off the ground by paying the first six months' rent for its quarters. Before the initial meeting was over, he had been elected president of the group.

On his return to England in 1913, Harry discovered that the club had made little progress during his absence. What had happened to plans for a clubroom? he asked Will Goldston. The magic dealer patiently pulled a letter from his files and showed it to Houdini. In it, Harry had objected to the high rental of the site proposed. Now the two agreed that their plans had been delayed long enough and suitable quarters soon were found at 2 Gray's Inn.

Speaking at the opening of the new clubroom, Houdini said: "Gentlemen. . . . When we first projected the club, we were told it was an illusion. Some kind people even used the word hallucination. . . . Members will find at the club all the publications relating to their art, . . . a writing room, a silence room, and, in the basement, a workshop and museum. Every magician will have facilities for carrying out experiments and demonstrating tricks and illusions . . . many friendships will be formed here; many a lame dog of a magician helped over a magical stile. But we are not lame dogs tonight; rather festive dogs, anxious to begin the festivities."

Among the congratulatory telegrams was one from Bess and his assistants. After he heard it he said: "Mrs. Houdini is the only handcuff that I never escaped from—or even tried to escape from."

At the club Houdini and Horace Goldin reminisced about their dime museum days in America. Goldin's trick-a-minute style had had a tremendous impact in British vaudeville. He became a headliner with his speedy presentations of big-scale illusions. He and Houdini had once applied for the same job during their struggling days. Sixteen shows a day at a dollar a day, plus the privilege of selling a souvenir pamphlet. When Harry was hired, Horace tried to sabotage him. He stood in the audience while Houdini was on the platform and showed card tricks to the people around him. "There," Goldin proclaimed to anyone who would listen, "don't you think they're just as good tricks as Houdini's? He's charging for his. I'm doing mine for nothing."

When the management of Hammerstein's Roof Garden asked Houdini to come to New York for a two-week engagement he accepted the booking, though it meant an extra round trip across the Atlantic. His mother, at seventy-two, was frail and feeble, and this would be his only chance to see her that year.

Challenges from the United States began arriving even before his ship docked. While still in mid-ocean on board the *Kronprinz Wilhelm* he received a cable. Captain Smith, whose convict ship *Success* was anchored off 79th Street and Riverside Drive, dared him to escape from one of that vessel's antique cells.

Harry's answer was: "Accept challenge any time mutually

agreed upon to undergo test. Want no favors, but demand fair play."

A page ad in the New York *Evening Telegram* June 1 carried a photograph of the old sailing prison and announced Houdini would be incarcerated aboard three days later. He was locked in massive irons and put behind a bolted door in a narrow cell once used to hold convicts aboard the sailing ship. It took him an hour to release himself. Then he dived through a porthole and swam ashore.

Cecilia Weiss sat in the front row at Hammerstein's and led the applause for her favorite son. She was thrilled with the reception accorded the American debut of his new feature, the Chinese Water Torture Cell.

The Hammerstein production was lavishly staged. The exotic scenic effects didn't appeal to the critic from the New York *Sun;* Houdini did. "It is his act and practically his act alone, which gives the present bill its one gleam of intense interest and originality. Owing to this man's wonderful flubdub and personality, one follows his entrances and exits as breath-batedly as if he were pushing himself through the small and hindermost entrance of a Yale lock. And he would get himself out of there—that's the wonder of the man."

Once Houdini had followed Ching Ling Foo at Keith's in Boston. Now the great Chinese magician, on another tour of the United States, was to replace Harry in the Hammerstein show. The night before Harry was to return to Europe, Ching invited him to a bon-voyage dinner in his apartment at the Hotel Bellevue. Howard Thurston, who had taken Kellar's position as America's leading illusionist; Theo Bamberg, of the famous Dutch family of conjurers; and Francis Werner, a past president of the Society of American Magicians, were the other guests.

On the deck of the *Kronprincessin Cecilie* Harry asked his mother what he should bring her from Europe. She couldn't think of anything she especially wanted or needed, but to play along at the parting game, she said she would like a pair of woolen slippers, size six. Back home, Cecilia observed the familiar ritual of winding the grandfather clock, which she never touched while her darling Ehrich was in the house.

Hardeen took Cecilia for a vacation at Asbury Park when he opened there at the Lyric Theater on July 14. The first day he leaped from the end of the fishing pier and escaped from manacles and chains in the ocean. At the theater he performed the old Houdini act: challenge handcuff releases, the strait-jacket, and the Water Can. That night in the Imperial Hotel Cecilia was stricken with paralysis. Dr. James Ackerman said her condition was serious. Her entire body was affected. She could not speak. Theo phoned his sister in New York. Gladys arrived the next morning. When Dr. Ackerman examined Mrs. Weiss again, he put her on the critical list.

Hardeen continued his performances at the Lyric. Wednesday night, July 16, he broke out of a challenge packing case, then hurried back to his mother's bedside. She was trying to say something about Houdini, but couldn't get the words out. She fell asleep. At fifteen minutes past midnight Cecilia Steiner Weiss was dead.

Across the Atlantic Houdini had opened at the Cirkus Beketow (later the Cirkus Schumann) in Copenhagen. Two members of the royal family, Princes Aage and Axel, were in the audience. "The Modern Proteus," who delivered his patter in Danish, was given an ovation.

At noon the following day, Thursday, July 17, Harry received the press in the circus vestibule. Bubbling with enthusiasm, he expressed his thanks for the wonderful reception the night before. Someone handed him a cable as he talked. He opened it, read the words, and fell unconscious to the floor. When he came to he sobbed: "Mother—my dear little mother—poor little mama." The reporters, moved by his grief, quietly left.

That night Director Beketow himself filled in for his absent star with the trained horses for which the circus was famous. At the hotel Houdini was in agony. A Danish specialist was called in. He said the shock of Houdini's mother's death had been followed with an attack of a "chronic kidney disease." He prescribed immediate hospitalization. Harry feebly objected. The doctor shrugged. Then only a long rest would bring about a cure.

Beketow sympathetically released Harry from his contract.

One thought was uppermost in Houdini's mind: he must see his mother before she was buried. He cabled Hardeen to delay the funeral. Return passage was booked on the ship which had brought him to Europe. The Copenhagen papers reported that the Danish specialist accompanied the party as far as Germany. There another doctor took over. In Bremen, Harry remembered Cecilia's last request. With tears welling in his eyes he bought a pair of woolly slippers, size six.

On arriving in New York, Harry found that the French gilt furniture had been rearranged on the first floor of his house for the funeral. He looked on his mother's face, then bent and pressed his ear to her body. The heartbeat that so reassured him as an infant was still. He put the slippers by her side. Sometime later that night he stopped the grandfather clock that Cecilia always wound while he was away. He felt as if his life had stopped too.

After the funeral Houdini visited the cemetery daily. Sometimes in the small hours of the night Bess would hear him call his mother's name. During the day he read and reread the letters Cecilia had written him through the years. Later he had the letters translated and typed in English so he could read them with less effort.

It was not until September that he could force himself back to work. He opened at the Apollo Theater in Nuremberg. His stationery now carried a wide black mourning border.

During his month at the Alhambra in Paris he met by chance the son of the great French magician Philippe, a contemporary of Anderson and Robert-Houdin, who had performed Chinese tricks in a flowing robe and conical cap. He had been the first European to achieve fame with the linking rings and the production of a huge bowl of water from a foulard. Houdini purchased the letters the magician had written to his son. As he began to recover from his grief, the old desire to present a big magic show returned.

While he was in Paris Houdini bought the entire illusion act of Hermalin, a British magician who was more noted for his excellent equipment than his ability to project his personality. Hermalin went through his routine as Harry watched. Then Houdini took over as Hermalin directed his movements. The apparatus was crated and shipped to Houdini's storeroom in England. After a brief holiday in Monte Carlo with Bess, he went to London for the Christmas season.

In Aberdeen, Scotland, Houdini made a pilgrimage to the grave of John Henry Anderson, "The Great Wizard of the North." Anderson was the master publicist of nineteenth-century magicians. Stencils on pavements heralded his performances, butter molds bore his likeness, song sheets carried his name. More than one hundred editions of his *Fashionable Science of Parlour Magic* were sold during his travels around the world. There was a legend that he had pasted his gaudy lithographs on the sides of the Great Pyramid at Giza.

Anderson, who had made and lost several fortunes, ended his career almost as poor as when he started. He was buried beside his mother. A few lines on a simple marker identified the grave. Distressed because Anderson's descendants were not keeping the plot in good condition, Harry started a Magicians Club fund to pay for its upkeep.

The evening of the Magicians Club supper in his honor, Houdini talked about Cecilia: "My mother was everything to me. It seemed like the end of the world when she was taken from me. Not until she lay dying did I realize how inexpressibly futile is a man's intelligence and determination when face to face with death. When her last hour came, I thought mine would soon follow. Everything seemed turned to dust and ashes for me. All desire for fame and fortune had gone from me. I was alone with my bitter agony. But time, the great healer, has brought me some measure of solace."

By mid-April the "king of escapologists" was ready to try for a new title. He had arranged with the theater managers who booked his Water Cell act for special all-magic performances during the week. For these gala occasions a typical handbill read:

The World-Famous Self-Liberator

HOUDINI

The Supreme Ruler of Magic
will present a

GRAND MAGICAL REVUE

In which he will prove himself to be
the Greatest Mystifier that History
Chronicles, introducing a number of
problems from his inexhaustible
repertoire

WHICH WILL BE SEEN FOR THE FIRST TIME ON ANY STAGE

1. The Crystal Casket. 2. Good-bye Winter. Vanishing a living, breathing human being in mid-air in center of stage, away from all curtains, and in full glare of the light, in less than One-Millionth of a Second. 3. Money from Nothing. In which HOUDINI solves for humanity that which has been the ruin of millions who try to get "Something for Nothing," obtaining £1,000 in genuine Gold and Silver, in the midst of the audience, in a manner never before shown by any performer past or present. 4. The Arrival of Summer. Materializing in a most inexplicable manner a FAIRY QUEEN GARDENER under strictest conditions possible. Everything open and above board, deceiving the Five Senses in one fell swoop. 5. Calico Conjuring. An object lesson for the Ladies. 6. Metamorphosis. Two human beings transported through space and walls of steel-bound oaken boards, outstrapping the rapidity of thought, after being bound, gagged and sealed by a committee selected from the audience.

Despite the bombastic billing, there was little new or startling in the Houdini magic revue. The Crystal Casket was a replica of Robert-Houdin's invention, which Harry had purchased from Charles DeVere, the Paris magic dealer. Coins disappeared from his fingertips and appeared in a suspended glass box. The best-received feat was his old standby, the substitution trunk. Bess, who hadn't appeared on stage since he had dropped it from his act, worked with him in this and other illusions. He had planned to include another Robert-Houdin invention in the program, having also acquired from DeVere a replica of the "automaton" which performed acrobatics on a trapeze. But the control strings had deteriorated with age and Houdini had neither the time nor the proper material to replace them.

Continuing his buying spree, he purchased in May a brilliant idea, "Walking Through a Steel Wall," from Sidney Josolyne, then decided to delay its initial presentation until his summer engagement at Hammerstein's in New York. And from Will Goldston's wife, Leah, he bought the original equipment for Buatier de Kolta's final creation, "The Expanding Cube." Houdini had seen De Kolta, one of the most inventive magicians who ever lived, years before in Berlin. The effect of the cube trick was staggering: A die, eight inches square, expanded instantly to become a cube, three-feet square, which was then lifted to reveal a girl beneath it. Houdini presented this illusion in the last showing of his magic revue at the Empire Theatre in Nottingham.

Despite the money and effort that went into it, the all-magic program was not a resounding success. Bookers who saw the show urged Houdini to concentrate on the Water Cell act, which was salable at top money.

When Houdini picked up his tickets back to the States on the *Imperator* at the Hamburg-American office in London, he was told in confidence that Theodore Roosevelt would be on the ship. He took a taxi to the *Telegraph*. The newspaper had started a series by the former President on his South American expedition. In a few minutes, with the help of a reporter friend, he had a copy of a Roosevelt map, as yet unpublished, and other facts still unknown to the public.

During Houdini's shipboard performance he asked the spectators to write questions on slips of paper. As Roosevelt wrote, Victor Herbert advised him to turn his back so that Houdini couldn't decipher the words by watching the motions of the top of the pencil. Harry then instructed the former President to fold his paper and drop it between two blank slates, which Houdini tied together. After the magician asked for "spirit" aid, the slates were parted to reveal a chalked map with an arrow indicating a point by the River of Doubt on one. The other slate now carried the words "Near the Andes" and the signature of W. T. Stead, the British spiritualist who had gone down with the *Titanic* two years before.

Roosevelt was astonished. His question had been, "Where was I last Christmas?" and Harry's answer had been correct and complete. The *Imperator* radio operator flashed the story to New York, by way of a relay station in Newfoundland.

Houdini scrawled a few lines in his diary June 14, 1914: "Roosevelt left about 9:30 at night but we did not dock until morning. I have 83 pieces of baggage. My good old Camera has been stolen."

In July, Houdini opened his third summer season at Hammerstein's Roof. Two escapes from submerged boxes in the East River alerted New Yorkers he was back in town. He began his second week with "Walking Through a Brick Wall." He thought a barrier of brick which the audience could see constructed before their eyes would be more effective than Josolyne's original concept of steel.

Twice daily bricklayers built a wall nine feet high in a steel frame on a wheeled base. To allay the suspicion that trapdoors might be used, a rug was spread on the stage and over this a large square of muslin was placed. The wall, inspected by a committee, was then rolled into position at the center of the muslin, with one end turned toward the audience. Houdini, in a long white coat, stood to the left of the wall. A six-foot-high, threefold screen closed him in. Spectators could see the bricks above and to the sides of the screen. Another screen was set on the other side of the wall.

Houdini waved his hands above his screen, shouting, "Here I am." As the hands vanished from view he added, "Now I'm gone." The screen was pulled away. No Houdini. When the other screen was opened, there stood the magician smiling enigmatically.

The "walking-through" was presented with thirty spectators ranged about the structure, leaving only the front unobstructed so the audience could have a clear view. The *Sunday World Magazine* devoted a full page to the new puzzler.

Meanwhile in England, P. T. Selbit, the illusionist, was performing the same illusion. He claimed it was his invention, not Josolyne's. Dr. A. M. Wilson, in the *Sphinx,* wrote that The Great Alexander, a mentalist, had performed the feat as far back as December 1898, in Dawson City, Alaska. Alexander penetrated a wall made of ice blocks, twelve inches wide. By Wilson's account, Alexander had also gone through solid wooden boards and sheets of iron, as well as bricks.

Houdini was unruffled by the hubbub in the conjuring fraternity. Who else had staged the illusion so sensationally, so effectively? No one! When the illusion had served its purpose, he passed it along to his brother Hardeen.

During his run at Hammerstein's the Proctor circuit

brought Cunning, "The Jail Breaker," to New York, hoping to take advantage of the inevitable wave of Houdini publicity. Cunning was still doing the challenge handcuff act which Harry had discarded six years before.

The advent of World War I, precipitated by the assassination of Austria's Archduke Francis Ferdinand at Sarajevo on June 28, 1914, had two immediately visible effects on Houdini. First, it became apparent to Harry as the conflict widened during the summer months that he had lost his foreign market for the duration. Instead of thinking about returning to England in the fall, he must begin making plans for an American tour. Then, less than three months after the Sarajevo incident, the fact of war was brought home to Houdini's company in personal terms as Franz Kukol received notice to report back to his native Austria for military duty.

As World War I gained momentum, the private conflict between Houdini and the editor of the *Sphinx,* the magic magazine, was entering its last stages. For eight years Dr. Wilson had either ignored Harry in his editorials or taken potshots at his pride:

Can anyone with a modicum of reason or common sense compare Houdini's or any other such act with that of David Devant, Servais LeRoy, F. E. Powell, Kellar or Thurston?

Magic is an art, a science that requires brains, skill, gentlemanliness and talent of a high order. Brick walls, torture cells, straightjackets, handcuffs, etc., demand nothing but physical strength and endurance, nerve, gall, bluster, fakes and fake apparatus, etc., ad libitum, heralded by circus band advertising. In my opinion magic is brought into disrepute by all such. Their place is in the side show or dime museums.

The former sideshow and dime museum attraction came face to face with his critic in Martinka's magic shop, June 1, 1915. After a heated exchange they parted with more animosity than they had when they met.

A few months later Dr. Theodore Blakesly, an amateur magician who admired both men, brought them together again in his Kansas City office during Houdini's week at the Orpheum. This time they talked over their differences without fire or fury. They left arm in arm to have dinner with Bess.

"I apologized to Houdini; he made amends," Wilson wrote. "Now we are friends, as we should have been years ago."

ABOVE THE STREETS

Hardeen seldom played practical jokes on his brother, but he couldn't resist the opportunity that arose when they were headlining at opposition theaters in Oakland, California, in November 1915. He had given the without-cover straitjacket presentation to Harry. Now Harry topped him—literally—by making the escape while suspended upside down in the open air. The day Houdini twisted and turned high above a downtown street to publicize his Orpheum appearance small boys distributed thousands of advertising cards to the crowd. They carried Hardeen's picture and the words: "All This Week at Pantages."

Harry invited Theo and his wife; Alexander Pantages, the theater magnate; and novelist Jack London to Thanksgiving dinner at his hotel. Hardeen waited for a chiding remark about his prank. It didn't come. After the mince pie and coffee, Houdini called for the check. He shook hands all around and left for the Orpheum, pausing only to give the bill to Hardeen.

The new straitjacket exploitation feat had been a success in Kansas City, Minneapolis, and the other cities on his western tour. In Minneapolis he spoke at the Advertising Forum. Advertising, he said, was vital to vaudeville. Unless people knew who was playing in a theater they wouldn't come. He held up a batch of front-page stories and photographs and said with a chuckle: "I get more advertising space without paying for it than anyone in the country."

Houdini's news sense was almost infallible. When he was told that Jess Willard, the world's heavyweight boxing champion was in his audience at the Orpheum in Los Angeles, he invited the boxer to come up and serve on the committee from the audience. There was no reply from the other side of the footlights.

"I will leave it to the audience, Mr. Willard," he continued as the applause broke out. "You see, they want to see you." From the balcony came a gruff: "Aw, g'wan with your act. I paid for my seat here."

"But, Mr. Willard," Harry continued, "I—" He was cut off with: "Give me the same wages you pay those other fellows and I'll come down." Houdini answered that the other volunteers were not paid for their services. "Aw, g'wan with the show," Willard bellowed and added something that sounded like "four-flusher, faker." This provoked hisses in the fighter's direction.

Harry quieted the audience. "Jess Willard," he said firmly, "I have just paid you a compliment. Now, I want to tell you something else. I will be Harry Houdini when you are *not* the heavyweight champion of the world." There were cheers and hearty handclaps. Willard attempted to reply, but the hoots of the spectators drowned out his words.

2,000 HISS J. WILLARD, CHAMPION DRIVEN FROM THEATER BY HOOTS AND CALLS was the headline of the Los Angeles *Herald*. The next day the paper ran another eight-column front-page banner: WILLARD LEAVES TOWN, SNEAKS OUT OF TOWN AS INDIGNANT FANS ROAST HIS CONDUCT.

In California, Houdini experimented with a "buried-alive" escape as a possible publicity stunt. Near Santa Ana early one morning he tunneled his way up from several shallow burials. Finally his assistants dug a pit six feet deep. He leaped to the bottom of it, stretched out on his back, covered his face with his hands. The earth was shoveled in. Feeling the heavy pressure of the sod, unable to see, Houdini had a moment of sudden panic. Suppose he blacked out or suffocated? He tried to call for help, but no one heard him. The earth trickled in his mouth, clogged his nose. Desperately he began to dig his way up. He clawed, tore, ripped, forced, pushed, crawled. As he saw a patch of blue above, he collapsed. Collins and James Vickery, his assistants, pulled Harry from the grave. He was covered with grime, his fingers were raw. "I tried out 'Buried Alive' in Hollywood and nearly (?) did it," he wrote. "Very dangerous; the weight of the earth is killing."

Danger sometimes came when it was least expected. Houdini had not been afraid to trade words with Jess Willard at the Orpheum, though at the time he thought the fighter might wait for him at the stage door. He was not as lucky with a

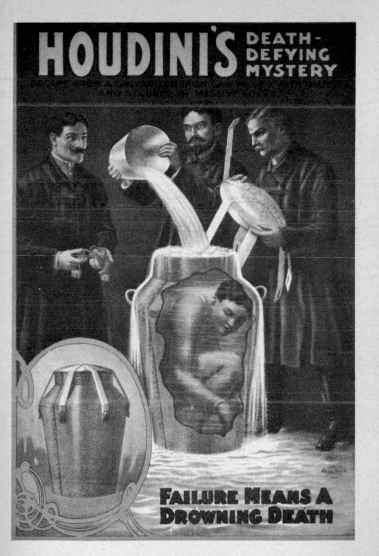

The escape from a padlocked can filled with water was introduced by Houdini, January 27, 1908, at the Columbia Theater in St. Louis. For more than four years it was the feature of his vaudeville act.

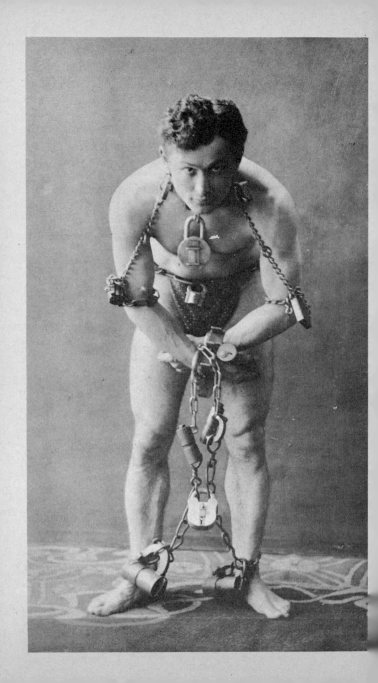

Ehrich Weiss, later to be world famous as Houdini, won these medals as a member of the Pastime Athletic Club track team in New York before his seventeenth birthday. Earlier he had been a runner for the Allerton Club.

After a successful "naked test," Houdini poses with the manacles from which he released himself. At twenty-six, he was a headliner on both the Orpheum and Keith circuits and had escaped from jails "in a nude condition."

Cecilia Steiner was twenty-two when she became Mayer Samuel Weiss' second wife in Budapest, May 27, 1864. Their son Ehrich was born there before they came to the United States. This photograph of Mrs. Weiss was taken many years later after one of Houdini's performances in Philadelphia.

A quick note from Bremen, Germany, before Houdini sailed for Mrs. Weiss' funeral in New York, acknowledged Will Goldston's cable of sympathy from London. Harry, who idolized his mother, collapsed in Copenhagen the day after his opening when he received the news of her death.

> Bremen July 22/13.
> my dear Goldston,
> Your wire has been forwarded, Thanks!
> I am very sick, and it will take a couple of months to get me back again, so I hope. Have canceled my work to end of Sept. We sail in morning for america.
> Regards
> H H
> cant write much, am too broken up over my darling mother. H H

Harry and Bess Houdini with their famous "Metamorphosis" mystery—a quick substitution feat using a box, a sack, and a cabinet. To the amazement of the audience, Harry escaped from a wrist tic, knotted bag, and roped and locked trunk in three seconds, and his wife took his place.

Mr. and Mrs. Harry Houdini pose for a formal portrait in Essen, Germany, in 1901. Their act in Europe was even more of an attraction than it had been in America. They had been married seven years when this picture was taken.

Silver replicas of the *Mirror* challenge handcuffs, from which Houdini had escaped in London, were presented to him in Brighton, England, by a representative of the newspaper in May 1904.

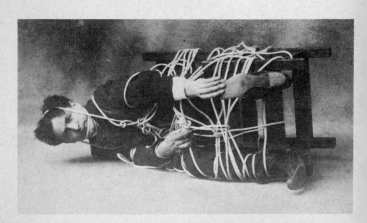

The first step in this "roped-to-a-chair" release was to tilt it over. Then, when Houdini freed a hand and slipped off a shoe, he was ready to squirm out of his bonds.

Police officials in Washington, D. C., apply official manacles, chains, and iron balls in their efforts to restrain the master escapologist.

Harry "Handcuff" Houdini had nothing up his sleeve when challenge irons were fastened on his wrists. Here four pairs of regulation handcuffs and a set of leg irons are locked in place prior to a stage demonstration of his skill.

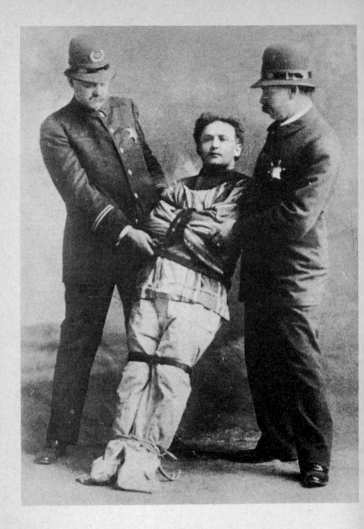

Another amazing feat: Once the straitjacket was strapped and the bag was roped, the challengers lifted Houdini and placed him inside a cloth-sided cabinet. He was free in minutes.

One of Houdini's special features was escaping from a ladder after he had been securely bound to it by short pieces of rope. Both ladder and ropes were supplied by the challengers.

Theo, Houdini's brother, worked his first theater dates abroad as "Harden." Then he added another "e" to his stage name and became "Hardeen" for the rest of his professional life. Harry called him Dash because he was such a sporty dresser.

Hardeen shows what the well-dressed "Handcuff King" wore for matinee performances. In the evening, he, like Houdini, performed in white tie and tails.

Houdini, who performed sensational feats high in the air and submerged in the sea, seldom took the wheel of a car. He bought an automobile in England, but driving made him nervous. Martin Beck, his American manager, Bess, and her pet dog Charlie are shown with him here in London.

Many circuses on the Continent had their own permanent buildings. Houdini, then the star of the Circus Busch, is seated in the automobile beside the driver. Harry was the strongest vaudeville attraction in Europe.

France's greatest magician, Jean Eugène Robert-Houdin. After Ehrich Weiss read the *Memoirs of Robert-Houdin*, his whole life—and even his name—was changed forever.

Alexander Herrmann was the most successful magician in America when Harry Houdini began his career as a mystifier. This remarkable Paris-born showman was acclaimed by both press and public as "Herrmann the Great."

Henry Evans Evanion, the great collector of magicana. Houdini arranged for a London photographer to take Evanion's last portrait. Before the British magician died, Houdini purchased most of his rare heralds, handbills, and engravings.

Will Goldston, the most prolific British writer on magic and a dealer in conjuring apparatus, was the founder of the Magicians Club of London. Houdini was elected its first president in 1911 and held the office for more than fifteen years.

ERECTED
BY
JOHN ANDERSON,
IN MEMORY OF
HIS BELOVED MOTHER,
MARY ROBERTSON,
WHO DIED 8TH JANUARY,
1830, AGED 40.
*Yes! She had friends when
fortune smil'd. it frown'd
they knew her not! She died.
the Orphans weept but liv'd to
mark this Hallow'd Spot.*
HERE ALSO RESTS THE ABOVE
JOHN ANDERSON,
"WIZARD OF THE NORTH."
DIED 3RD, FEBRUARY, 1874,
AGED 60

John Henry Anderson's relatives were too poor to pay for the upkeep of the great magician's grave in Scotland. Houdini started a fund to maintain it. Anderson, a world-traveler who was billed as "The Wizard of the North," made and lost several fortunes but was almost penniless when he died in 1874.

Harry Kellar, Alexander Herrmann's principal competitor, was later one of Houdini's closest friends. Kellar (R.) gave Houdini "Psycho," an "automaton," while he was in California making a motion picture.

Howard Thurston (L.), who succeeded Harry Kellar as America's greatest illusionist in 1908, poses with the world's most famous escape artist.

Fellow members of the Society of American Magicians: standing, left to right: B. M. L. Ernst, Houdini's lawyer; T. Nelson Downs, "King of Koins"; Frank Ducrot, the magic dealer; Dr. A. M. Wilson, editor of *The Sphinx;* Hardeen, Houdini's brother; and Frederick Eugene Powell, dean of the society. President Houdini is kneeling in the foreground.

Ching Ling Foo, China's most famous conjurer, has a visitor during his engagement at the theater in Brighton Beach, New York.

Chung Ling Soo (William Ellsworth Robinson, an American) and his wife Suee Seen (Dorothy, also an American). Chung Ling Soo was fatally shot while performing the dangerous bullet-catching feat in England.

Houdini was a pioneer airman. He was photographed here as he made his first flight over a German Army exercise field near Hamburg, Germany, on November 26, 1909.

Houdini had taken his biplane to Melbourne in the hope that he would be the first to fly in Australia. This photograph shows him at the controls of his Voisin after a successful flight in 1910.

CHALLENGE!

Thousands of handbills alerted the public that the "Elusive American" had accepted yet another challenge. Sometimes he met six dares in a single week.

COPY OF LETTER. *November 8th, 1910*

HOUDINI, Islington Empire, N.

Dear Sir,

Having watched your performance several times and making note of the manner in which you release yourself from various Restraints, we, the undersigned, having seen more than

100 YEARS' SERVICE IN METROPOLITAN POLICE DEPT.

between us, and knowing how to thoroughly fasten anyone, we hereby Challenge you to escape out of a Full-length Restraint that we have made from Heavy Sacking, bound with Leather and fastened with Canvas Belts and heavy Buckles and Straps   This restraint will

ENCASE YOUR ENTIRE BODY

from your Neck, down to and including your Feet, and we believe we can so secure you in the above-mentioned Restraint that we deem it a physical impossibility for you to release yourself therefrom.

The only condition under which we will bring the Restraint, and put you to the Test is, that you must make the attempt to release yourself

IN FULL VIEW OF THE AUDIENCE

to show you have no concealed confederates or traps in the stage,

Awaiting your reply, yours, etc.,

THOMAS J. BARTROP, Ex. P.C., 27 years' service, 12 Grove Villas, Poplar,
JAMES VINING, Ex. P.C., over 25 years' service, 29, Vesey Street, Poplar,
FREDERICK OATES, Ex. P.C., 25 years' service, 101 Abbott Rd., Poplar, B
ELLIS PAGE, Ex. P.C., 25 years' service, 86 Sussex Street, Poplar.

Houdini Accepts

the above Challenge on condition that any Straps or Fastens at the neck must be fixed so that during his efforts to release himself there shall be no danger of Strangulation.   Test to take place at the

ISLINGTON EMPIRE

On FRIDAY. NOV. 11th (2nd HOUSE).

HARRY HOUDINI THE JAIL BREAKER

INTRODUCING HIS <u>LATEST</u> & <u>GREATEST</u>

PRISON CELL & BARREL MYSTERY

HOUDINI is strapped & locked in a barrel placed in a police cell which is also locked and in less than 2 seconds changes places,

£100. WILL BE PAID TO ANYONE FINDING TRAPS PANELS OR FALSE DOORS IN THE CELL

Devils and a fairy godmother had nothing to do with Houdini's escape from a padlocked barrel and a locked wooden "cell," but they attracted attention from passersby who saw the lithographs.

The Water Torture Cell was Houdini's most puzzling stage escape. This half-sheet heralded the new attraction during his engagement with the Corty-Althoff Circus in Munich, Germany, in October 1912.

And I am a T.T.

Brewers Challenge Houdini!

MR. HARRY HOUDINI,
Empire Theatre, Leeds.

Dear Sir,—

We herewith **challenge you to allow four of our Employees to fill that tank of yours with beer,** and if you accept our defiance, name your own time. Our men will be at your disposal with the required amount of the beverage.

Awaiting the favour of an early reply.

JOSHUA TETLEY & SON, LTD.,
BREWERS, LEEDS.

CHALLENGE HAS BEEN ACCEPTED

FOR

SECOND PERFORMANCE

TO-NIGHT, THURSDAY, FEB. 9TH

AT

EMPIRE THEATRE.

The above Challenge and Acceptance is unique from the fact that it is positively the first time that such an affair has ever taken place in any part of the world.

A local brewing company, Joshua Tetley and Son, Ltd., in Leeds, England, challenged Houdini to escape from his Water Can when it was filled with beer. "And I am a T.T. (teetotaller)," he typed at the top of the challenge handbill.

The "burglar-proof" safe which Houdini penetrated on December 4, 1908, was just large enough to hold him. Note his typed comment that the release was made in fourteen minutes.

I escaped in 14 minutes.

Burglar-Proof Safe
Challenge to
HOUDINI

J. R. PAUL,
Locksmith and Safe Expert,
11 Ray Street,
Farringdon Road, E.C.

HOUDINI,
Dear Sir,

I have in my possession, a GENUINE OLD BURGLAR-PROOF SAFE, weighing about 8-cwt., which will easily hold a Human Being.

I would like to know, whether (you being locked up inside this Safe), there is any subterfuge by which, with your knowledge of locks, you could discover a method of escaping therefrom—WITHOUT DESTROYING OR INJURING the Lock or Safe.

If you would care to make this attempt in private you can do so at any time at my Works; but should you wish to do so Publicly, I will bring the Safe to the Euston or any other place you may designate, at your convenience.

I am, Sir,
Yours faithfully,
J. R. PAUL.

Houdini accepts the above Challenge, and invites Mr. Paul to

BRING THE SAFE
to the
EUSTON PALACE
on
Friday Evening next, December 4th, 1908
when he will make an attempt to perform this
UNHEARD-OF FEAT
in the SECOND HOUSE.

NEW ORLEANS ITEM
CHALLENGES
HOUDINI
"Sporting Chat"
of THE NEW ORLEANS ITEM
Dares Houdini

of the Orpheum Theatre to allow himself to be manacled by a member of the Police Department, selected by the Item, and then

to DIVE INTO the MISSISSIPPI RIVER

releasing himself under the water, which is a test Houdini claims to be able to do under all conditions.

Having accepted this defie, the test will take place at the

FOOT OF CANAL STREET,

Houdini allowing himself to be heavily manacled, and will leap into the Mississippi River from the gang plank of the

Steamer "J. S."

moored at the foot of Canal Street, Sunday, at 12 o'clock, noon.

The Leap can be plainly seen from the Levee

SUNDAY, NOV. 17th, 12 NOON SHARP !
REMEMBER THE DAY AND DATE !

Five thousand spectators saw Houdini dive, manacled, into the Mississippi River, Sunday, November 17, 1908, on a dare from a New Orleans newspaper columnist. In thirty seconds from the time he entered the water he was free.

Two attractions in the nation's capital—the Washington Monument in the background and Houdini suspended upside down in a straitjacket in front of Keith's Theater.

A moment after Houdini has wriggled from a straitjacket and let it fall to the ground.

The master of escape is caught in mid-air by a photographer as he dives, while handcuffed, from the wall of the Paris Morgue into the Seine, April 7, 1909.

Houdini was the first magician to produce an eagle —and make an elephant disappear.

Houdini—the magician and showman. Note his bare arms. He yanked off his sleeves, which were attached by snap fasteners, moments after he appeared on the stage.

The great publicist was one of the first to use radio talks for theater promotion.

Houdini and Senator Arthur Capper in Washington. The Senate, as well as the House, voted on a bill to outlaw "fortune-telling" in the District of Columbia. Neither bill was approved.

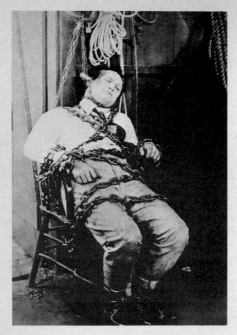

Chain escape, movie style. Note the strangulation twist around the neck.

Even barbed wire doesn't faze Houdini in this sequence from one of his films.

Although he rescues the heroine before she is swept over Niagara Falls in *The Man from Beyond*, the star himself had to struggle against being caught in the current.

The waterwheel, from which Houdini escapes after being lashed to it by the villains of *Haldane of the Secret Service*, adds a quaint touch to this between-takes shot.

A jail escape was one of the most exciting scenes in Houdini's movie, *The Grim Game.*

Houdini, the movie producer, with his cast and crew. Jim Collins, his chief stage assistant (right, wearing a straw hat and bow tie), passes out sandwiches. In the center of the picture, leaning on a funnel, is the star of the film.

Mina Crandon, the wife of a noted surgeon, was known to the public as "Margery the Boston Medium." Houdini claimed Margery used her left foot to press the lid of a bell box during her dark room séances. He duplicated her feats in his lectures and stage performances.

Mrs. Benninghofen, the reformed medium, showed Houdini how she gained the use of one hand in a dark room, though the sitter was sure that both were touching his. With the free hand she manipulated a metal trumpet and made it seem to be floating in the air.

During a lecture on mediums and their methods at the Police Academy in New York, Houdini demonstrates that he can slip his foot from a specially made shoe and use it to ring a bell on the floor. The sitter, whose feet are on Houdini's shoes, is unaware of the deception.

"Genuine" spirit photograph taken by Alexander Martin in Denver. Sir Arthur Conan Doyle endorsed Martin's phenomena. Though a friend of the magician for several years, he refused to speak to Houdini when the latter persistently spoke against spiritualism as a fraud.

Houdini produced his own spirit photographs by the method he claimed Martin used—double exposures. Here he appears with his own spirit to show how even the eye of a camera may be deceived.

The photograph Houdini couldn't explain. He and the photographer swore that the plate had not been scratched or altered. The strange "streak of light" (left) was not visible when the picture was taken in Los Angeles but appeared when the plate was developed.

Nino Pecoraro (L.), an Italian medium, amazed Sir Arthur Conan Doyle with his manifestations while tied to a chair. Houdini (R.) did the tying when Pecoraro was investigated by the *Scientific American*. Result: no manifestations.

The final Houdini séance was held at the Knickerbocker Hotel in Hollywood on Halloween, October 31, 1936—the tenth anniversary of the great magician's death. Standing behind the table are Mrs. Houdini and her friend Dr. Edward Saint. The others in the picture were members of the Pacific Coast Association of Magicians.

seemingly harmless bit of magic. A spectator was asked to cut a strip of cloth in half. The man accidentally slashed Harry's right hand as well as the cloth. The wound bled profusely. Houdini finished the trick, tossing out the strip to show that it had been restored. He wore a rubber glove to protect the injured hand when he made his escape from the Water Cell.

The week before Christmas Houdini accepted a double dare from a casket company at the Salt Lake City Orpheum. He was sealed in a coffin; it was locked inside a steel burial vault. Neither, the challengers discovered, could restrain him.

He perfected a device that would release a deep-sea diver from his heavy suit in an emergency. "So my work as an entertainer has served as something better after all, that is, if there is really anything better than making people forget their worries."

The war in Europe had seemed as remote as the moon to most Americans during the early months of the conflict. German submarine attacks on unarmed vessels brought it closer to home. BREACH WITH GERMANY OVER U-BOATS IMMINENT was the headline of the Washington *Times* on April 19, 1916, the day Houdini was suspended in a straitjacket in front of the Munsey Building in the nation's capital. Woodrow Wilson, addressing a joint session of Congress, demanded that the German government cease submarine warfare upon American merchant ships. "Friendly relations," the lead story said, "hang upon a slender thread of hope." Despite the crisis, there still was space on page one for the beginning of a long article headed "HOUDINI GETS OUT OF JACKET 100 FEET IN THE AIR." An eight-column photograph, on page two, showed "the biggest crowd ever assembled in Washington at one place except for the inauguration of a president." The spectators were watching Harry's aerial contortions. The graphic account of the two-minute, thirty-second release carried a surprise near the end.

"For the last thirty years or thereabouts," Houdini was quoted, "I've been getting out of all sorts of things human ingenuity has devised to confine a human being. . . . I've about made up my mind that this is the last stunt I'll perform. . . . See these gray hairs? They mean something. I'm

not as young as I was. I've had to work hard to keep up
with my profession. I'll still be entertaining for many years
to come. But I intend to do it along lines not quite so spectacular. As an escapist extraordinary, I feel I am about
through."

Saturday morning the forty-two-year-old "escapist extraordinary" was recognized from the Senate floor as he entered
the visitors' gallery. Vice President Thomas Marshall waved
from the presiding officer's chair. Several senators looked up
to see who merited this special attention. They too acknowledged his presence. Soon a page brought a message. Mr.
Marshall would like to see Mr. Houdini in his chamber. The
Senate was recessed as Harry diverted the nation's lawmakers
with his card tricks.

A year before, President Wilson had met Houdini after
his performance at Keith's. He commented: "I envy your
ability to escape from tight places. Sometimes I wish I were
able to do the same." That night, April 22, the chief executive,
his wife, and a guest sat in the Presidential Box at Keith's
Theater again. They cheered and applauded along with the
rest of the audience. It was, Harry told reporters, the happiest
day of his life.

In Baltimore the next week, fifty thousand onlookers
jammed Baltimore and Charles Streets as the escapologist
dangled from a rope attached to a cornice of the Sun Building and stripped away a five-buckle restraint. The *Sun* reported it was the biggest street mob since the Great Baltimore
Fire of 1904.

Harry stayed in the news during his summer vacation.
An article said that Houdini was looking for a live, sixteen-
foot shark. If he could find one, he would give a public
demonstration of the shark-fighting technique he had learned
in the Solomon Islands. Fortunately, no sharks of the proper
size were offered, and he had a comparatively quiet vacation.

In August, before going back on the road, Houdini entertained the prisoners at Sing Sing, the first important magician
to give a show within the prison walls since Alexander
Herrmann had performed there in 1896. Houdini held rapt
attention for three hours. The films of his escapes brought
envious sighs. Playing cards rose from an isolated pack at
his command. A rabbit was pulled from an empty box.
There was an unexpected reaction when he found a borrowed

watch, which a moment before had been conjured away, in the center of a loaf of bread.

"When I broke the loaf in half, two convicts grabbed the bread and ate it. It was white bread and I think they get only gray or black. . . . Next time I'll produce it in the midst of a pound cake."

Never did he have a more completely enthralled audience. Every move of his handcuff, straitjacket, and wooden crate escapes was carefully observed. His methods inspired at least one onlooker, a lifer, to make a successful break a few weeks later.

That fall a Baptist minister who had seen Houdini perform in Rochester preached a sermon on "Houdini and the Art of Getting Out of Things." Other clerics followed his example. The New York *Journal* ran an editorial on the subject, which said in part: "a distinguished clergyman has chosen Houdini's magical performance as a text for a sermon. He uses it to emphasize the fact that vice is a straitjacket that holds its victims, one that even the greatest magician could not overcome."

Sarah Bernhardt was on her last tour of the United States. John Drew, the distinguished actor, presented her with a bronze statuette at a special matinee in the Metropolitan Opera House. It was, he said, a sincere tribute from her admirers in the American acting profession. But the admirers neglected one thing: payment for the casting. The Gorham Company sent Madame Bernhardt the bill. When Houdini learned of the incident early in 1917, he sent a $350 check to the company. Madame Bernhardt told him she appreciated his gesture, but insisted that he keep the bronze. It was given a place of prominence in his living room.

The outdoor upside-down straitjacket release drew even larger crowds in the spring than it had during the fall and winter. Theaters reported Houdini's grosses were hitting a new high.

The greatest crowd ever assembled in Providence, Rhode Island, fifty thousand people, saw Houdini's open-air escape there. Twenty-two boys who played hooky from the Hope Public School to attend the midday exhibition were suspended. In other cities the police reported that the huge street throngs gave pickpockets the best opportunities they had had in years.

Houdini welcomed local magicians to his dressing rooms

wherever he performed. He attended meetings of independent magic clubs and invited them to affiliate with the Society of American Magicians. Largely through his efforts, assemblies of the society were formed across the United States. No conjurer before or since has been president of the Society of American Magicians and the Magicians Club of London simultaneously. Harry achieved this dual honor after his unanimous election as president of the S.A.M. at its annual meeting in June.

On June 12, 1917, two months after the United States declared war on Germany, Houdini registered for the draft. The New York *Clipper* posed the question: "Could Houdini, who gets out of everything, escape from military service?" The army was not interested in the forty-three-year-old escape king. In a burst of patriotism, Harry announced he would cancel his vaudeville bookings and work for the war effort.

He headed a show for the Red Cross in Brooklyn. Two ambulances were bought with the profits. He performed for the Army Athletic Fund at the New York Hippodrome. There he said he would escape from a chair in less time than it took to tie him up. The tying took five and a half minutes; his escape, seven. "Whew," he said when he was free. "They must have thought they were tying up the Kaiser."

As president of the S.A.M., Houdini arranged for the society to join with the Junior Patriots of America in staging a benefit performance at the Hippodrome for the wives and families of the men who lost their lives on the torpedoed U.S. transport *Antilles*.

He had tried, when he played the Palace Theater a year earlier, to get permission from Police Inspector Thomas V. Underhill to stage his straitjacket escape over Broadway. The request was refused. Now Elsa Maxwell, later to become America's most famous party-giver, secured a permit. The S.A.M. gave her a gold medal in appreciation.

Handbills announcing the *Antilles* benefit were distributed to thousands who craned their necks along Broadway to see Houdini's traffic-stopping stunt. Wives of S.A.M. members sold Thrift Stamps and War Bonds in the street. Harry expressed his gratitude to Miss Maxwell's friend, the mayor, by shouting "Vote for Mitchel" as he swung by his feet.

Despite this endorsement, the mayor was defeated in his bid for reelection.

Houdini's persuasive powers brought Harry Kellar, the dean of American magicians, from retirement in Los Angeles to make a "farewell appearance" at the benefit show. The evening at the Hippodrome began with seven magicians working side by side on the stage. For an eye-catching finish to their act, they produced a red banner with S.A.M. on it in gold letters. They strung it out from man to man and marched off.

Raymond Hitchcock, the musical comedy comedian, offered a burlesque conjuring act. Other magicians rolled up their sleeves before they worked their tricks. Hitchcock turned up his trouser legs. Arnold De Biere, a noted magician, acted as his assistant. Julius Zancig and his wife sent and received thoughts. Takasi produced his Oriental assistant from an empty sedan chair, linked and unlinked steel rings, tore and restored tissue paper.

Then Houdini took the spotlight. He was there, he said, to introduce America's greatest illusionist, who had made the trip from the West Coast to aid a cause close to his heart. A roar of welcome greeted the tall, bald, suntanned Kellar. A table floated in the air when the sixty nine-year-old magician touched it with his fingertips. He was tied in a cabinet. He produced "spirit" phenomena. This was not just another Davenport Brothers routine. It was a master performance by a great artist who conjured up memories as well as "ghosts."

Kellar bowed and turned to leave the stage. The applause was deafening. Houdini stopped him. He signaled for silence. Kellar walk off after his last performance? Ridiculous! He should leave in high honor by sedan chair. Members of the society brought out Takasi's ornate prop. Kellar sat on the cushioned seat. The chair was shouldered by the magicians and paraded around the stage. Suddenly the stage was filled with men who showered Kellar with flowers. The audience stood, joined hands and sang "Auld Lang Syne" as Kellar, with a final wave of his hand, was borne off into the wings.

There was more show to come. Houdini performed his trunk illusion and the Water Cell escape. Louise Homer sang "The Star-Spangled Banner." A detachment of French sailors drilled with flags of the two red, white, and blue nations whipping in the air. But the evening had reached its peak when the aging Kellar made his final bow.

Hippodrome producer Charles Dillingham was impressed by Houdini's staging of the affair. He asked him to create something spectacular in the way of illusions for his *Cheer Up* revue in January.

THE BIGGEST ILLUSION

The Vanishing Elephant made its first disappearance on the stage of the New York Hippodrome on January 7, 1918. Other magicians vanished doves, ducks, rabbits, horses, and donkeys. Houdini was the first to spirit away a live pachyderm. His friend Charles Morritt, whose "Disappearing Donkey" baffled audiences in England, conceived the idea. When Morritt described the illusion to Harry, he immediately bought the exclusive worldwide performing rights.

Jennie, a 10,000-pound elephant said to be the daughter of Barnum's Jumbo, and her trainer vanished from a wooden cabinet when Houdini fired a pistol. Curiously, no one seemed to notice that the trainer vanished as well as the elephant. The fact that a live elephant disappeared on a brightly lighted stage was overpowering.

Sime Silverman described the mystery in a *Variety* review headed HOUDINI HIDES AN ELEPHANT:

Houdini puts his title of premier escape artist behind him and becomes The Master Magician. The elephant was led on the stage by its trainer with Houdini watchfully standing by for another escape if the Asiatic product declared war. Nothing happened excepting Houdini made the elephant do a little magic by making a piece of sugar disappear. Houdini supplying but one piece through the high cost of sugar by the lump. In the immediate vicinity was a "cabinet" that would not fit an ordinary stage, but would Houdini's four-legged subject. The attendants turned the cabinet around. It only required fifteen of them to do it. Nothing there, open back and front. One would swear he was looking at the back drop directly through the cabinet. The trainer marched the mammoth in a circle around his lodging house and then led the brute into it. Curtains closed. Curtains opened. No elephant. No trap. No papier maché animal. It had gone. . . . Mr. Houdini has provided a headache for every child in New York. . . . The matinee crowds will worry themselves into sleep nightly wondering what Houdini did with his elephant.

Hippodrome patrons knew the animal could not have gone through a trap. Beneath the stage was the famous Hippodrome pool. Later in the show Houdini escaped from a box lowered beneath its surface. The critic from the Brooklyn *Eagle* noted: "The program says that the elephant vanished into thin air. The trick is performed fifteen feet from the backdrop and the cabinet is slightly elevated. That explanation is as good as any."

In the *Sphinx* Clarence Hubbard wrote his impression of the new illusion for the magic fraternity: "The Hippodrome being of such colossal size, only those seated in front got the real benefit of the deception." When the cabinet was opened, Hubbard couldn't see inside. He had to take Houdini's word for it that the animal had disappeared.

Some magicians said the elephant vanish wasn't much of a trick, but when pressed to explain it, couldn't. Three illusionists announced they would have their own disappearing pachyderms next season. One, Harry Blackstone, claimed he had invented the illusion but he offered not a shred of evidence to prove the statement.

Jennie, the 10,000-pound elephant, wore a bright blue ribbon around her neck and an alarm clock "wristwatch" on her left hind leg. The audience could see her until the very last second, Houdini said. The Hippodrome staff had their own pet names for Jennie. The dancers called her "The Ballet Master"; producer Charles Dillingham referred to her as "Miss 1917." The stagehands, burdened by extra work, said: "Here Comes Old Man Gloom."

Houdini was booked for a month and a half with the Vanishing Elephant. He stayed nineteen weeks at the Hippodrome—the longest theater engagement of his career. He could boast he had presented the largest and the smallest stage feats in the history of magic. One with an elephant, the other with needles and thread.

"Houdini May Be a Millionaire, That Is, If the Princess Nicholas Legacy Materializes," a Brooklyn newspaper reported a week after "Princess Alexandria Gladstone Nicholas" died in Rochester, New York, in February 1918. Harry met the lady in 1908 when he was researching the life of Washington Irving Bishop, a pioneer thought reader, who had collapsed during a demonstration at the Players Club in New York in 1889. The doctor who was called in pronounced the mentalist dead and an autopsy was performed. "Murder!" charged Eleanor Fletcher Bishop when she learned of the dissection of her son's body. She said the mentalist always carried a document which warned he was subject to cataleptic attacks which gave the appearance of lifelessness. Apparently this paper was missing when the physician ordered an autopsy. She instituted criminal proceedings against the three medical men involved. After hearings, which created a sensation in the press but no evidence of malfeasance, the indictments were dismissed.

Mrs. Bishop was ill and without income when Houdini visited her. She told him she was the daughter of a British nobleman and the cousin of Gladstone, the British prime minister. She said she had been known as "the Florence Nightingale of America" during the Civil War. The mentalist was the son of her first husband, Nathanial C. Bishop, a millionaire banker. Harry paid her bills and sent her money when she needed it. Mothers, especially mothers of mystery performers, had a special place in his heart.

She could never repay Houdini's kindness with cash, but she could leave him her share of General Carlos Butterfield's suit against the government of Denmark. He claimed the Danes had destroyed his ship illegally in Mexico in 1854. Mrs. Bishop saved the general's life when she stopped him from committing suicide. In gratitude, the officer gave her a third in his claim against Denmark. She in turn left her share in the potential settlement to the performer who had befriended her in her last years. The claim was never settled.

Houdini made a novel contribution to the war effort in February. He opened a special room at the Hippodrome and kept busy between shows teaching men in uniform how to escape from German handcuffs should they be captured overseas.

In March, Houdini announced that he had arranged a gigantic War Benefit performance at the Hippodrome. The Society of American Magicians would cosponsor the event

with the Showmen's League. Never, he said, would a show
be better publicized. Ruth Law, the aviator, would fly from
Chicago and land on the Hippodrome Roof. Kirby Speedy,
the daredevil diver, had offered to leap from the top of the
Woolworth Building into a four-foot-deep tank of water.
James J. Corbett, former world's heavyweight boxing champ,
was to be master of ceremonies.

Just as the publicity campaign got under way, the magic
world was shocked by news from London that Chung Ling
Soo had been killed while performing his famous bullet-
catching feat. Houdini, capitalizing on the headlines created
by Soo's death, promptly announced that he would attempt
the dangerous trick himself at the S.A.M. Showmen's League
event.

Despite the Chinese name, Chung Ling Soo was actually
an American, William Ellsworth Robinson. As a young man
he had worked as an assistant for both Harry Kellar and
Herrmann the Great. He had seen a statement issued by
Ching Ling Foo's manager. One thousand dollars would be
paid to any magician who could duplicate the Chinese
performer's production of a giant bowl of water. Robinson
practiced until he could not only do the bowl feat but Foo's
entire act. When he applied for the money, he learned that
the challenge was just a press blurb. Ike Rose, a theatrical
agent, told Robinson that Ching Ling Foo's act was in great
demand in Europe, where the Oriental had never played,
so he crossed the ocean to begin a new career.

After a disastrous debut in Paris, Robinson opened—as
Chung Ling Soo—in England. He was an overnight sensation. He had shaved his head, he wore Chinese robes, and
talked through an interpreter. The public accepted him as
Chinese. He soon had the most elaborate and successful
oriental conjuring act ever staged. He preceded Houdini at the
Alhambra Theatre in London in 1900.

When the real Ching Ling Foo came to England, he challenged the copyist, Chung Ling Soo, to a battle of magic at the
office of a London newspaper. Houdini, who had become
friends with Robinson after a chance meeting on a London
bus, taught Robinson his method for the needle-threading
feat—just in case Ching included a similar trick in his routine. Robinson, as Chung Ling Soo, came to meet the
challenge at the appointed time, but Ching never showed up,

so Chung won by default. Houdini was there to see the contest that was never staged.

Robinson was shot on the stage of London's Wood Green Empire while performing the bullet-catching feat—in which he caught live, marked bullets in a plate held in his hand. He had presented the feat onstage hundreds of times before. The bullet that killed him was fired March 23, 1918, and he died the next day in a hospital. The coroner's verdict was "misadventure."

When Harry Kellar learned that Houdini planned to perform Soo's bullet-catch at the Hippodrome, the old magician pleaded in a letter:

Now, my dear boy, this is advice from the heart. DON'T TRY THE D——N Bullet Catching trick no matter how sure you may feel of its success. There is *always* the biggest kind of risk that some dog will "job" you. And we can't afford to lose Houdini. You have enough good stuff to maintain your position at the head of the Profession. And you owe it to your friends and your family to cut out all stuff that entails risk of your life. Please, Harry, listen to your old friend Kellar who loves you as his son and don't do it.

Houdini was so moved by Kellar's words that he dropped the feat from his proposed routine.

The night of the benefit actor Lee Carillo, who had been advertised to replace James J. Corbett, didn't arrive at curtain time. Houdini took on the task of emcee. War Bonds totaling $54,000 were sold. A capacity audience applauded Madame Adelaide Herrmann, the widow of the great magician, as she presented her elaborate vaudeville act. Alexander Herrmann's wand was auctioned off for $250. Later the bidder couldn't be found. Houdini escaped from his Water Torture Cell. The entire First Battalion of the 71st Infantry marched on stage for the finale.

Before the elephant vanished for the last time at the Hippodrome, Houdini signed with B. A. Rolfe of Octagon Films to star in a movie serial. Two years earlier Harry had produced the special technical effects for Pathé's *The Mysteries of Myra*.

He was so excited by the possibilities of his escapes on film that he had written a script, "The Marvelous Adventures of Houdini, the Justly Celebrated Elusive American." When Harry sent Rolfe a copy, the producer explained that Arthur B. Reeve and Charles Logue, coauthors of *The Perils of Pauline, Exploits of Elaine,* and *The Clutching Hand,* already had been hired to prepare a scenario.

The Master Mystery went into production at Yonkers, New York. Houdini played the part of Quentin Locke, an undercover investigator for the Justice Department. He was employed in the research laboratory of International Patents, Inc., a firm financed by industrialists to buy new devices from inventors and keep them off the market—if they proved practical. This way the giant manufacturers would be able to retain control of their markets without retooling their plants.

In the story the daughter of one of the owners of International Patents, Inc., fell in love with Locke, who had little time for romance. Her father wanted to reform, but his partner, the chief villain, was fighting to gain control of the business for himself. A Chinese gang lord, an imported strangulation expert, and the cinema's first mechanical monster—an automaton—teamed up with the bad guy in this melodrama. They even used a gas, which produced "Madagascar madness."

Houdini, as Locke, was matched against them all. He escaped from a straitjacket, various manacles, and an underwater diving suit. He fought his way up from a pit covered with gravel and debris, broke out of a jail cell, and the straps of an electric chair. The film thrust him into all sorts of dramatic situations that would never have been possible onstage. He was tied inside a huge water tank, where water gushed in over him. He was bound at the bottom of an elevator shaft, as the car inched slowly down to crush him. Ensnared in coils of barbed wire, he had to free himself before a flow of acid burned away his body.

In one episode he hung, thumbs tied, in a locked room. With his legs he got a scissor hold around the neck of the automaton's emissary, choked the man, then kicking off a shoe, he went through the man's pockets with one foot until he found a key. Holding the key between his toes, he swung and fitted it into a nearby door, then turned the knob with his feet. When the door opened, Harry, still hanging by his thumbs, "walked up it" with his feet, mounted the top, then released his hands.

In another scene he dangled by his roped neck with his hands tied behind him. Houdini released his hands, reached up and took a firm grasp on the rope above his head so he would not be strangled. Next he swayed back and forth until his feet touched the chandelier. Astride the light fixture, he unloosened the rope from his neck and jumped down to safety. Later Houdini was suspended head downward over a vat of sizzling acid. The rope attached to his feet ran over a rafter to the knob of a door. If the heroine opened the door he would be lowered into the acid. He solved this one by freeing his hands and swinging like a human pendulum until he could reach the rafter. He pulled himself up on it and untied his ankles—in the nick of time, just as the door swung open.

Though he received no screen credit as a writer, Harry was constantly called in to help the scenarists concoct more diabolical dilemmas to showcase his acrobatic skill and escapology expertise.

One of the strangest torture instruments in the serial was a garroting machine. He was shackled to a board. The rope around his neck went through a hole in the wall to a control wheel. When the strangler in the next room turned the wheel, the rope tightened around Houdini's windpipe. Harry rapidly divested himself of the handcuffs. He revolved like a human clock hand as the strangling wheel turned. Eventually he spun faster than the wheel, obtained slack in the rope, and eased his neck free.

Before the fifteen-part serial ended, Houdini revealed that the "automaton" was manipulated by a hidden man, discovered that the second female lead was his long-lost sister and he was set to marry the good partner's daughter. Harry broke three bones in his left wrist during the rough-and-tumble movie-making action in Yonkers. Even so, he was back at the New York Hippodrome in August. Fractured wrist and all, he escaped at every performance from a suspended straitjacket.

How, he had wondered, during the months of movie work, could he hope to top last season's Vanishing Elephant? Finally he hit upon a patriotic production spectacle as the answer. His magic act opened on a bare stage. He put a sheet of glass on the top of a small table and a transparent fish bowl on that. To the water in the bowl he added red and blue liquids, then mixed them together. The top was sealed with a paper drumhead. Baring his right arm to his elbow, he plunged his hand through the paper and whipped out a cascade of silk streamers—four hundred feet long and forty inches wide.

As the music built to a crescendo, Harry produced a succession of giant flags which extended like a huge necklace from one side of the stage to the other. He moved to center stage and reached into the folds of the Stars and Stripes to pull out a live, wing-flapping American eagle. The wartime audience gave him an ovation. Houdini presided at the next meeting of the Society of American Magicians with the eagle perched majestically on his shoulder.

The eagle was added to the pets that abounded in the Houdini household. One of Harry's major sorrows was that his marriage had produced no children. Both he and his wife were fond of youngsters. He seldom refused an invitation to appear at an orphanage and he constantly performed extemporaneous tricks for the children who recognized him on the street or came backstage to meet him. There were always canaries, dogs, and rabbits in the house on West 113th Street. When a bird died, Bess suffered for weeks. The loss of Charlie, their Russian Pomeranian—Bess said the dog had been a present from Grand Duke Sergius of Russia—was a family tragedy. Harry trained Bobby, the fox terrier that replaced Charlie, to escape from a pair of miniature handcuffs. He also could wriggle out of a tiny straitjacket and pick up selected cards from a pack spread on the floor. Bobby, Houdini claimed, was "the greatest somersault dog that ever lived." When Bobby died in December 1918, Harry wrote an obituary for his pet in *M-U-M*, the magazine of the S.A.M., which he edited as president of the society.

One of Houdini's 1918 plans was to open a permanent theater of magic in New York, along the lines of the entertainment John Nevil Maskelyne had introduced in London in 1873. After forty-five years, "Maskelyne's Mysteries" still was doing excellent business at St. George's Hall. An extra Houdini touch was to be a display of historical conjuring apparatus, automatons, and colorful lithographs, prints, and programs from his collection. Oscar S. Teale, a past president of the Society of American Magicians, drew up a set of plans for the building. Houdini worked out costs and routines for the shows.

His friend Charles J. Carter had purchased Martinka's magic shop in 1917 with the profits his illusion show had earned abroad. Now, to Houdini's surprise, Carter leased the Belmont Theater and advertised that he would open his own "Temple of Magic." With a staff of insufficiently rehearsed assistants, little advertising, and less publicity, "The Eminent Prestidigitateur Carter, Direct from an Eight-Year Tour of the World," faced a Broadway audience. "He could have toured the globe another eight years and not been missed by Broadway," was the opinion of the New York *Clipper*. Harry put his plans aside for a more propitious time.

The late fall and early winter months were filled with hospital shows for wounded soldiers. Margaret Marsh, Houdini's leading lady in *The Master Mystery,* asked why he didn't revive his Vanishing Elephant. Harry, deadpan, explained that Herbert Hoover had ruled that elephants, as well as other resources, should be conserved. "I made two disappear a day, that is twelve a week. Mr. Hoover said that I was exhausting the elephant supply of the world."

Publicity stories for *The Master Mystery* revealed that Houdini's nine-month-old eagle, "Miss Liberty," was a he, not a she, and gave its real name—"Josephus Daniels Abraham Lincoln." The bird, the only tame eagle in the United States, was named after Old Abe, an eagle that had been carried on a flagpole in the Civil War. Houdini hoped his eagle would ride up Fifth Avenue perched on a flagstaff when the boys came marching home. With November came the armistice in Europe, but "Miss Liberty" did not spearhead the reception when the troops returned. Skilled as he was at gaining publicity, this was one event that Houdini could not dominate.

A week after the war was officially over, Houdini established a record of sorts by making fifteen appearances in a single day to promote his film serial in New England. A car waited by the stage door to speed him from movie house to movie house in Boston, East Boston, Brookline, Newton, Cambridge, and East Somerville. This tour was heralded as his first appearance in the area at "popular prices." Extensive newspaper ads, billboards, and handbills preceded the whirlwind tour. Business was fantastic. At one theater alone, the St. James in Boston, five thousand people were turned away from the door.

Houdini's contract for *The Master Mystery* called for an initial payment of $20,000 and half of the net profit. The serial had worldwide distribution. After the film had been in circulation a year, Harry sued for his share of the earnings, which he estimated at $32,795.18. When the suit came to trial he was awarded precisely that amount. By that time income from the film thriller had soared to $250,000. He filed another suit for his share of the additional money.

The star of *The Master Mystery* was confronted by a minor mystery in his own home. When Houdini was in Scotland, Bess had hired a maid, Bethel May Dove, and brought her back with them to New York. Bethel May was a conscientious worker and seemed to enjoy her work in the Houdini household. She was twenty-one and almost a part of the family. One night Bess went to Bethel May's room to give the girl her instructions for the next day. Ten minutes later Bess passed the door again and noticed that it was open. She walked back, looked in. Miss Dove was gone; so were her clothes and her wardrobe trunk. Harry told the police he thought she might have run away to marry a soldier. He knew exactly how his elephant disappeared, but the vanishing Dove baffled him.

The wrist broken during the filming of *The Master Mystery* no longer ached. Houdini thought a ridge around the break made it stronger than ever. He signed a contract for a movie to be made in Hollywood by Paramount-Artcraft Pictures, with Jesse Lasky as producer.

HOLLYWOOD STAR

Shooting began on Houdini's first feature-length Hollywood film in the spring of 1919. The scenario for *The Grim Game*, by Arthur B. Reeve and John W. Grey, was tailored to present the escape king at his daredevil best. He broke out of a jail cell, climbed the outside of the building to reach a dangling rope, and used it to slide to the street. Captured after a fight, Houdini was taken to a rooftop, strapped in a straitjacket and suspended head down over the side. He released himself, fell into an awning, then dropped to the ground. Then he rolled under the wheels of a moving truck, grasped the underside and rode away beneath it. Later he was caught in a rope-sling bear trap and tossed into a well.

The script also called for Houdini to make a plane-to-plane transfer in midair. As the aircraft maneuvered into position they collided, became locked together and spiraled toward the earth. Director Irvin Willat, in a third plane, kept his camera running. The two flying machines disengaged before they crash-landed in a bean field. Miraculously, no one was seriously injured. The story line was revised to include actual footage of the aerial accident in the film.

One of Houdini's best-kept secrets was that he was not involved in the crash. His left arm was in a sling at the time. He had fallen a mere three feet during a jail escape sequence and fractured his fragile left wrist again. His double for the plane-to-plane descent was Lieutenant Robert E. Kennedy.

Several other doubles were used for Houdini during the more hazardous feats in the movie. These were dummies with painted faces. They were dressed in striped shirts and dark trousers to match the clothes he wore. The dummies were filmed in long shots, then studio-made close-ups of the star were inserted to create the illusion that he performed breathtaking feats that not even a Houdini would risk.

While the broken wristbone was healing Houdini visited Harry Kellar, who lived six miles from the studio. He had tea with the famous magician on his seventieth birthday. Intrigued by Kellar's stories of his adventures around the world, Houdini asked for and received permission to write the retired illusionist's biography. It had been thirty-three years since Kellar's *A Magician's Tour, Up and Down and Round About the Earth* had been compiled by a journalist. Many of Kellar's best anecdotes were not in it. Harry used his good right hand to fill more than a hundred pages with notes. The Kellar biography proved to be another of Houdini's uncompleted projects.

After *The Grim Game* was finished, Harry returned to New York to take over the management of Martinka's magic shop. He had formed a company to purchase it before he went to the coast. And he worked on another book—*Miracle Mongers and Their Methods*. Playbills, portraits and old prints of stone-eaters, poison-swallowers, fire-resisters, and other performers of phenomenal feats were culled from his collection to illustrate it.

To no one's surprise, Houdini was elected to a third term as president of the Society of American Magicians. Traditionally a past president's medal was given to each outgoing president when he completed his term of office. The council decided not to wait in Harry's case. Perhaps they thought it would be a lifetime job. They presented him with the most elaborate award the society had ever made. The usual red-and-gold insignia was rimmed with thirty small diamonds and emeralds were embedded in the eyes of the two snakes which formed a circle around the letters S.A.M.

When *The Grim Game* opened at the Broadway Theater in New York, the publicity campaign featured the plane accident in midair. Houdini offered a thousand dollars to anyone who could prove that the collision had been faked. Like all Houdini challenges, it was a safe offer.

Harry scarcely had time to go through the stock of Martinka's magic shop and put aside the choice pieces for his personal collection before he returned to Hollywood to star in another Lasky picture. The filming of *Terror Island* began in September. Harry almost persuaded Kellar to make the thirty-minute flight with him to Catalina Island where location scenes were shot. But Kellar changed his mind as soon as he saw the plane. He said he'd be delighted to go—if he could keep one foot on the ground.

The new film followed the old formula: fast action, fantastic escapes, and spectacular stunts. After he saw the finished product, Kellar wrote: "What particularly left an impression on my mind was the fight in the submarine . . . where the water compartment was left open and the boat was being flooded. . . . The scene where you rescue the girl from the safe . . . I just sat there and enjoyed it and shouted at the villain like a gallery kid. To me it was all real and I forgot I was looking at a movie."

Motion pictures were now Houdini's major interest. He sold his share of Martinka's magic shop. Another of his ventures, a film developing corporation, was losing money, even though he had persuaded his brother Hardeen to leave the road and manage it. Kellar, an investor in the project, advised Harry to give it up. He wouldn't listen. An increasingly large share of his income went to keep the business afloat.

It had been almost six years since Houdini had toured Britain, and theater managers there were now asking him to honor contracts he had signed before the war. *The Master Mystery* had been a success in England. A new demand had risen for his act. This time he would not only be a vaudeville headliner, but an American movie star making personal appearances. He sailed in December 1919 on the *Mauretania*.

In postwar Britain entertainers were required to register with the police as they entered and left cities. Ration cards were issued for sugar and butter. Meat was almost impossible to find. "But I will say," Houdini wrote, "that if one knew how to go after it, it was obtainable."

Mourning clothes, worn by women, were reminders of the tragic years. Shops, however, were doing brisk business, and the demand for luxury items was at a new peak. Prices had risen everywhere. As his expenses mounted, Harry demanded and got bigger salaries.

The last week in February 1920, during his engagement at the Empire Theatre in Edinburgh, Harry took Bess to visit the grave of the Great Lafayette. A versatile magician, who had shared billing with Houdini in the United States some twenty years previously, Lafayette could paint, juggle, act, and make lightning-fast changes in costume and character. In a hilarious burlesque of Ching Ling Foo, he produced a giant bowl of water as well as pigeons, ducks, and a small Negro boy.

Houdini had given Lafayette a dog when the two magicians worked in Nashville, Tennessee, in 1899. Lafayette, who lived alone, developed a strong attachment to the animal, which he named Beauty. As his fame grew, so did his love for his *"gheckhundt."* Lafayette became the highest paid illusionist in vaudeville. He toured with his own company, orchestra, and scenery. His feature illusion, "The Lion's Bride," was presented in the form of a playlet, the climax being a startling change of a live lion to Lafayette.

Beauty died in Edinburgh in May 1911. Lafayette performed at the Empire Theatre with tears streaking his greasepaint. A fire broke out during his act on May 9. The asbestos curtain was lowered, but the stage became a blazing trap. Eleven bodies were found in the charred ruins. One was recognized as Lafayette because of the costume and sword. The British King and other notables expressed sympathy. Houdini sent a floral arrangement in the shape of Beauty's head. Then another body was found. This was positively identified as Lafayette. The other corpse had been that of his stage double, a man named Richards. When Houdini heard of the strange mix-up, he said: "He fooled them in life and in death. I envy him."

Harry and Bess stood by the monument where Lafayette and Beauty lay buried. "We had brought flowers in pots. . . . I said, 'Lafayette, give us a sign you are here.'" Both pots overturned, as if a spirit hand had swept them to the ground. Houdini set them upright. Again they crashed to the ground. "This time they fell with such force that the pots broke." A spiritualist would have concluded that the ghost of the great illusionist had made its presence known. Houdini had a more rational explanation. "It was all very strange, yet I do not attribute what happened to anything other than the high wind which was blowing at the time." The photograph Houdini had taken that winter day in Piershill Cemetery bears out his conclusion. Harry and Bess are shown by the Lafayette monument. The wind has whipped open the bottom of Bess' coat.

At the suggestion of Will Goldston, Houdini made an outline for a book, *Magical Rope Ties and Escapes.* Another project, which took more of his time, was research for a history of spiritualism. In the aftermath of the war the cult had grown. The British press reported that such noted figures as Sir Arthur Conan Doyle were firm believers in spiritualism. Houdini could not understand how Doyle, who had shown such keen powers of reasoning and deduction in his Sherlock Holmes stories, could be deceived by simple tricks in dark rooms. At the same time, Harry was appalled by the callousness with which professional mediums took advantage of grief-stricken widows and mothers, who flocked to séances in the hope that they might talk with and perhaps see their departed loved ones. He began attending as many as two séances a day to gather material for his history.

After Houdini met Doyle he wrote Kellar from Portsmouth on April 20: "I had lunch with Sir Arthur Conan Doyle Thursday and he saw my performance. He was so much impressed that there is little wonder in him believing in Spiritualism so implicitly."

He talked with Carl Hertz, the illusionist who had appeared for the prosecution at the Ann O'Delia Diss Debar trial in New York. Hertz had helped send the medium to jail by duplicating in court the deceptions she had used to gain title to lawyer Luther B. Marsh's Madison Avenue mansion. Houdini also listened to Stuart Cumberland describe séances he had attended. Widely known as a "thought reader," Cumberland's technique was to hold a spectator's wrist as he sought to find a hidden object. His fingers detected changes in the pulse beats when he approached his goal. Washington Irving Bishop had used a similar method. Cumberland was a bitter critic of spiritualism on the lecture platform and in his books.

Houdini visited more than a hundred mediums during his British tour. Letters from Sir Arthur gave him entrée to sittings where otherwise he would have been unwelcome. He found no evidence that the communication with the dead was anything more than self-deception or conscious trickery. "The more I investigate the subject," Houdini wrote, "the less I can make myself believe." In March he injured his right ankle while escaping from the Water Torture Cell. During a week of doctor-prescribed recuperation, he put his notes in order. He felt there was a pressing need for a debunking book on spirit phenomena by someone who was an expert on trickery—and he thought he was that someone.

In Newcastle, Houdini was the subject of an unusual article in the *Illustrated Chronicle*. A reporter had been attracted by a noontime crowd which gathered in front of St. Nicholas' Cathedral. All eyes were fastened on the lofty spire. The reporter looked up but saw nothing unusual. A girl nearby explained the rapt interest. She said the people were waiting to see Houdini who was in the church. Any minute now he would climb the spire; after that he was to be put in a box and thrown off the high level.

Shortly after five o'clock the reporter passed the cathedral again. The street was still filled with people staring upward. He asked an old man why he was there. Again he heard that Houdini was about to perform a spectacular feat. Meanwhile Harry was in his dressing room at the Hippodrome preparing for his performance. He had not announced an outdoor stunt that day. The first he heard about the rumor was from the reporter.

The theatrical papers reported that Houdini was booked at the London Palladium for the highest salary ever paid a single performer—$3,750 a week. Houdini was greeted with a roar of approval when he walked onstage. Will Goldston, who saw the show, said that at the end of his routine Houdini had to beg off—after four bows.

The perennial president of the Magicians Club of London was honored with a banquet at the Savoy Hotel ballroom. The Great Raymond, who once had aroused Houdini's ire by ordering a Water Can from a manufacturer without his permission, apologized and admitted that Houdini had invented the escape. During his speech Raymond said: "Harry Houdini was born, as I was, under the Stars and Stripes. He saw them a little bit ahead of me and he has been ahead of me ever since."

Harry thanked Raymond for his compliments and expressed his appreciation for the illuminated scroll presented to him in a silver box. He talked about movie-making more than magic. He had been filming street scenes during his British tour which he planned to use in one of his pictures. Movies made his life easier, Houdini told the club. In the past when he had worked out a sensational stunt—such as a bridge jump or an open-air straitjacket release—he had to repeat it in every city he played. Once he put the feat on celluloid, it could be shown and reshown to millions of people all over the world.

When the Magicians Club moved to new quarters above

Bennion's Restaurant in Great Chapel Street, Houdini talked more about his plans for the future. In the years to come he would confine his activities to picture-making and writing. But before he retired from the stage he would make a farewell tour of the world with his own full-evening magic spectacle.

The six-month tour of Britain had been the most successful ever for him. His luck held on the ship home: for once he was not seasick. He used the time to correct the manuscript of the book on rope ties and to work on the notes for the volume on spiritualism.

John William Sargent, a gray-haired, goateed past president of the Society of American Magicians, had been in charge of the Houdini collection during his absence overseas. He was to have catalogued the books. Reluctantly, Sargent admitted the task was too much for him. For almost three years he had been Houdini's private secretary. He enjoyed his work in the treasure house of magic, but the collection had grown to such staggering proportions that Houdini needed a trained librarian.

The new addition to the staff was a seventy-four-year-old scholar, Alfred Becks. The British-born librarian had close ties with the theater. Once he had been the man Professor Tobin cut in pieces, then put back together. That was before Tobin sold the feat to Dr. Lynn. Becks had been a secretary to Dion Boucicault, the playwright, and Lotta Crabtree, the actress. For thirty years he had worked in the office of A. M. Palmer, the theatrical manager. His interest in dramatic literature led him to Harvard, where he catalogued the Robert Gould Shaw collection. It had taken him two years to catalogue the Evert Jansen Wendell library and prepare a list of the duplicates for public sale. Houdini estimated it would take Becks a year to get his collection in workable order.

Becks moved to the house on West 113th Street. Each morning he hobbled down the stairs to the rooms that held Houdini's books and memorabilia. A maid would bring him his lunch. Often hours would pass before he would tear himself away from his cataloguing to eat. Precisely at five o'clock he would go to his room and change his clothes. Though his working hours were over, he almost invariably returned and, except for a dinner break, continued his labors until nine.

After Sargent died at the age of sixty-eight in September, Julia Sawyer (Sauer), Bess' niece, became Houdini's private secretary. Oscar S. Teale gradually took over the research for and the editing of Houdini's literary projects, which Sargent had formerly handled. John William Sargent had been a reserved, gentlemanly collaborator. The bald, bespectacled Teale was frequently testy and outspoken. He too had been a past president of the S.A.M. Though he spent most of his life as an architect, he had been passionately interested in magic since boyhood. Teale had known Houdini for years, worked for him at Martinka's magic shop, and was always ready to take on anyone who was critical of Harry or his performances.

Houdini was the featured attraction at the Field Days staged for the New York Police Department Hospital Fund at Sheepshead Bay in late August 1920, but he turned down offers for Keith and Orpheum tours for the fall and winter. He had decided to retire from vaudeville and produce his own films. He formed the Houdini Picture Corporation— Harry Houdini, president.

THE MAN FROM BEYOND

The president of the Houdini Picture Corporation took just ten days to write the scenario for his first production. The star of the film, Houdini, would be chopped from a block of ice, where he had been frozen a hundred years before, defrosted, and given the assignment of trying to cope with the complexities of twentieth-century life.

Most of the footage for *The Man from Beyond* was shot at Fort Lee, New Jersey. The arctic scenes, however, were filmed during the winter at Lake Placid. And in May 1921, the company traveled to Niagara Falls for the big rescue sequence. Burton King, who had directed Houdini's serial *The Master Mystery*, artfully blended shots of the thundering falls with Houdini's dramatic rescue of the heroine before her canoe reached the brink. It was said later that dummies had been used for some shots and that Harry had a concealed safety line attached to his waist. But no such trickery was apparent in the finished product. The reels of *The Man from Beyond* were processed and printed at Houdini's Film Development Corporation plant. Editor Houdini supervised the cutting and editing.

The Film Development Corporation had taxed his bank account for almost three years. Harry transferred $5,000 to it before he sailed to England; he sent another $10,000 from London. Further, the production costs of his movie far outstripped his estimate. To build up his capital he took advantage of the box-office war then raging between Keith and Shubert interests. He signed for nine weeks with Keith at $3,000 a week for the first four theaters, then $3,500 a week for the last five. His act opened with films of his bridge jumps and closed with the Water Cell escape. In between he performed the needle-threading feat and talked of his adventures. Periodically he accepted challenges to escape from wooden boxes.

The tour began in Boston, always a good city for him.

More than twenty-five feet of publicity appeared in the papers.
In the past other escape men had used his name, now a
woman billed herself as Lady Houdini. A letter of complaint from Bess was printed in *Billboard:*

> This is very unfair to me, as there is only one Houdini
> and I have been married to him for a quarter of a
> century, and I therefore would ask in fair play, that, as
> I have managed to have an inescapable hold on Houdini,
> all others of the gentler sex keep away from the name
> which rightfully belongs to me.

Houdini won a thousand-dollar bet for the Knights of
Columbus by getting out of a straitjacket during his engagement at the Palace Theater in New York. An agitated policeman tried to stop the stunt when Houdini already was in the
air, dangling over Broadway. The officer hadn't been shown
the special permit for a charity performance. Harry shouted
down: "See the theater manager. I'm busy."

"I am working very hard, drawing bigger than ever," he
wrote in late January 1922, "but must acknowledge that the
publicity I have received in motion pictures is the prime
cause of the big crowds. . . . Every week is like an ovation. . . . Despite my enormous salary, they are engaging me
for five more weeks."

The world premiere of *The Man from Beyond* was held
in April at the Times Square Theater. The film had its faults,
but critics agreed that one scene alone was worth the price
of admission. "It has a whale of a punch," *Variety* said.
"Houdini does a sensational rescue of the heroine in the
Niagara rapids, and it has a kick that would carry any audience." Quincy Martin, in the *World*, "quivered at the views
of the couple battling in the rapids on the verge of the
cataract and almost cheered when they made the crawl to
safety." Harriet Underhill proclaimed in the *Tribune:* "There
is no fake about this; Houdini actually does it."

Houdini, the showman, was taking no chances with the
opening of his first movie production. He made personal
appearances at the Times Square Theater featuring the Vanishing Elephant, which had not been seen since his long run
at the Hippodrome. He included other spectacular feats in his
act. A fur-clad girl stood on the topmost of three stacked

tables. He climbed a ladder to cover her with a cloth. When he pulled away the covering, he shouted, "Good-bye winter!" The girl was gone. He swallowed needles, brought them up threaded. He escaped from a straitjacket and caused knots to appear and disappear in a silk scarf. Surrounded by the committee of volunteers that had come on stage for this series of tricks, he took off his thumb, waved it and replaced it. A wooden structure, shaped like a pyramid, was shown empty. He fired a pistol, shouted "Welcome summer!" Up popped a girl garlanded in flowers.

Houdini borrowed elephants for the vanishing feat from the Ringling Circus. Before the elephant—either Fannie or, more often, a smaller pachyderm named Baby—entered the wooden cabinet, the rear curtains of the stage were raised. When the animal disappeared, the audience saw a bare brick wall through the box. There was a sound reason for this new presentation at the Times Square Theater. Had the curtains stayed in place, the far end of the cabinet would have been flush with the backdrop on the shallow stage, instead of fifteen feet away from it as was the case at the larger Hippodrome. The combined Houdini-on-film and in-person show ran three weeks, giving Harry good reason to believe his future as a movie producer-impresario was assured.

Sir Arthur Conan Doyle, who had arrived in New York for a country-wide lecture tour on spiritualism, came with his family at Houdini's invitation to see *The Man from Beyond.* Doyle's verdict: "The very best sensational picture I have ever seen . . . it holds one breathless . . . one of the really great contributions to the screen."

He was less enthusiastic about Harry's library when he had lunch at the house on West 113th Street. The magic section, he admitted, was outstanding, but the books on spiritualism were written mostly by people who held antagonistic views. Where were the monumental epics by the believers? Houdini was apologetic. Some might be in the crates stored in the basement. If Sir Arthur would give him a list of the books he should read, he would get them. Why, he would even devote a complete floor of his home to volumes on the subject.

After lunch Sir Arthur read the letters in Harry's collection by D. D. Home and Ira Davenport, two of the author's personal heroes. Doyle discounted the hundreds of letters Harry Kellar had written, though Kellar had been with the Davenport Brothers on an American tour and had made his first success with a reproduction of their cabinet séance.

Harry and Bess attended Sir Arthur's lecture at Carnegie Hall. The tall, portly, moustached writer displayed a "spirit photograph" which had been taken during a séance in London at the home of Sir William Crookes, the eminent scientist. "Katie King" was so obviously a flesh-and-blood woman in white drapery that Harry squirmed in his seat. How could this intelligent man believe in such utter nonsense?

Doyle declined Houdini's invitation to the annual S.A.M. banquet at the McAlpin Hotel until Harry assured him that none of the performers would ridicule spiritualism. Then he announced he would have a little surprise for the magicians. Sir Arthur sat with the other special guests: Adolph S. Ochs, the publisher of *The New York Times;* Melville Stone, the founder of the Associated Press; and Bernard Gimbel, the department store owner.

Doyle volunteered to assist Max Malini during a card trick and he came up for Houdini's trunk feat. Harry borrowed Sir Arthur's coat and put it on before his hands were bound behind his back and he was tied in the bag and locked in the trunk. A few seconds later he was out. When the trunk and bag were opened, there was Bess inside, all but swallowed up in Sir Arthur's huge jacket.

Now came Doyle's surprise. A movie projector was wheeled in, a screen erected, and the lights extinguished. Realistic prehistoric monsters were projected on the screen. These man-made dinosaurs would later appear in the film version of Sir Arthur's story *The Lost World.*

In June, Doyle, resting from the rigors of his lecture tour, invited the Houdinis to visit him at Atlantic City. They checked in at the Ambassador Hotel in a room adjoining his suite. Doyle had read a biography of the Davenport Brothers which Harry had given him. This convinced him more than ever that the Davenports were genuine mediums. Houdini told Sir Arthur of his visit with Ira. In Australia in 1910 he had placed a wreath on William Henry Davenport's grave and talked at length with William Fay, who had worked with the brothers. When he met Ira Davenport in Mayville, New

York, in 1911, the older brother had been amazed by Houdini's knowledge of his career. Ira admitted frankly that he was an entertainer, nothing more. He taught Harry the secret of the rope tie he used to free his hands whenever he needed them to ring a bell or play a musical instrument.

But Doyle persisted in his belief. What about the time the boys, still in their teens, were lifted by invisible hands from a street in Buffalo and deposited in a snowdrift sixty miles away? Doyle asked. It was just a fable, Harry answered. This did not shake Sir Arthur's convictions; he had made up his mind and was not about to ch nge it. While conceding that they might have resorted to trickery when their powers were weak, as other mediums had, Doyle insisted until his dying day that the Davenports were genuine mediums, not conjurers.

As they sat in chairs by the sea, Doyle showed Houdini a photograph of a corpse in a coffin flanked by male and female spirits. Could anyone be so heartless s to fake ghostly forms in such a setting? he asked. Harry agreed it would be sacrilegious but refrained from adding he was familiar with photographic techniques which were used to produce such pictures. Sir Arthur mentioned the wonderful spirit photographs taken by a London medium, Mrs. Deane. Again Houdini diplomatically chose to avoid a controversy with his friend. A recent letter from England had informed him that Mrs. Deane was detected in fraud, as she switched marked camera plates for her own.

Sir Arthur approached the Houdinis on the beach late the afternoon of June 17, 1922. Lady Doyle had asked him to invite Harry to an automatic-writing séance. He told Bess that with Harry alone, there would be a better ch nce for success. In the Doyle sitting room the curtains were closed. Lady Doyle sat at a table. On it were pencils and writing pads. Doyle bowed his head in prayer, asking d'vine aid, then covered his wife's hands with his own to generate spiritual power. Houdini closed his eyes, honestly trying to blot out all worldly thoughts. Sharp rapping noises made them open wide. Lady Doyle was striking a pencil against the top of the table as if impelled by an electric current. The unseen forces, she said, were more powerful than they had ever been before. "Do you believe in God?" she asked. Her hand hit the table three times. Her spirits always rapped three times to answer yes. She marked a cross on the pad. She asked if the invisible presence was Houdini's mother. She beat on the table three times more. Touching the point of her pencil to the pad, she wrote rapidly:

"Oh, my darling, thank God, thank God, at last I'm through. I've tried, oh so often—*Now* I am happy. Why, of course, I want to talk to my boy—my own beloved boy—Friends, thank you with all my heart for this. You have answered the cry of my heart—and of his—God bless him a thousand fold for all his life for me—never had a mother such a son—Tell him not to grieve—soon he'll get all the evidence he is so anxious for—Yes, we know—tell him I want him to try to write in his own home. It will be far better so."

With Lady Doyle writing quickly, the spirit message followed on:

"I will work with him—he is so, so dear to me—I am preparing so sweet a home for him which one day in God's good time he will come to—it is one of my great joys preparing it for our future—I am so happy in this life—it is so full and joyous—My only shadow has been that my beloved one hasn't known how often I have been with him all the while, all the while—here away from my heart's darling—combining my work thus in this life of mine.

"It is so different over here, so much larger and bigger and more beautiful—so lofty—all sweetness around me—nothing that hurts and we see our beloved ones on earth—that is such a joy and comfort to us.

"Tell him I love him *more* than ever—the years only increase it—and his goodness fills my soul with gladness and thankfulness.

"Oh—just this—it *is* me.

"I want him only to know that—that—I have bridged the gulf—that is what I wanted, oh so much. Now I can rest in peace.

"Now soon—"

Sir Arthur interrupted. Perhaps Houdini had a question for his mother? Normally Harry would have asked: "Tell me the name you called me when I was born?" or any of a dozen other séance-stopping challenges. Not wishing to embarrass the Doyles, he concentrated on, "Can my mother read my mind?" a query that had been suggested by Sir Arthur. Lady Doyle's pencil started scrawling again:

"I *always* read my beloved son's mind—his dear mind—there is so much I want to say to him—but I am almost overwhelmed by this joy of talking to him once more. It is almost too much to get through. The joy of it—thank you, thank you, thank you, friend, with all my heart for what you have done for me this day—God bless you too, Sir Arthur, for what you are doing for us—for us over here—who so need to get in touch with our beloved ones on the earth plane—

"If only the world knew this great truth—how different life would be for men and women.

"Go on, let nothing stop you—great will be your reward hereafter—Good-bye—I brought you, Sir Arthur and my darling son together—I felt you were the one man who might help us pierce the veil—and I was right—

"Bless him, bless him, bless him, I say, from the depths of my soul—he fills my heart and later we shall be together—Oh, so happy. A happiness awaits him that he never dreamed of—tell him that I am with him—just tell him that I'll soon make him know how close I am all the while—his eyes will soon be opened—Good-bye again—God's blessings be on you all."

Lady Doyle put down her pencil. Houdini was uncomfortable. First the Christian cross at the top of the paper on a message ostensibly from his Jewish mother had bothered him; then the flow of words in English. His mother knew only a few words of the language and could neither write nor read it. She had always written him in German. By sheer coincidence the séance had been held on her birthday. The message hadn't mentioned it!

The spirit had told him to try for messages at home. He asked Lady Doyle just how he should go about it. She told him to keep his mind clear, take a pencil and let it write. He picked up a pencil, touched it to a pad and wrote the name "Powell."

Sir Arthur was thunderstruck. A friend named Ellis Powell had died recently. Here—on Houdini's first attempt at automatic writing—he had made contact! The answer to the escape king's amazing skills was now clear beyond doubt. Houdini was not a trickster at all—he was a medium!

Harry had another explanation. Frederick Eugene Powell, the American illusionist, had been in his mind during the weekend. Powell's wife was ill; the magician was thinking of hiring an attractive girl to take her place. Harry had been in correspondence with Powell and had talked to Bess about him.

No! The message had been from the British Powell, Doyle insisted. Houdini was trying to hide his psychic powers. Despite Harry's protestations, Sir Arthur was convinced that he, by accident, had discovered Houdini's "secret."

Later the Doyles were guests at the Houdinis' wedding anniversary party at the Earl Carroll Theater. Raymond Hitchcock, the star of *The Pinwheel Revue*, introduced Sir Arthur and Houdini from the audience, then asked Harry to come on stage to perform one of his marvels. B. M. L. Ernst, Houdini's lawyer, shouted: "Do the needles!" Out from Houdini's pocket came five packages of needles and a spool of thread. Stagehands, chorines, and the cast flocked on stage to see the trick. When it was over, there was time only for the final production number of the revue.

Two days later the Doyles boarded the *Adriatic* for their return passage to England. Among their bon-voyage messages was one from Houdini. He wished them a quick return to American shores.

Young Richard Ernst, the son of Houdini's lawyer, for a few minutes at least, shared Doyle's opinion that Houdini had occult powers. A sudden cloudburst on the Fourth of July at the Ernst summer home in Sea Cliff, Long Island, sent the boy and his friends scurrying to the magician. Richard implored the wizard to stop the rain so that he could set off his fireworks. Harry obligingly extended his arms heavenward and commanded the storm to cease. It did. After the Roman candles and sparklers had been exhausted, Richard informed Houdini that the rain would have stopped by itself.

Never one to ignore a challenge, even from a youngster, Harry again lifted his hands and dramatically called for the rain to start again. Down came another shower. The children ran for shelter and asked the rainmaker to call off his deluge. Houdini, unlike most gamblers with fate, ignored their cajolings. He was wise enough to quit when he was ahead.

Though Houdini and Doyle had parted on cordial terms,

it was perhaps inevitable that their opposing views on spiritualism would lead to a personal clash. In an article that appeared in the New York *Sun* on October 30, 1922, under the title "Spirit Compacts Unfulfilled," Houdini wrote: "My mind is open. I am perfectly willing to believe, but . . . I have never seen or heard anything that could convince one there is a possibility of communication with the loved ones who have gone beyond."

Still treading lightly because of his friendship with the Doyles, Houdini mentioned neither the séance in Atlantic City nor Sir Arthur. Nevertheless, the article made Doyle "rather sore" and he sent a bristling letter to Harry, criticizing him for ignoring the contact Lady Doyle had made with Mrs. Weiss and Houdini's own automatic writing of the name Powell. Houdini attempted in his reply to show the British spiritualist why he could not accept his conclusions. Once more he failed; apparently nothing could shake Sir Arthur's faith.

INVESTIGATING THE SPIRITS

The Man from Beyond opened at the Rialto Theater in Washington in mid-August 1922. Instead of promoting the film with the usual escape stunts, Houd ni made personal appearances in which he warned the public against spiritualistic frauds. He used projected slides to demonstrate his points and wrote a daily column in the Washington *Times* answering readers' questions about psychic racketeers. The gross for the engagement was $9,000. In Detroit at the Madison Theater Houdini appeared in person the first day of the film's run and featured his straitjacket escape. The box-office figures there mounted to $12,000. Later a record-breaking opening audience of 4,700 at the Globe in Boston assured a holdover for a second week.

Harry would have had to have been triplets to keep up with the demands for personal appearances with his film. He organized road companies. Houdini Unit No. 1 premiered at the Roosevelt Theater in West Hoboken, New Jersey, early in September. It was headed by Frederick Eugene Powell, the distinguished performer, whose name Harry had written instinctively at the Doyle séance in Atlantic City. With Powell on the show was Virginia Carr, a mentalist. Houdini made a special appearance with them in the middle of the week. He was a popular figure in Hoboken; his Film Development Corporation plant was there. Six policemen on motor-cycles met the car carrying Harry and Bess at the ferry landing and, with sirens screaming, escorted them to the theater, where the city's mayor introduced Houdini to the soldout house. A pretty girl presented him with a massive bouquet of American Beauty roses. He promptly passed them to Bess.

Houdini wore a straw hat. After the show a mob of boys surged around him at the stage door and yelled that straw hat days were over. He laughed and sailed his headpiece in

180

the air. Seconds after the hat had landed in the crowd, it was torn to bits as his fans scrambled for souvenirs.

The Houdini Unit No. 2 opened in November at Steinway Hall in New York. It featured Frederick Melville's "radio-operated mechanical man" and Gemester, who escaped from handcuffs and a locked barrel. Houdini Unit No. 3 starred Mystic Clayton, the crystal gazer. The combination of Houdini in *The Man from Beyond* and a live mystery attraction was paying off handsomely.

The manuscript for a new book, *Houdini's Paper Magic*, was sent to E. P. Dutton & Company, the firm which had published his *Miracle Mongers and Their Methods*. He dedicated the volume to John William Sargent, his late secretary, who had done most of the research and editing. Meanwhile Oscar Teale was at work checking the facts in Houdini's manuscript on the history of spiritualism.

Houdini, the film producer, was in a quandary. He faced a choice of three scripts for his second independently produced movie: *Il Mistero di Osiris or The Mystery of the Jewel*—a story of old Egypt; *Yar, The Primeval Man*—the adventures of a caveman; and *Mysterious Mr. Yu or Haldane of the Secret Service*. It was a difficult decision; he had written them all himself. Finally *Mr. Yu* was selected and the title was shortened to *Haldane of the Secret Service*.

In this movie, Heath Haldane (Houdini) fights a gang of counterfeiters which has been chasing Adele Ormsby (Gladys Leslie). The thugs throw the Secret Service man into the Hudson River, and he is rescued by a passing tug. Reviving quickly, Haldane swims to an ocean liner, the *Aquitania*. "Man overboard," someone shouts. A rope is lowered and our hero pulls himself up, hand over hand, to the deck. Haldane goes on to track down spurious bank notes in Hull and London (using footage shot in England), then visits an Apache café in Paris, where he learns that the counterfeit money is being produced in an old monastery in a French village. The "monks" trap him, lash him to an outsize waterwheel. "Bound to the swirling wheel of death, hands and feet manacled, rushing torrents of water engulfing him," he escapes. He rounds up the gang, unmasks their "Chinese" leader as the girl's father. The picture ends with the heroine safe in Haldane's arms.

Houdini was no Valentino. His shy, restrained love scenes

produced few sighs in the picture houses of the world. His films were sold on sensation value. Regrettably, there was nothing in *Haldane* to match the Niagara Falls rescue in *The Man from Beyond* or the fantastic escapes of his earliest films. He read the reviews with dismay. He compared his cost sheets with the income statements. Sadly, he removed his pending productions from the active file and brought his career as a picture producer to an abrupt finish.

He fought desperately to recoup some of his investment with an extensive exploitation campaign for the film. Giant cutout figures of Houdini, manacled in a diving position, were made available for theater-front display. Thousands of small slips of paper bearing the message—"This lock is not HOUDINI-proof. He could pick it as easily as you pick a daisy. See the Master-Man of Mystery HOUDINI in 'Haldane of the Secret Service.' A picture that will thrill you to your marrows"—were inserted in the keyholes of doors in cities where the film was shown.

Harry devised a novel street stunt. Two men carrying identical black satchels met on a busy downtown street. One man shouted that the other had taken his bag. When their dispute had drawn a crowd, one of the satchels was opened, and the two men whipped out a big cloth banner and held it up for all to see. The banner carried the name of the film and the house where it was showing. Houdini also sought to push the accident angle which had boosted interest in *The Grim Game*. Reporters were told that the giant waterwheel had broken as it whirled him around. He said he was almost drowned before he got free from the wreckage. Yet even with the financial fiasco his movie-producing period had its compensations. The films built up Houdini as a public figure and raised his theater and vaudeville salaries higher than they had ever been before.

The widespread interest in spiritualism which had been stimulated by Sir Arthur Conan Doyle's lectures led the *Scientific American* to offer two prizes for phenomena: "$2,500 for an authentic spirit photograph made under strict test conditions and $2,500 for the first physical manifestations of a psychic nature produced under scientific control." A committee was created to investigate the evidence submitted by contenders for the awards: Dr. William McDougall, professor of psychology at Harvard; Dr. Daniel Fisk Comstock, late of the Massachusetts Institute of Technology; Dr. Walter Franklin Prince, research officer of the American Society for Psychical Research; Hereward Carrington, prolific writer on the subject—and Houdini.

The committee was Houdini's idea. He had been approached by the magazine to write a series of articles on spiritualism but, because of his theatrical commitments, could not accept the offer. He suggested instead the formation of an investigation committee on which he would serve without a fee—if he were granted the "right to select or reject" its other members. Houdini did not exercise his power of approval to limit committee membership to people he knew would agree with him. Houdini's personal opinion of Carrington, for example, was that the writer was an opportunist who professed to believe in spiritualism because the "pro" books he wrote sold more copies than "anti" volumes.

Before Houdini left on a cross-country vaudeville tour, he promised to cancel his bookings whenever he was called for an investigation. The Water Torture Cell was still the feature of his act; the open-air straitjacket escape continued to tie up city traffic and draw capacity crowds for his performances.

Thousands of Missourians watched his struggle in the air in Kansas City in January 1923. Most of the front page of the *Post* was taken up by the story and photographs of the exploit. A week earlier in St. Louis, Mayor Henry W. Kiel gave Houdini the key to the city. He was the first theatrical personality so honored.

In April it was the Los Angeles Society of Magicians' turn to pay homage to Houdini. After their banquet a man named Robinson, a Glendale pharmacist, performed an original trick. He intended to change a crumpled piece of cigarette paper into a live moth but he found to his dismay that he had crushed the moth, which now lay lifeless in his hand. Uncannily, just at the moment the dead moth was shown, another moth appeared from nowhere, flew around Robinson's head and disappeared. "A believer might well have decided it was the astral body of the dead insect which appeared or that in some way the powers of darkness had conspired to assist the magician," Houdini said. "Of course, it was a coincidence but a miraculous one. I was myself startled and so was everyone else, the performer possibly most of all. I have never seen anything like it in my experience with the art of conjuring."

Spiritualism was very much on his mind. He was shown an unusual photograph in Los Angeles. Above the open coffin of Mrs. Mary Fairfield McVickers, in the First Spiritualist Temple, hovered several misty spirit faces.

Nine months earlier the seventy-three-year-old medium had predicted that if a photograph was taken at 5 p.m. on the day of her funeral, she would appear in ghostly form. The picture had been taken, according to Mrs. McVickers' instructions, on March 23. The circumstances, Houdini felt, warranted an investigation. He went to the church on April 11. Studying the wall, which was behind the coffin in the photograph, he found that what had appeared to be faces on the print were irregularities in the surface, visible only when he stood some distance away.

Nathan B. Moss, a Keystone Press photographer, took ten pictures in the church. Harry had purchased the plates himself and was in the darkroom when they were loaded in Moss' camera. Later when Moss processed the plates he noticed a strange streak on the second negative. In front of a black cloth panel, to the left of the church's altar, was a jagged line of white which culminated in what seemed to be a luminous point. Moss had no explanation for it. He was so perplexed he offered a hundred dollars to anyone who could duplicate the weird shaft of light under exactly the same conditions. Houdini dispatched copies of the photograph of the medium's funeral with the "faces" in the background and the picture which had been taken during his visit to the church to Sir Arthur Conan Doyle, who had arrived in New York for the start of another lecture tour. Doyle agreed that the wall was responsible for the illusion of the "faces." He was more interested in the white streak, though not convinced it was psychic in origin. He suggested a scratch on the plate could have produced the effect.

This would have been a simple, logical explanation, but both Houdini and the photographer swore the plate had not been scratched. Camera experts who studied the negative could offer no solution. This was one of the few times in Houdini's life that he admitted he had no satisfactory explanation for a mystery.

During Sir Arthur Conan Doyle's first American lecture tour Houdini, with difficulty, had avoided a public controversy with his friend. Now, as headlines again carried Sir Arthur's "spirit truths," counter-arguments from the magician member of the *Scientific American* committee made the wire services.

Their paths crossed in Denver. The Doyles and their children were Houdini's guests at the Orpheum Theater. Harry sent a box of candy to their ten-year-old daughter and a bouquet of violets for Lady Doyle. In his dressing room after the show Harry and Sir Arthur were at odds as to whether or not spirit photographs could be made by trickery. The next day Doyle, when they met, stated emphatically that the Zancigs were genuine telepathists. Harry knew better. In 1906 the Zancigs had been with his short-lived road show. Julius was a member of the S.A.M. To prove the point for posterity, Houdini later bought the act from Zancig, complete with all spoken and silent cues, and added it to his collection.

The Denver *Express* of May 9, 1923, ran a story headed:

DOYLE IN DENVER DEFIES HOUDINI AND OFFERS TO BRING DEAD BACK AGAIN

Sir Arthur Conan Doyle, here to preach his gospel of spiritism, is going to back his psychic forces with $5,000 against the skepticism of Harry Houdini, the magician, who recently asserted that all séance manifestations were fakes. The famous writer so asserted on his arrival from Colorado Springs late yesterday when informed Houdini was also in Denver.

"Houdini and I have discussed spiritism before," said Sir Arthur. "I have invited him to attend a sitting with me, each of us backing our beliefs with $5,000. I have even offered to bring my dead mother before him in physical form and to talk to her. But we have never got together on it."

The Doyles met the Houdinis that evening in the lobby of the Brown Palace Hotel. Sir Arthur was apologetic. The paper had put words in his mouth. Harry was understanding.

He had not seen the story, but he knew reporters sometimes misquoted their interview subjects. He was sorry he would have to miss Sir Arthur's lecture at the Ogden Theater because of his own performances at the Orpheum, but Bess would accept the Doyles' invitation to attend and she would tell him about it later.

On Doyle's recommendation, Houdini and his assistant Jim Collins went to see Alexander Martin, a Denver photographer whose pictures of the living also showed faces of the dead. Martin, an elderly, bearded man, posed Harry in a straight-backed chair with Collins standing behind him. When the plate was developed, the print showed four ghostly faces in the background: two bearded men, an Indian, and a shrouded woman. The next day Harry returned for another sitting. This time he sat alone. Five "spirit extras" appeared on the print—four bearded men and one who wore a moustache. Three of the "spirits" wore glasses! Apparently even in the Land Beyond opticians were working. The "spirit" with the moustache was the late Theodore Roosevelt.

Harry was amused, but unimpressed. He believed that Martin was using a double-exposure technique. Before his arrival Martin could have cut the heads from other photographs, put them on a black background and exposed the plate, masking the area in the center. With this prepared plate, the ghostly visitors would "materialize" when Martin photographed his subject. Later Houdini made his own spirit photographs in New York. In one he clasped his own astral body in his arms and in another Abraham Lincoln appeared with him.

There had been no rush of applicants for the *Scientific American* prizes. It was easy for a photographer to produce puzzling pictures on his own plates in his studio or a medium to conjure up phenomena when surrounded by hymn-singing friends. Why should they risk their reputations being tested by observers who were well versed in psychology, physics, and the use of trickery?

The best-known psychics claimed harmony was essential for a successful séance. A single doubter in the circle would shatter the spiritual calm required to attract friendly Indian guides and shadowy forms of those who had once had substance.

George Valiantine was more daring than his fellows in the business of otherworld communication. He had given two séances for the *Scientific American* while Houdini was on the road. The first had been unimpressive. During the second a trumpet floated in the dark, lifted by an astral Indian, according to the medium. The trumpet tapped various sitters, whacked a spectator's head, then crashed to the floor as Fred Keating, a young magician friend of Hereward Carrington's, made a grab for it.

The third test, which Houdini attended, brought science into the séance room. Unknown to the medium, men in an adjoining chamber were following his movements with light signals, a Dictaphone, and a stopwatch. Valiantine's chair had been wired. Whenever he left his seat a light flashed on in the control room and a note was made of the time. By comparing the times Valiantine vacated the chair and the times phenomena were recorded in the séance room, it was obvious that the medium, not the spirits, had been raising the ruckus. *The New York Times* quoted Houdini in its story on the exposure.

J. Malcolm Bird, an associate editor of the magazine who acted as secretary to the investigating committee, was annoyed. The *Times* reporter should not have written the story, until he, Bird, had printed an article in the *Scientific American.* Bird resented being scooped.

When the *Times* followed up with an interview with Houdini, Bird went wild—and with reason. The medium-trapping system had been devised before Houdini, who was busy on the road, came on the scene. Yet to the public it appeared that the magician had exposed Valiantine.

In California, Sir Arthur Conan Doyle was upset by another newspaper story. Quotes from Houdini in the Oakland *Tribune* were "full of errors." He had to "utterly contradict" them. Perhaps Sir Arthur had forgotten he had been misquoted in the Denver *Express*. Harry replied that he had given the Oakland writer material for a single article, which had been expanded into a series. The friendship between the two men was reaching the breaking point.

Houdini spent more time attacking mediumistic frauds than arranging challenge escapes during his fall vaudeville tour. In late September he addressed a psychology class at the University of Illinois on "The Psychology of Audiences" and "The Negative Side of Spiritualism." The latter subject took up most of his hour. In October he gave an illustrated lecture on mediums and their methods for the arts and sciences department at Marquette University in Milwaukee.

The *Scientific American* committee, meanwhile, was preparing to investigate Nino Pecoraro, a young medium who produced manifestations which he attributed to the spirit of Eusapia Palladino, herself a controversial medium who had died but five years previously. There was some reason to think that the committee might give Pecoraro a comparatively sympathetic hearing.

Sir Arthur Conan Doyle, in the course of his first American lecture tour, had attended a séance held by Pecoraro, and had been tremendously impressed as the medium, while bound with wire, caused a bell to ring, a tambourine to spin in the air, and a toy piano to play. Hereward Carrington, a member of the *Scientific American* committee, had once been Palladino's manager and he had arranged Pecoraro's séance for Doyle.

Doubtlessly worried that Pecoraro would have too easy a time of it, *Scientific American* publisher Orson Munn urgently requested Houdini, then playing in Little Rock, Arkansas, to return to New York. Since Munn told no one else what he had done, Houdini was able to make one of the dramatic entrances that he so much enjoyed. The other committee members had hardly recovered from their surprise when Houdini almost literally exploded.

He had learned that the investigators planned to tie Pecoraro with a single long rope. It was simply impossible, Houdini declared, to bind a person securely with only one rope; any amateur escape artist knew the release. Houdini had often performed the feat on the stage and had explained the method of escape in an illustrated article in the June 1918 issue of *The Ladies' Home Journal*. J. Malcolm Bird suggested a coat sweater be used to restrain the medium. Houdini was off again. Even a simpleton knew that a sweater "had the elasticity of a rubber band."

Harry slashed the long rope into short pieces. After he had finished tying Nino, the Italian no longer was a contender for the prize. When an expert did the binding, his darkroom manifestations ceased.

Houdini returned to his theater tour in the Midwest. The Pecoraro episode was an interesting addition to his lectures on spirit fraud at the University of Wisconsin and Notre Dame. The college talks were rehearsals for a lecture tour booked by the Coit-Albee Lyceum. His antifraud campaign had been a spare-time activity during the Orpheum tour. Now he was free—at least for twenty-four one-nighters—to devote his full energy to counteracting Sir Arthur Conan Doyle's propaganda.

Why would a man of fifty, at the head of his profession, with more offers for first-class theaters at top salaries than he could play, accept a string of single-night lecture dates? Houdini took on the discomfiture of a series of sleepless nights because he was genuinely disturbed by spiritualism's growing hold on the gullible, eager-to-believe American public. Houdini felt he had found his real purpose in life. His years as an entertainer and a student of deception had prepared him to be a public benefactor, an effective crusader against the cheats and charlatans who fleeced the bereaved.

The death of his beloved mother had almost shattered his life. He had gone to séances hoping to hear her soft voice and encouraging words again. The shabby deceptions he encountered in séance rooms sickened him. He was willing to believe; he wanted to believe. He had formed pacts with John William Sargent, his secretary, and other close friends. The first to die was to try desperately to reach the survivors. No word had ever come from Sargent or the other men who had "passed over." His rage against fraudulent mediums grew in intensity.

The people who attended Houdini's lectures came more to see him perform than to hear his denunciations of spiritist scoundrels. He found he had to mix entertainment with his message to make it palatable. To say that a medium employed a trick slate was not enough. He had to show how the slate was used. The actual demonstration drove his point home and delighted his listeners in the process. To ensure full auditoriums he broke out of challenge packing boxes at some stops along his route.

In Erie, Pennsylvania, Harry Kellar's hometown, Houdini flashed a picture of the great magician on the screen and gave Kellar such a glowing tribute that the audience rose en masse and cheered. Booked for an hour and a half at the Carnegie Music Hall in Pittsburgh, he talked for two hours and fifteen minutes. In Cleveland, when mediums baited him from the audience, he held the stage and his own for two hours and a half.

The publication of Houdini's book *A Magician Among the*

Spirits in 1924 brought violent attacks from believers, cheers from nonbelievers, and an end to his friendship with Sir Arthur Conan Doyle.

He wrote that he treasured Doyle as a friend. Sir Arthur was a "brilliant man," he had a "great mind"—except where spiritualism was concerned. Houdini respected Doyle's beliefs and was convinced he was sincere, but the British author refused to accept the fact that many of the mediums he had endorsed were frauds.

Houdini listed instance after instance of mediums that Sir Arthur trusted though others had found them fraudulent. He quoted at length the written message Lady Doyle said came from his mother in Atlantic City. He told why he couldn't believe it was from her.

Doyle had been fascinated by Houdini the man, but when his friend attempted to destroy his religious beliefs and held him up to ridicule, any further amicable relationship was impossible.

He never wrote or spoke to him again.

REVELATIONS

Not since Frank Podmore's explosive *Modern Spiritualism*, published in 1902, had a book created such a stir in psychic circles as Houdini's *A Magician Among the Spirits*. Houdini produced ample evidence that the founders of spiritualism had not only deliberately deceived the public but later, as if adding insult to injury, had drawn paying crowds to attend lectures at which they explained how the public had been tricked. Houdini's book was loaded with awkward facts that most true believers either had not known about or preferred to forget.

The self-confessed charlatans included even the Fox sisters, the two girls who, after attracting attention by rapping out messages in Hydesville, New York, in 1848, went on to popularize spiritualism both in the United States and abroad. Quoting from an account that he had found in the New York *World*, Houdini described a performance by Margaret Fox Kane at the New York Academy of Music on October 21, 1888. Demonstrating the method she had used to trick her followers, she slipped off her right shoe and put her foot on a wooden stool. "The entire house became breathlessly still and was rewarded by a number of little short, sharp raps—those mysterious sounds which have for forty years frightened and bewildered hundreds of thousands of people in this country and in Europe," the *World* account continued. Three doctors studied the movements of her foot as Margaret rapped. They "agreed that the sounds were made by the action of the first joint of her large toe."

Catherine Fox Jencken was in a box adjacent to the stage that night, cheering her sister on. Less than two weeks before, Catherine had admitted in print: "Spiritualism is a humbug from beginning to end. It is the greatest humbug of the century."

Ira Eratus Davenport and William Henry Harrison Davenport, the first successful stage mediums, went from the United States to England in 1864 and then across the Continent as far as Russia. Believers said the manifestations the Davenport Brothers produced while tied in their cabinet were the work of spirits. Ira had confessed to Houdini that he used a trick rope tie which enabled him to free his hands and retie them at will. He taught the trick to Harry and suggested they team up for a tour of Mexico and South America.

The Italian medium Eusapia Palladino had been endorsed by leading European scientists. One of Houdini's friends, Joseph F. Rinn, whom he had known since his Pastime Athletic Club days, had been "clad in black even to a head covering and smuggled into the room under cover of darkness" when she sat for a group of Columbia University professors in New York. Rinn saw Palladino strike a table leg with her shoe to produce raps, watched as she put her foot under the table leg and lifted it until it was "floating in the air."

Another friend, Remigius Weiss, bored holes in the floor, ceiling, and doors of the Philadelphia room where Dr. Henry Slade, the popular slate medium, was to give a séance. Concealed observers reported Slade's methods. They "saw how he (Dr. Slade) with his foot upset chairs, kicked a book (extending over the edge of the table)." Weiss then visited Slade and duplicated his séance. He threatened to have the medium arrested unless Slade signed a confession. The confession "that all his pretended Spiritualistic manifestations were and are deceptions, performed through tricks," was printed in Houdini's book.

Belief in spiritualism, Houdini wrote, led to insanity and tragedy. A Barnard student, in love with a spirit, committed suicide to join her lover. A San Francisco man shot his sons because his dead wife sent him a message saying she wanted the children with her. The only affirmative statistic Harry included was attributed to medium John Slater. More than five hundred spiritualists had served with the American Army overseas during World War I. None of them had been wounded, or even attacked by cooties.

While *A Magician Among the Spirits* was drawing fire from the psychics, another book, *Elliott's Last Legacy,* was causing Houdini embarrassment in magic circles. Dr. James William Elliott, physician-turned-magician, died before he could complete a book on his methods. Clinton Burgess, a New York performer and a collector of magicana, wrote Elliott's father of his wish to carry out his friend's project. The elder Elliott sent Burgess money and material to help him with the work. Burgess advertised in the *Sphinx* for advance subscriptions for the volume.

When the demand for his performances slackened, Burgess used the money for living expenses. After he ran out of funds, he came to Houdini in desperation. Houdini had known Burgess for years. He had employed him both as a researcher and writer. Harry agreed to publish the volume and assigned Oscar Teale the task of preparing the chaotic manuscript and illustrating the tricks.

When *Elliott's Last Legacy* appeared in 1923, Houdini's name was printed in large letters on the cover and spine of the book. "Compiled by Clinton Burgess," in small type, was below Editor Houdini's name on the title page. Burgess never spoke to Harry again. Houdini's detractors accused him of taking advantage of his hard-pressed friend.

Burgess and a friend, Albert Guissart, sent letters attacking Houdini to magic journals in England, France, and Germany, and to the *Sphinx* in Kansas City. Oscar Teale answered the onslaught. His rebuttal provoked further accusations from Burgess and Guissart. Eventually Houdini, after consultation with his lawyer, B. M. L. Ernst, pressed charges against Burgess at the Society of American Magicians for conduct unbecoming a member. The hearing was postponed several times at Burgess' request. He didn't appear when a final date was set. The council voted to expel him. Thereafter Burgess was the bitterest and most vocal of Houdini's expanding circle of magician critics.

Joaquin Maria Argamasilla, son of the Marquis de Santa Cara of Madrid, came to the United States in 1924 with impressive credentials as a psychic. His ability to see through metal had baffled committees appointed by the Royal Academy of Science and the Spanish Academy of Medicine. He had been investigated by Dr. Charles Richet in Paris. Richet, whose medical research won him a Nobel Prize in 1913, could find no clue to Argamasilla's methods. Nor could Dr. Walter Franklin Prince, research officer for the American Society of Psychical Research and member of the *Scientific American* committee. In May, Houdini, who had completed another lecture tour, was in New York.

With newspapermen and other observers present, he challenged the nineteen-year-old Spaniard. He offered two metal boxes of his own design to test the penetration powers of the medium. One was a tin container wound with two strong wires twisted at the ends. The other was locked by a bolt held in place by a thumb nut. Houdini defied Argamasilla to reveal the contents of the boxes. Argamasilla refused to try; he said he would work only with his own silver and steel boxes. A close scrutiny of those props convinced Houdini that the hasp on one and the lid on the other were so constructed that a clever performer could take a fast peak inside without the spectators being aware of the simple move. Houdini volunteered to duplicate Argamasilla's feats with the psychic's own special boxes; the Spaniard's manager would have none of that.

As always, Houdini, the showman, was quick to make use of his experience and to capitalize on someone else's notoriety. He could and did reproduce Argamasilla's demonstrations of X-ray vision with hunting case watches. Thereafter, seeing through metal became one of Houdini's favorite impromptu tricks. Reporters were instructed to set their pocket watches to any time and close the lid. In a few seconds, using Argamasilla's technique, Harry would call off the hour to which the hands had been set.

Argamasilla faded from the psychic scene.

Dr. A. M. Wilson, the editor of the *Sphinx,* was to have been the guest of honor at the annual S.A.M. banquet in New York. Houdini rose to express his friend's regrets and to explain his absence. Wilson was making a radio speech that evening in Kansas City.

Busboys wheeled in a receiving set. Houdini switched it on. Wilson's voice, blurred by static, filled the McAlpin Hotel ballroom. Wilson spoke about the age of marvels in which they lived. Sending pictures by telephone wires was nothing compared to wonders yet to come. One day, he predicted, human bodies would be broadcast from one place to another. He was working on this experiment himself. He would try it tonight! The front of the box flew open, out scrambled the bald, moustached doctor in person.

Harry had arranged for Wilson's dramatic appearance. His assistants folded him in the box, with a microphone, just before the radio was brought in from the McAlpin kitchen.

Daisy White, who worked at Frank Ducrot's magic shop, was so moved by the familiar voice "coming from Kansas City over the radio" that she cried. Magician John Mullholland's first thought when he saw the man emerge was that he was an actor impersonating Wilson. Richard Van Dien, the secretary of the society, wrote: "The radio box outfit broke open and out tumbled Dr. A. M. Wilson, absolutely looking the picture of a man that had been transported by radio. His eyes blinked, his hair was disheveled, his coat mussed up." The sudden materialization was the hit of the evening.

Houdini also came in for special attention at the banquet. As the society's seven-term president, he was tendered a testimonial gift. He was visibly moved as Howard Thurston presented him with a miniature half-length portrait of his mother. Harry praised it as a true-to-life image. He said it was eleven years ago that week he suffered the greatest loss of his life. He had made enemies but his great friends outnumbered them. He had lived straight without fear of anyone. Each year on the anniversary of Cecilia's death he went to the grave to mark the hour of her passing—fifteen minutes past midnight. This year he would take the portrait with him.

Conjecture in June as to who would be nominated for the second highest elective office in the nation caused the New York *World* to suggest: "Why not fill the empty place for the Vice-Presidential nomination with Houdini? A clap of the hands, forty-eight nations vanish . . . no trouble at all for a magician."

The editor of the Circumnavigators' Club's *Log,* James H. Birch Jr., went further in a letter to the Burlington (New Jersey) *Daily Enterprise:* "Now, as the Democratic party seems to be at a loss for a candidate, I suggest that they nominate Harry Houdini for president of the United States for no matter what platform they build, he could stand and run on it and if he or his party should get in trouble of any kind, President Houdini could 'get out of it easily,' as he has always been able to do. Hurrah for Houdini for president. Vote for Houdini for president! Rah! Rah! Rah!"

Good psychics were as hard to find as presidential candidates. Sir Arthur Conan Doyle wrote, in a letter from London to J. Malcolm Bird at the *Scientific American,* that he had met a marvelous medium in Boston during one of his lectures there. She was not a professional. Her séances were not open to the public. Only friends of the family attended.

She was the wife of a distinguished surgeon and her credentials, social and psychic, appeared impeccable. Doyle was certain that her powers were real; obviously, he reasoned, she had nothing to gain—and everything to lose—by cheating.

MARGERY THE MEDIUM

In the spring of 1923, Dr. Le Roi Goddard Crandon purchased a book with a provocative title, *The Psychic Structures at the Goligher Circle*. That night the former professor of surgery at Harvard Medical School began reading Dr. W. J. Crawford's account of his scientific experiments with a family of mediums in Belfast. Dr. Crandon became so engrossed that he stayed with the book until dawn. Was it possible for a strange substance, of which he had never heard, to extrude from a human body and lift a heavy table? The author of a textbook on aftersurgery procedures was impelled to dig deeper into this fascinating subject.

Mina, the surgeon's wife, was twenty-six—half his age—blond and personable. Her good looks and vivaciousness made her a popular hostess in the less staid circles of Boston. She had been married once before, to Earl P. Rand, a man who ran a small grocery store. Mysticism had never been a part of her life, either in Canada where she was born or Boston. She enjoyed sports, had played in an orchestra, worked as a secretary, and for a time was active with a church social group. After her marriage to the wealthy doctor she shared the amenities of his spacious house on Beacon Hill and his yacht.

Her husband's newfound interest in the supernatural amused her. To humor him she went to a clairvoyant. The psychic told her she had strong, latent mediumistic powers. Dr. Crandon was delighted. As he read voraciously on spiritualism and occult research he passed along the basics of mediumship to his wife.

By May Dr. Crandon decided it was time to develop Mina's psychic potential. After dinner one evening, four family friends were invited to a room on the top floor of their Lime Street house for an impromptu séance. Until then it had been used to store books which overflowed from the library on the floor below.

197

They sat around a table which had been constructed to the exact dimensions of the one used by the Golighers in Ireland. After turning off the lights, the Crandons and their guests placed their fingertips lightly on the tabletop. At first nothing happened. Then, as Mina summoned up her powers, the table began to move. It vibrated, danced from side to side, slid across the floor, tipped up and balanced on two legs, Dr. Crandon was gratified, the guests were jubilant. Clearly the spirits had arrived at No. 10 Lime Street!

The career launched that night was to be unprecedented in the annals of spiritualism. The more her husband read about the marvels of mediums, the more versatile Mina became. It was as though Dr. Crandon had but to read about some extraordinary, bizarre manifestation and she could duplicate it.

By mid-November when J. Malcolm Bird, of the *Scientific American*, arrived for his first séance on Lime Street, Mina had progressed from simple table-turning and uncanny raps to the production of mysterious bugle calls from an invisible instrument and strange rattling sounds from an unseen chain. Flashes of light streaked across the séance room and observers said that Mina stopped clocks in distant rooms by mere concentration.

Delving into more arcane realms of the uncanny, she became adept at materialization. Guests were perplexed when objects appeared under seemingly impossible circumstances in the séance room. A two-dollar bill came from nowhere. A live pigeon flew into the chamber, apparently penetrating its solid walls.

The startling happenings occurred when Mina was in a trance. She spoke then with a voice deeper than her own. The voice identified itself as Walter Stinson, Mina's older brother, who had been killed in a train wreck.

Walter was loud, sarcastic, and frequently profane. His vocabulary was sometimes so shocking that this alone convinced many academic and professional friends of the family that the words came from a spirit. Certainly Mina would not have uttered them.

It was a period of universal interest in spiritualism. In France and England distinguished scientists were scrutinizing psychic phenomena. Dr. Crandon was curious as to how foreign investigators would react to Mina. In December, he and his wife sailed for France.

At the Paris home of Dr. Gustave Geley, director of the Institute Metapsychic Internationale, Nobel-prize winner Dr. Charles Richet and his associates were present when Mina made a table cavort and a cloth-sided cabinet collapse. *"Bien,"* the excited Frenchmen cried, *"encore!"*

In London, Mrs. Crandon made an excellent impression when she went into a trance for the British College of Psychic Science and the Society for Psychical Research. She was invited to give a private séance for Sir Arthur Conan Doyle and his wife. A dried flower, which had been on the mantelpiece when the lights were extinguished, was found at Lady Doyle's feet at the end of the sitting. This had been a favorite feat of the celebrated D. D. Home.

Mina sat for the cameras of Mrs. Deane and Charles Hope, two of Britain's best-known spirit photographers. Every plate exposed had either misty faces around her head or mysterious blobs of light. The Crandons, triumphantly successful abroad, returned to Boston.

In April 1924 the *Scientific American,* which until then had attracted only obvious cheats, expanded its offer in the hope of persuading worthier mediums to compete for its prizes. The magazine announced it would pay all the expenses of any first-class psychic who would come to New York to be tested.

Dr. Crandon read the article. The prize money didn't interest him, but he did want to encourage psychical investigation in the United States. He wrote J. Malcolm Bird saying he would pay the fares for the publication's committeemen if they would come to Boston and sit with his wife. They would be welcome to stay as guests in his house. He regretted he could not come to New York because of his medical practice. This was a curious statement. Mina—not the doctor—was the medium. Could she not work without him?

Dr. William McDougall, the Harvard professor of psychology, was the first committeeman to attend one of Mina's séances. Bird, the secretary to the committee, was a frequent visitor. Bird wrote two enthusiastic articles in which he extolled the mediumship without identifying Mrs. Crandon. He gave her the pseudonym Margery, and it was as Margery that she became known to the public.

Houdini had been engrossed with his own affairs. In June he was startled by a letter from Bird: "As you will observe when you get your July *Scientific American,* we are engaged in the investigation of another case of mediumship. Our original idea was not to bother you with it unless, and until, it got to a stage where there seemed serious prospects that it was either genuine or a type of fraud which our other committeemen could not deal with. . . . Mr. Munn feels that the case has taken a turn that makes it desirable for us to discuss it with you. . . ."

Houdini confronted Bird in publisher Munn's office. "Do you believe that this medium is genuine?" At least half the time, was the answer. Did Bird think she merited the award? "Most decidedly," he replied.

Houdini was stunned. The publication was considering endorsing a medium he had never seen. It was imperative, Houdini told Munn, that the two of them attend one of Margery's séances immediately. Bird and committeeman Hereward Carrington had enjoyed the warm hospitality of No. 10 Lime Street. Could either offer a fair appraisal of Margery's mediumship under these circumstances? Houdini thought not. Determined to keep their dispassionate distance, he and Munn booked rooms at the Copley Plaza Hotel. They did accept a dinner invitation from the Crandons when they arrived in Boston Wednesday, July 23, for their first meeting with the blond charmer.

Dr. Crandon was a gracious host and an interesting conversationalist. Bird had said Margery was a beautiful woman. Houdini found her attractive, sensuous, and confident.

It was so hot that night that the men—Crandon, Houdini, Munn, Bird, and R. W. Conant, who worked in committeeman Comstock's laboratory—removed their coats in the upstairs séance room. Bird confessed to Houdini that the room itself had never been thoroughly examined. Harry set about to remedy that. There was no door to be locked between the room and a hallway leading to the stairs. He inspected the props—a megaphone, a three-sided cabinet, a phonograph which usually played Margery's favorite melody, "Souvenir," and a bell box. The fourteen-inch-long wooden box contained batteries and a bell. A slight tap on the flap at the top would complete an electrical circuit and make the bell ring.

Margery and four of the men sat in chairs forming a circle. She asked them all to link hands with one another. The medium was between Houdini and her husband, with Munn and

Conant rounding out the circle. Bird sat outside the circle, his right hand clasped around the linked hands of Margery and the doctor. Margery's right foot was pressed against her husband's left. Her left foot was firmly against Houdini's right foot. These body contacts were to prove that the medium's hands and feet were "under control" when the manifestations began. After the lights were turned off, Walter's voice broke through the darkness. He whispered, whistled, and talked, "Houdini was touched several times on the inside of the right leg," Bird wrote in his report. "He did not announce it, but Walter did so for him, specifying the place touched."

Nothing much had transpired but there was an intermission to allow the medium to rest. When they resumed in the dark, Walter asked that the bell box be placed on the floor between Houdini's feet. Then Walter directed Bird to put a luminous board on the top of the bell box. There was an interval with the lights on as Bird went to look for the board. Then the lights were switched off again and Walter called for control. Walter said the megaphone, which no one could see, was in the air. He asked in which direction he should hurl it. "Toward me," Houdini answered. The megaphone landed with a crash. Then there was more clatter as the cabinet fell over backward.

The lights were on for the third pause. Bird had found the luminous board. He put it on the bell box before the lights were extinguished. After several minutes, the board began to move. One end tipped up, eight inches or so above the box. It fell back in place before the fourth intermission. During the final segment in the dark, Walter called for the table, which had been in front of Margery, to be taken from the circle. This was done while a red light was switched on. In the dark that followed, the luminous board again moved and the hitherto quiet bell rang several short peals and one long one. Walter said "Good night." The séance was over.

Bird drove Houdini and Munn back to their hotel. He stopped briefly on Beacon Street so they could discuss what they had seen. "Well, gentlemen," Houdini said, "I've got her. All fraud, every bit of it. One more sitting and I will be ready to expose everything." There was still one manipulation he must work out; the megaphone episode puzzled him. Bird said a committeeman had suggested it might have been on the medium's shoulder. Houdini shook his head and sat quietly. Then he smiled knowingly, as though the answer had just come to him. "I've got it. The megaphone must have been on her head!" he said emphatically. What about the luminous board that moved? The bell that rang? Harry laughed. Margery's agile little foot was the answer. He proceeded to explain in detail how he knew.

Earlier in the day he had worn a rubber surgical bandage on his right leg beneath his knee until the skin became tender; he removed it shortly before he left for Lime Street. He had rolled up his trouser leg before Margery put her foot against his. Small leg motions might go undetected through thick trousers, but his sensitive skin picked up the action every time Margery moved a muscle. He had felt her leg sliding as she inched her foot behind his to tip the luminous board on the bell box. He was aware of the move when she pressed down with her toe on top of the bell box.

The falling of the cabinet? Simple. While Bird was out of the room looking for the luminous board, Walter called for control a moment after the lights went out. Margery quickly lifted the megaphone with her right hand, put it on her head, tilted the cabinet with the same hand, slipped her right foot under the closest side of the cabinet and later, with a deft, sure kick, toppled it backward.

The next day Houdini and Munn returned to Lime Street. In the séance room, alone with the publisher, the magician demonstrated that his explanations were practical.

That night the tests resumed in Dr. Comstock's apartment at the Charlesgate Hotel. His secretary, Gladys Wood, searched Margery before the séance and made a statement: "She removed most of her clothes and I examined her and them carefully. She wore a loose green linen dress into the séance room and I examined this carefully before she put it on. She also removed her shoes, and I examined her feet and shoes carefully. She then put on her shoes again. She also took down her hair, which I searched."

Dr. Comstock sat outside the circle recording his observations with a Dictaphone. The action started at 8:45 p.m. Walter's voice called for a card table to be substituted for the heavy table around which the circle was formed. The card table was put in place with the bell box on it.

Background music was supplied by a phonograph. Dr.

Comstock noted when it was started and stopped. The first manifestation in the dark was the movement of the threefold screen behind Margery. At the end of the séance it was found closed almost flat, but still upright.

The card table was the center of interest. It tipped in the dark and fell toward Houdini, but did not upset. At 9:45 it toppled over completely, spilling the box to the floor. At 10:07 the bell box was put, at Walter's suggestion, between Houdini's feet. At 10:12 the bell shrilled several times in the blacked-out room. Walter shouted for Munn to straighten up. The publisher admitted he had been bending over. The bell rang at 10:30. It sounded again thirty seconds later. Walter instructed Munn to tell the bell how many times it should ring. It rang five peels at his suggestion. Walter's usual "Good night" concluded the sitting.

Dr. Comstock, Houdini, Munn, and Bird went to another room to discuss the manifestations. Houdini said he had released his grip on Munn's hand in the dark and reached under the table as it was tilting. He felt Margery's head below the table lifting it. He had quickly withdrawn his hand and felt for Munn's ear in the dark, then leaned over and whispered: "Shall I denounce and expose her now?" The publisher whispered back that he should wait.

Houdini, who had rolled up his trouser leg again, revealed that Margery's stocking had caught on the garter of his right stocking. When she complained that the buckle was hurting her, he had unfastened it. After that he could feel her leg moving as it extended toward the bell box.

Harry was all for calling the newspapers immediately and exposing the trickery. The other men voted him down.

Munn and the magician took the night train to New York. Bird stayed on as the Crandons' guest. During the journey the publisher said that the September issue had already gone to press carrying an article by Bird praising Margery's mediumship. Houdini advised him to stop the presses. When the public learned that Margery was a fraud the article would be embarrassing. At first Munn objected to the extra cost of remaking the issue, but he finally agreed to do it and the Bird article was deleted.

There is an interesting and hitherto unpublished sidelight on Houdini's first clash with the Boston medium. The magician came to the store where Willard B. Greene, an amateur magician and old friend, worked. Houdini claimed he had detected Margery in every trick: "She's the slickest ever. Can I use the phone in the back room?" Houdini called the United Press. When the office answered, he suddenly hung up. "It wouldn't be fair to Munn," he said. He started to leave, then asked Greene if he would like to meet the medium. Greene followed him to the automobile parked at the curb. Margery had been sitting there all the while. They chatted briefly as Houdini sat by her side and the car drove off.

Later in the day Houdini returned alone. He gave Greene a roll of film. "Don't let this out of your sight while it's being developed," he said mysteriously. "As soon as you make the prints, send them and the negatives to me in New York by registered mail."

Greene waited impatiently while the film was processed. Then he studied the prints carefully. For the most part they were commonplace group shots of the medium, Houdini, and two men, who he learned later were Bird and Munn. The final print, however, was interesting. There was a strange blur above Margery's head—almost a halo.

When Houdini's pamphlet on Margery was printed it carried one of the pictures, but not the one with the halo. Greene asked his friend why he hadn't used the dramatic shot. Houdini answered that his camera bellows had developed a leak when the last picture was made. He had discovered it later. Since believers in spiritualism might think the haze was ectoplasm, he hadn't published the photograph.

"You know as well as I do, Willard, that she's a fake. Why should I help build her following?"

Two committeemen, Houdini and Dr. Walter Franklin Prince, had been disturbed by Bird's early articles in the *Scientific American* lauding Margery's talents. They were even more annoyed by his statements to the press. Bird was not a committee member. He was an employee of the magazine. The committee should be independent of the publication. They met with Munn and voiced their complaints.

If, the publisher said, Margery was using trickery, as Houdini charged, the committee must prove this to the public. Houdini was given the assignment to construct a device which would prevent the medium from using her head, hand, and foot in the manner he had explained.

Harry promised he would have a foolproof device ready for

the next series of investigations, which were scheduled for August. Most of his life he had coped with challenge restraints, now he would have the opportunity to present an unbeatable challenge himself.

THE FRAUDPROOF BOX

J. Malcolm Bird offered to take Houdini's "fraud-preventer" to Boston in his car, but Harry, trusting no one, brusquely answered that he would carry it himself. He and Collins, his assistant, lugged it to Dr. Comstock's apartment early on the morning of August 25, 1924. It was an odd-shaped box that might have been a crate for an old-fashioned slant-top desk. There was ample room inside for the medium to sit comfortably on a chair. Semicircular sections were cut out of the hinged front and the top panel so that when the cabinet was closed, a hole was created to hold the occupant's neck. Her hands could be extended through holes in the cabinet sides so that committeemen could "control" them. Provision also was made for panels of wood to be nailed over the side openings should the committee wish to test her with her hands inside the box.

After Dr. Crandon and his wife inspected the contraption, they withdrew and held a hasty conference. When they returned, the doctor insisted that Margery must have a tryout in the device with her friends before she submitted to the committee's tests. With reluctance, the committeemen agreed.

The doctor made a formal statement: "The psychic does not refuse to sit in the cage made by Houdini for the committee; but she makes the reservation that she knows no precedent in psychic research where a medium has been so enclosed; and she believes that such a closed cage gives little or no regard for the theory and experience of the psychic structure or mechanism."

Crawford, in his book on the Goligher Circle, had used the term "psychic structure." Margery's followers now believed that a pseudopod extended in the dark between her legs and was responsible for the manifestations in the dark.

The familiarization séance with the new box was held behind closed doors as the investigators waited in another room. In thirty minutes Dr. Crandon ushered his friends out and the committee in. Bird, who was not present at this séance, wrote one version of what happened; Houdini, who was there, offered another. Both agree that the sloped front of the box broke open in the dark. Dr. Crandon said that Walter had been responsible. If one believes in spiritualism, this is a reasonable explanation. Houdini said Margery forced the panel with her shoulders. It had been held in place only by two narrow strips of brass. With the front open, Margery could have leaned forward and reached the bell box, which was on a table in front of the box, with her head.

The verbal clash between the Crandons and Houdini became so heated that Walter's voice called for a recess. Margery's friends trooped in to replace the investigators and temporarily psychic harmony was restored.

When the committeemen were invited to return, Walter was in a querulous mood. He wanted to know how much the magician was being paid to stop the phenomena. Harry replied he was losing money, since he had to pass up a theater date in Buffalo in order to come to Boston for the séance. Time passed; there were no manifestations. Eventually Walter told Dr. Comstock to take the bell box under a light and examine it. Comstock reported that a small, round eraser, the sort that is usually on a pencil, was wedged under the flap. He estimated that four times the usual pressure on the lid would have been necessary to make the bell ring.

Houdini stated at once, for the record, that he had not put the eraser there. The séance ended with no further attempts for phenomena.

At the postmortem meeting the other members of the committee said that Houdini had not fulfilled his obligation to construct a fraudproof box. Harry replied he hadn't expected Margery to break out of it. He vowed he would have the box in proper condition for the séance the next night.

The eraser in the flap of the bell box? Margery or her friends could have put it there to discredit Houdini.

For the second séance, the box was heavily reinforced. Four staples, hasps, and padlocks had been added. An unexpected visitor was J. Malcolm Bird. Munn had instructed him to stay away from the Charlesgate Hotel. He wanted to know why. Houdini and Dr. Prince unburdened themselves. Bird had given the Crandons information about the committee's discoveries in July. He had released unauthorized statements to the press. Before he was ushered out, Bird was permitted to resign as secretary to the committee.

Bird and Houdini are again at variance in their accounts of the August 26 séance. Bird, who believed Margery produced genuine phenomena but who was not there, said Houdini was satisfied with Miss McManama's search of the medium's body. Houdini, on the other hand, wrote he had objected to the superficial examination. But Dr. Crandon would not permit a physician to be called for a more thorough probe of his wife's anatomy.

The record of the séance is lacking in important detail, as many séance records are. Apparently a pillow was placed under Margery's feet in the box, but it is not known who suggested that this be done or who put the pillow there.

Houdini held Margery's left hand as it extended through the hole on his side of the box. On the other side, Dr. Prince took her right hand. This was a most important procedural change; until this time, Dr. Crandon had "controlled" his wife's right hand!

Harry repeatedly cautioned Dr. Prince not to release Margery even for a moment. Margery asked why he made such an issue of this.

"I'll tell you," Houdini answered, "in case you have smuggled anything into the cabinet-box you cannot now conceal it as both your hands are secured and as far as they are concerned you are helpless."

"Do you want to search me?" Margery inquired.

"No, never mind, let it go. I am not a physician."

Walter's voice sounded in the dark room: "Houdini, you are clever indeed, but it won't work."

Walter said that there was a ruler beneath the cushion on which Margery rested her feet. While Houdini had not been in the room just prior to the sitting, Walter said that his assistant had, insinuating that Houdini had arranged to have it hidden there. His voice became loud, abusive, and profane: "Houdini, you Goddamned son of a bitch, get the hell out of here and never come back. If you don't, I will."

The box was unlocked. A new carpenter's ruler, a two-foot-length folded in six-inch sections, was found under the pillow. Dr. Comstock offered the opinion that it may have been left there when the box was being repaired. Orson Munn brought

Collins into the room to be questioned. Collins said his ruler was still in his pocket. He pulled it out and showed it.

Houdini dictated a statement to the stenographer: "I wish it recorded that I demanded Collins to take a sacred oath on the life of his mother that he did not put the ruler into the box and knew positively nothing about it. I also pledge my sacred word of honor as a man that the first I knew of the ruler in the box was when I was so informed by Walter."

No one knows how the ruler came to be in the cabinet. In his biography of Houdini, William Lindsay Gresham quoted Collins as admitting, years later, that he had hidden the ruler in the box on Houdini's instructions. The source of this story, though not given by Gresham, was Fred Keating, a magician who had been a guest of the Crandons in their house on Lime Street at the time Carrington was investigating the medium. Keating, however, was not unbiased. Several days before Gresham spoke to him, Keating had seen an unpublished manuscript in this author's collection in which Houdini, while praising Keating as a magician, had commented in unflattering terms on Keating's abilities as an investigator of psychic phenomena. In this writer's opinion, the story of Collins' admission is sheer fiction.

Unfortunately, the investigators did not check thoroughly the possibilities of fraud. If the ruler had been taken to a laboratory for analysis, fingerprints or traces of body secretions might have been found. The *Scientific American* committee was not that scientific.

The day of the third and final August séance, Munn, Prince, Houdini, and the Crandons had dinner together. Houdini wrote later that Margery said she had heard he planned to denounce her from the stage of Keith's Theater. If he did, her friends would give him a thrashing. She didn't wish her young son to read one day that his mother had been a fraud. Houdini, who usually had a soft spot in his heart for mothers, was unmoved.

"Then don't be a fraud," he answered.

Dr. Comstock had a medium-control device of his own that night. It was a shallow wooden box into which Margery and an investigator, sitting face to face, put their feet. A board was locked in place over their knees. The sides of the box were open except at the bottom and top so the restraint wouldn't interfere with a "psychic structure." When the medium's hands were held, and the bell box was on the floor by the box, she was under excellent control.

While the committee waited for the bell to ring and other manifestations to occur, according to Houdini's account, Dr. Crandon remarked:

"Some day, Houdini, you will see the light, and if it were to occur this evening, I would gladly give ten thousand dollars to charity."

"It may happen, but I doubt it," Harry replied.

"Yes, sir," the doctor repeated, "if you were converted this evening I would willingly give ten thousand dollars to charity."

Dr. Comstock's fraud-control was effective. When Margery's hands were held by someone other than her husband and while her feet and legs were immobilized, no phenomena were produced.

It was a totally blank sitting. Houdini had not been converted and Dr. Crandon still had his ten thousand dollars.

CRUSADER

For eight weeks in the fall of 1924 Houdini lectured across the United States. Booked by the Affiliated Lyceum and Chautauqua Association, the tour of one-nighters took him to small towns he had never played as well as to the big cities where he was a vaudeville favorite. His contract called for $1,500 a week, plus transportation. Boston, Philadelphia, San Francisco, and Los Angeles were exceptions. In these cities he was to receive 50 percent of the net profits. His contract specified that the words "hocus" and "fakery" were not to be used in advertisements. He considered them "too vulgar."

In Denver, the crusader challenged the Rev. Josie Stewart, who had been exposed in New York by the *Scientific American* committee, to take the stage and prove to her home-town audience that she was not a fraud. She specialized in spirit messages that appeared suddenly on what previously had been blank cards. The cards given to her by the *Scientific American* investigators had been identified secretly with pinpricks. When the spirit writing appeared, the pinpricks vanished, proving, the committee charged, that the medium had switched cards. Now Harry declared to the packed Denver house that he would give her the night's receipts if she could produce any psychic phenomena that he couldn't duplicate. She produced no manifestations, but she put up a verbal battle, during which her followers tangled with Houdini's supporters. The next day the Denver *Post* story was headed: HOUDINI STARTS NEAR RIOT.

The Rev. Vincent W. Wilson, of the Church of Divine Guidance, taunted the lecturer from the audience in San Francisco. "Step up here," Houdini demanded, "and give us evidence of the spirit world." Wilson replied that he couldn't produce proof then and there. He explained that the spirits didn't work that way. HOOT SPIRITUALIST PASTOR the *Bulletin* reported next day.

Houdini visited the unique house in San Jose built by Mrs.

211

Sarah L. Winchester, widow of the Winchester arms magnate. Describing the visit, Houdini wrote: "Her spirit guide told her that as long as she kept adding to her home she would live. For thirty-six years she kept building and building. I walked through the house at midnight with Mrs. Houdini and know that she will never think we live in a big house. Mrs. Winchester built 160 rooms, there are over 200 doors, 10,000 windows, over 150,000 panes of glass. Some of the windows must have cost over $2,000.

"There are forty-seven fire places, one room especially built to hold a séance has a wardrobe in which she had different colored robes and whenever she wished to talk to any particular spirit she would don the colored robe required. . . . It was the greatest house I ever saw, meaning it is the largest dwelling place ever built."

The recipe for immortality, however, had not worked. Mrs. Winchester was dead and her sprawling mansion just an empty showplace when Houdini visited it.

The next day at Stanford University in Palo Alto, Houdini examined the paraphernalia once used by Charles Bailey, an Australian medium whose specialty was apporting—passing objects from outside his séance room into the chamber. Margery had limited her livestock productions to a single pigeon. Bailey conjured up many birds, sometimes in their nests, a snake, a turtle, and a crab. His most startling apport was an eighteen-inch-long live baby shark. Harry inspected a pair of slates still covered with the late Melbourne medium's spirit messages. The magician's reaction: "The locked slates can easily be written on by having a slate pencil secured on an umbrella rib." If the slates were wedged apart, the writing instrument could be inserted without opening them.

Houdini's tour took him into the Tennessee valley. He drew five thousand people in Chattanooga. "*Times* panned me. Expected escapes. No mention of the thousands of dollars to charity from the show." The Morristown lecture in a high school was attended by "about 300, mostly young people." In Johnson City he received $750. "Sponsors lost $357.57." Of Chapel Hill, North Carolina, Houdini wrote: "College boys. Great audience. Gave me the college yell." He almost had a fight with a belligerent saloonkeeper in Frederick, Maryland. The man charged Collins, his assistant, had passed information to him during the performance.

All the while he was garnering publicity in a new Sunday tabloid section, "Red Magic," "edited by the World-Famous Houdini." Published by the New York *World,* the supplement was syndicated to other newspapers. Its name came from the color of the ink. Papers that carried the section in black and white called it "Home Magic." Harry's agreement, signed October 6, 1924, specified "that none of the material used . . . shall expose any of the fundamental principles of magic." He was editor in name only; he had neither the time nor the desire to assemble the weekly assortment of games, tricks, and puzzles.

The Margery story continued to get a big play in the press. Dr. Crandon's criticism of the *Scientific American* committee, which issued a preliminary report hinting at a less than favorable verdict, made the front pages in Boston and was picked up by other papers. Houdini retorted in print that he could reproduce every Margery marvel he had seen. A rumor spread that Houdini had been dropped from the committee. "Not true," roared Harry. "Not true," echoed Orson Munn, the publisher.

The spirit world converged to put the hex on Harry. On December 19, 1924, Walter, Margery's spirit voice, predicted that the mediums' greatest enemy had less than a year to live. Other ethereal voices in other séance rooms chimed in. The magician would not be alive by the end of 1925. If, Harry shot back, he died within the next twelve months, it would be God's will, not Walter's. The mediums, he charged, were trying to silence his attacks with ominous prophecies.

His Christmas Eve performance at Sing Sing featured the exposures of Margery he had demonstrated on his lecture tour. But the feat that got the biggest response—as usual—was an escape. He was out of a packing case, made by the prisoners, in just twelve minutes by a stopwatch.

Houdini reinvaded Margery territory on January 2, 1925. He gave Mayor Curley of Boston five thousand dollars in bonds as photographers took pictures. The bonds were to be awarded to any medium, Margery included, who produced physical phenomena which he could not duplicate. Symphony Hall, where once Sir Arthur Conan Doyle had presented his lectures endorsing spiritualism, was nearly full for his appearance. Occupying a hundred chairs on the crowded stage was a committee Houdini had invited as his guests—ministers, reporters, detectives, magicians, and public-spirited citizens.

This was a new Houdini to the Bostonians who had seen him so often at Keith's. He was a bit stockier, the once-dark, curly hair was thinner and sprinkled with gray, his demeanor was more serious. Only the flashing, hypnotic eyes were the same. He spoke slowly, accenting every syllable. He had no intention of attacking anybody's religion, he began. Everyone should be allowed to worship as he saw fit—as long as he stayed within the laws of his country and didn't injure others. He remembered watching an East Indian swing from a hook impaled on his back. That was in keeping with the man's belief. He harmed no one. He had seen another Indian mystic who clenched his arm so long that his fingernails had grown into his flesh.

Houdini said he was not a skeptic. He longed to believe in a spirit world that would bring him a word from his beloved mother—or from any of the others with whom he had made pacts before they died. His enemies, Houdini lamented, dismissed him as a mere itinerant magician, a showman, a vaudevillian. He had to pressure his way to success, but simultaneously for thirty-five years he had studied spiritualism, investigating mediums day and night. Like his father, he was a scholar. He had two wonderful libraries in New York—one of them the largest in the world on witchcraft and magic. He owned the fourth largest dramatic collection. Recently he had added twenty packing cases of books bought in Boston from the late editor of the spiritualist paper *The Banner of Light*.

Anyone could talk to the dead—but the dead would not answer. Inmates of lunatic asylums listened to strange voices, saw phantoms. A million dollars had been spent on psychic research in sixty years without producing any convincing results. Since 1854, Harvard University had a standing offer of five hundred dollars for a genuine case of mediumship. That very day, he said, he had posted five thousand dollars with the mayor, but there had been no takers. Not even from the same mediums who regularly showed manifestations—under their own fixed conditions—for a dollar or two.

Sir Arthur Conan Doyle, Sir Oliver Lodge, and men like them were menaces to mankind, Houdini declared. (There were gasps in the audience.) They were great and to be much respected in their own fields, but they were not qualified to pass judgment on pickpockets and burglars. Why, with six or seven magicians he could show feats of so-called psychic phenomena which would defy scientific explanation.

He paused to unfasten a letter file, then called off a long list of court cases involving spiritualism. The Clara Barton case, the Rand case, the case of Sarah L. Winchester, who kept adding rooms to her house on the advice of a spirit medium. He had been there, had seen the bushel baskets of keys, the ten thousand windows.

A college professor once said he had seen a pencil stand on end and write a message at a séance. "No honest lead pencil would do such a thing," Houdini commented. "I'm not denouncing spiritualism. I'm showing up frauds. If there is an honest medium, trot her out."

Admitting that he had posed as a medium himself, as a foolish and hard-pressed young man, Houdini told how his faked message from a murdered man in Kansas had panicked an audience.

He showed a letter in which Lady Shackleton denied that Sir Arthur Conan Doyle could have heard from her explorer husband. He told of Lady Doyle in Atlantic City writing page after page purporting to be from his dear mother. His mother, who had been educated in Europe, could speak five languages, but no English. Sir Arthur, when he learned this from Houdini, had blandly asserted that his mother had gone to college in heaven and learned English!

After this rambling discourse, the house lights were turned off and slides of such famous mediums as the Fox sisters and the Davenport Brothers were flashed on the screen. Houdini summarized their careers, explained that their feats were mere tricks, not the result of spiritual powers. After the lights went back on, Houdini demonstrated how the mediums had worked some of their swindles. A man from the audience was invited to come up on the stage. He sat down with Houdini at a table, such as might be used at a séance, and examined a slate the magician gave to him. It was blank. But after the man held it beneath the table, a message appeared on it. A medium, Houdini told the audience, would call this a spirit message. But it was merely a trick. Then he showed how he had switched slates under his chair before the man grasped the slate beneath the table. The audience rocked with laughter.

"Now for a message from Walter," Houdini continued. He marked numbers—one, two, three, four—on the sides of two slates, he tied the slates together and had a man in the audience hold them over his head. He displayed a dictionary and asked another man from the crowd to insert a card between two pages. This done, Houdini ordered the spirits to write the page numbers and the first and last words on each page. The slates were opened. Inside were the page numbers, 116 and 117, and the first and last words on each of those pages, as well as two pictures, one of Margery's brother Walter and the other of the wreck in which he had been crushed between a railroad engine and a car. An irate spiritualist jumped up in the audience and shouted: "That's a trick." Of course it was a trick, Houdini answered. He was doing just what a medium would do.

He digressed. He vouched for three *Scientific American* committeemen, McDougall, Prince, and Comstock. He had scorn for Hereward Carrington, J. Malcolm Bird, and Dr. Crandon. He charged Carrington with being a confederate of Margery and Bird with carrying secret committee information to the Crandons. He read a letter advising him not to have a Christian Scientist on his stage committee. This brought an immediate murmur of disagreement from the Scientists in the audience. He said it would be terrible if that denomination espoused spiritualism. "Don't worry," came the response from the other side of the footlights.

Two spectators were invited to the stage. One sat to his left, the other to his right. Both had their heads covered with lightproof hoods to simulate conditions in a dark séance room. Each man held one of Houdini's hands, each controlled one of his feet. "Is the megaphone on the floor near you?" he asked the man on his right. The spectator released his hand, touched the megaphone, said it was there and took Houdini's hand again. "Stretch back in your chairs." The men did as they were told.

He bent forward, put his head under a table and lifted it so that only two legs were still on the floor. Then he pulled his head away. The "levitated" table bumped back in place. The audience howled its approval. "That's exactly how Margery did it," Houdini shouted. "If it isn't, I lose five thousand dollars."

Once more Harry asked the man on his right to make sure

the megaphone was by his side. The man released the magician's hand, verified the position of the trumpet. In the few seconds this action took, the delighted audience saw Houdini pick up the megaphone as the spectator's hand left it, jam it on his own head and have his hand ready for the spectator's grasp. Neither hooded volunteer was aware of what had happened. The man to Houdini's left was told that the megaphone was floating in the air over their heads. Did he wish it to drop near him? He did. Harry turned in his direction and with a shake of his head sent the megaphone his way. The audience dissolved in laughter.

Houdini demonstrated how the bell box on a table could be rung with his forehead while his hands and feet were held by the hooded volunteers. He also made it ring while it was suspended by strings. The stockslike enclosure he had designed to hold Margery was brought on stage, its first appearance in Boston since his last séance with the medium. He told how Margery, locked within it, could not use her hands or feet to ring the bell box. He told how Walter had called him a vile name during the sitting, how he had insisted it be put in the records. He displayed a spirit hand on the end of a lazy-tong device, and demonstrated how a person, some distance away, could be touched with it. He had obtained the device in Berlin. The medium who used it was sentenced to a four-year jail term for fraud. He exhibited two paraffin hands, purportedly produced by spirits. He coaxed another man up from the audience. The man sat at one end of a table, Houdini at the other. The man put his feet on Houdini's under the table and held Houdini's hands across the top.

A dinner bell rang under the table. A tambourine jangled. Control had not been broken, the volunteer said; he could still feel Harry's hands and feet. The bell rang again. Houdini's assistant lifted the tablecloth. The audience laughed. The man's feet were still on Harry's shoes, but he had slipped out of his right shoe. His stocking was cut away at the toes, permitting him to grab the dinner bell between his big and second toes. As he shook his foot the bell rang.

Houdini started an open forum. One member of the audience asked: "Do you deny you are in the pay of the Roman Catholic Church?" "Preposterous," he answered, "I believe I'm stopping people from going to the madhouse. The Catholic Church wouldn't do such a thing in the first place and I wouldn't in the second." The man who had been so annoyed by the slate trick had questions about it. Harry asked Sam Bailey, the Boston magic dealer, to verify that trick slates had been used. They sold for $1.50. "Why have you collected so many books on spiritualism?" "Because I hoped there might be one grain of truth in one of them. But I've found nothing."

A woman halfway back in the hall asked: "Are there no true spiritualists?" Houdini started to answer, but the woman continued with more questions. She had to shout over an uproar in the audience. "Let her be heard," came several demands. She was invited to the stage. She said she was Mrs. Frances—a spiritualist and proud of her faith. She abhorred fraud, but people should think for themselves. Houdini should be fair.

"Name one genuine medium," Houdini challenged. She repeated her own name. Houdini said he had never had her tested. "And you never will," she snapped. "You can't get any business here," a voice from the rear advised.

"I know one trick you can't do, Houdini. Fill this hall twice, the way Conan Doyle did," another voice from the back chimed in. This prompted more questions about Doyle. Sir Arthur, Houdini explained somewhat sadly, was an honest but deluded man. Doyle went to a séance in a frame of mind to believe, and he believed. Even the simplest trick of magic would baffle him. "I contend this," Houdini said, "nobody can get communication from the dead. That's all."

Asked whether Moses and Elias appeared to Jesus on the mountaintop, Houdini replied: "I'll talk Bible to you privately."

"What is ectoplasm?" He replied: "A peculiar slimy b-r-r-r stuff which oozes from the medium's body and takes form, they say." He was asked: "Was it difficult to produce?" He answered: "Give me eight magicians around a table and we'll produce two elephants. Are there any more questions? Anything more you want to see?" Houdini asked. Silence, until a voice from the gallery expressed the mood of the majority: "Do some more tricks."

In the audience that night were Mayor and Mrs. Curley and many other celebrities. Few recognized Anna Eva Fay, who had once been the most talked-about psychic worker in Europe and the United States. Sir William Crookes, the distinguished British scientist, had no explanation for her phenomena. Now she was on Harry's side. Privately she told him precisely how she had worked her tricks. The newspapers had hinted that friends of the Crandons would try to break up the meeting, that Houdini had bodyguards present. The threat did not materialize, the only excitement had been onstage.

The antispiritualism show continued on to New York, opening in condensed form as an act on January 12 at the Hippodrome, where in other years Houdini had vanished elephants and produced eagles. For the New York run he revived the cabinet séance he had used with the California Concert Company many years previously. While tied to a chair inside a cabinet, he made bells ring and a tambourine jangle. When a knife was tossed inside, the "spirits" cut him loose. He presented Margery's megaphone-tossing stunt with two blindfolded spectators touching his hands and feet. He rang a bell under a table with his toes. And he made a bell box ring while locked in the "fraudproof" crate which had been built to hold Margery. A black cloth was used to enhance the drama by hiding his operating procedure from the audience. But he openly showed how a two-foot ruler could have been used by Margery—if her right hand had been released. It was easy to slip the open ruler out through the neck-hole until it was within reach of the box on the table. A little chin pressure on it forced the box top down to make the bell ring.

Each day Houdini successfully predicted the big news stories which would break in the papers the next morning. Later he revealed that he had had a direct wire to the New York *World*. As cable dispatches from abroad arrived, they were relayed to him at the theater. His engagement was extended. To spark business for the fourth week, he returned to the old exploitation route—escaping from a submerged box in the Hippodrome pool. When the Albee Theater opened in Brooklyn, he doubled there. A police escort sped him from one stage door to the other. His act at the Albee featured escapes. "I take two baths every day," he noted. "One after the straitjacket in Brooklyn so I am fresh when I get to the Hippodrome."

Houdini's six weeks at the Hippodrome ended on George Washington's birthday. *Variety* had called him a master magician when he made the elephant disappear. This time the accolade went further. He was, the theatrical paper proclaimed, "the master magician of all times."

The long-delayed *Scientific American* committee report on

Margery was released in February. Hereward Carrington claimed that the Boston medium had produced genuine phenomena. Houdini branded her a fraud. Dr. Walter Franklin Prince said her supernormal powers had not been proved; Professor McDougall shared this opinion. Dr. Comstock said he had never seen a manifestation under strict scientific control. By a 4-to-1 verdict, Mrs. Crandon did not merit the award. As far as the magazine was concerned the case was closed.

THE MYSTIFIER

A dispatch from London early in 1925 reported that Gilbert Murray, Regius Professor of Greek at Oxford and president of the British Society for Psychical Research, and the Earl of Balfour, a past president of the society, had completed 259 experiments in thought transference with remarkable results.

During one of the tests the professor had left the room in which several friends had gathered. His daughter Agnes told the guests she was imagining a scene in which Prime Minister Gladstone at 10 Downing Street was chiding Lloyd George for having made an indiscreet speech in Paris.

When Professor Murray returned he said: "I see a dignified man severely reproving somebody—giving him an awful dressing down. I should think it was Mr. Gladstone—it's something political. I can't think whom Mr. Gladstone would be likely to rebuke. Oh, he's rebuking Lloyd George."

The editorial department of the New York *World* was impressed by the story from London. They could not conceive of the distinguished scholar or his associates using trickery. Telepathy seemed the only rational explanation. Houdini was asked for his opinion by his old friend Ralph Pulitzer, the publisher. Telepathy, the magician stated flatly, was impossible. He could duplicate the tests by perfectly natural means.

He invited Pulitzer; Walter Lippmann, the paper's chief editorial writer; Bernard M. Baruch, former chairman of the War Industries Board; Dr. Edward J. Kempf, a psychiatrist; Arthur Train, the novelist, and several other people to his house for a demonstration. Harry was escorted up the stairs to his office. One of his guests stood guard outside the closed door. In the living room Walter Lippmann said he was concentrating on Lord Curzon in the British Foreign Office in January. No impression of this thought reached the magician. The experiment with Bernard Baruch was more successful. He pictured the words "Don't give up the ship." Houdini reported that he visualized a great body of water and many shipwrecks.

After Dr. Kempf chose a subject, Houdini bounded down the stairs. He had received a vivid mental image of black oxen stampeding on a western plain. A hungry man on horseback was shooting the oxen. No, he amended, they weren't oxen, they were buffalo. Hungry people were surging about. The man was giving them buffalo meat. The man had piercing eyes and long hair. Dr. Kempf was visualizing the Buffalo Bill statue in Wyoming.

Pulitzer and Lippmann went with Houdini to the top floor as the other guests concentrated on another target. They stripped the magician. There was no concealed apparatus on his body. Then they locked him in a wooden box which they had examined and placed on two chairs. Harry was wrapped in a blanket when he returned to the living room. He received, he said, the image of something associated with a famous theatrical family. He paused, then identified the family. It was the Barrymores. There was an object—a painting—by Zuloaga. He thought it was a portrait of Jack Barrymore. Again Houdini was uncannily close to the mark. The selected painting was a Zuloaga portrait of the actor's wife.

Though he didn't reveal to his guests how he performed his "telepathic" feats, Houdini stressed that thought transference was not involved. His purpose had been to show that Professor Murray's tests could be duplicated without a sophisticated audience discovering the method.

The house on West 113th Street had been wired by a magician friend, Amedeo Vacca. Hardeen, Houdini's brother, had been with the guests downstairs. When they chose a subject Hardeen repeated the words as if to fix them in the minds of those present. His voice was carried by a transmitter to the office upstairs. The box in which Houdini had been locked had a receiver ingeniously concealed inside.

The success of Houdini's spirit-exposure act at the New York Hippodrome was repeated on his Keith tour. He featured escapes his first week in Cleveland, during the second he was "Unmasking Spirit Frauds." Reporters from local papers in the cities he played joined his corps of psychic investigators, which until then had been his wife; Julia Sawyer, Bess' 22-year-old niece; his stage assistants, and friends. Eventually he hired private detectives who devoted their full time to the task.

During his Cleveland engagement, Harry, wearing shabby clothes and thick-lensed glasses as a disguise, went with County Prosecutor Edward B. Stanton and reporter Louis B. Seltzer to George Renner's home on Superior Avenue. In his séance room on the second floor, the medium showed his clients four spirit photographs. Houdini's name was mentioned. Renner called the magician a four-flusher. "I once paid two dollars and a half to see him. He's a big frost and a faker. They chased him out of Massachusetts. When he says spiritualism is a fake, he lies, folks. Tonight we will prove that spiritualism is genuine and Houdini is a faker."

Three other visitors, not members of the Houdini party, joined the circle around a big table. "Move closer," Renner instructed, "each of you put your hand on the knee of the person next to you." He made sure his instructions were carried out.

"Young man, you look a little frightened," Renner said to Seltzer. "There is no need to be. If the spirits brush you on the cheek, don't be afraid. If the guitar or the trumpets float over your head, keep quiet. They will not harm you."

The medium continued: "Folks, you will hear tonight from Jimmy Nolan of Anderson, Wisconsin. . . . Are you ready?" Renner stood up, fastened two frames covered with opaque paper to the windows, then draped rugs over the three doors to the room. He returned to his seat in the circle and switched off the lights. It was not long before a booming voice broke the silence: "This is Jimmy."

There were raps, voices purporting to be the father of a sitter, and an Indian chief. Then the guitar began to play in the dark, apparently floating up and overhead. It returned to the table, the music stopped, and the lights were turned on. Renner was in his seat, his hands on the knees of those next to him, as they had been earlier.

Making motions toward leaving, Seltzer said he wanted to pay for himself and his two friends. Renner accepted the three dollars, but protested that the séance had barely started. Once more the room was darkened. A spirit voice sang "Nearer, My God, to Thee" and "Jerusalem," and the sitters joined in.

A whooshing sound through the air indicated that the trumpets were airborne. Then came clanks as they dropped back on the table. A flashlight stabbed through the dark and spotlighted the medium. He blinked his eyes. His hands were covered with soot. There were dark streaks on his face.

"Mr. Renner, you are a fraud," announced Houdini. "Your hands are full of lampblack. The trumpets are also full of lampblack. That's where you got it on your hands." Reporter Seltzer turned on the lights. Houdini told how he had taken a can of lampblack from his pocket in the dark and coated the trumpets.

"I have been a medium for forty years," Renner shouted angrily, "and I have never been exposed."

"Well," replied the magician, "you are now."

"Who are you?" asked the flustered Renner.

"My name," said the lampblack-applier, removing his glasses, "is Houdini." He introduced the country prosecutor and the reporter, whose story made the Cleveland *Press* front page the next day.

Renner was arrested, tried and found guilty of obtaining money under false pretenses. He was fined twenty-five dollars and sentenced to serve six months in jail.

In Cincinnati, Houdini challenged Mrs. Laura A. Pruden, a medium noted for her ability to produce messages on slates. Sir Arthur Conan Doyle was one of her many admirers. Harry offered five thousand dollars if she could give him an authentic message from the spirit world or reveal the words he himself would write in her presence. Mrs. Pruden, who had enjoyed a comfortable two-dollars-per-person séance business for many years, was wise enough to ignore him.

In mid-April Houdini was saddened by the death at seventy-nine of Alfred Becks, the librarian he had hired five years before to catalogue his collection. At the time Harry thought the job would be completed in a year, but he reckoned without considering his acquisitive nature. Scarcely a week went by without substantial additions to his hoard: rare books, play-bills, letters, and not infrequently complete collections which he purchased from other men—anywhere from a few dozen items to several thousand.

Becks was a collector too, despite his limited means. Once he made the mistake of telling Houdini about a set of rare books on the theater which he hoped to purchase when they came up for auction. Houdini developed an overwhelming urge to buy the volumes himself. He sent a representative to the sale. It was a sad old man who reported to his employer that someone had raised the bid beyond the sum he could afford. Houdini guiltily smuggled the books into his house and hid them in the basement. He knew he had been cruel and unfair, but he was never remorseful enough to present the treasures to his disappointed librarian.

Partly to atone for this wrong and partly because he missed his hardworking librarian, Houdini arranged a far more elaborate funeral for Becks than he would have done otherwise. Harry kept his emotions under control at the ceremony but back in his library the tears came. He wiped them away and brought up from the basement the books Becks had longed for. He unwrapped them, flicked through the pages. As he added the volumes to his drama section, the memory of the dedicated old man filled him with remorse. Again he wept.

Also in April, Houdini, Will Rogers, and Ann Pennington were among the headliners who contributed their services for an "All-Star Cabaret" charity benefit at the Fifth Avenue town house of Mrs. Vincent Astor. The proceeds of the April 14 show went to the Lenox Hill Neighborhood Foundation. On the program he mailed to Oscar Teale, Houdini wrote: "This was one of the ultra finest audiences I have ever played to and the V. Astor home the finest I've ever played in." After he signed his name he added an afterthought: "I played in my own home, whereas [it] was not as sumptuously furnished, it was richer in happiness."

Bess, who had not appeared in the act since "Metamorphosis" was last shown on the road, worked with lightning speed when he included the trunk substitution feat in his routine at the New York Hippodrome in June. A new feature was a slate-writing exposure. He revealed how a girl concealed in a specially built table could write through a trapdoor in its top on the underside of a blank slate placed on its surface. The story of how he had trapped Renner, the Cleveland medium, delighted the spectators as he pantomimed the incident.

He lectured, as a special instructor, at the New York Police Academy later in the month. His lecture "How to Catch Fake Spiritualists" was attended by a hundred student detectives. He astonished them by feigning a trance and revealing personal details about their lives. Then he explained: "Before I came into this room I got all this information from one of your

men. It is just as easy for mediums to get it. . . . It is pure
fraud and so simple that no one should be baffled, though
everybody is."

Houdini explained how psychics produced darkroom phenomena and instructed the police in the best methods for
gathering evidence when raiding séance rooms. One of his
tips was: "Don't grab the ectoplasm high up or around the
waist. Tackle it. . . . Don't grab it from the front. Grab it
from behind and you'll get the medium too."

The new police instructor appeared in court—not as a
prosecutor, but as a defendant—in late July. He had been
served with a summons when he arrived at WOR for a radio
interview. Acording to the charges, Harry had entered a shop
on Broadway that sold radio equipment to protest the firm's
use of the name Houdinia. The company was trading on his
reputation, Houdini asserted. Allegedly, he used abusive language and in the ensuing melee several chairs and a chandelier
were broken. There was little doubt that this happened as
charged, but, as a representative of the firm didn't appear at
the hearing to press the charge, the case was dismissed.

Howard Thurston, Kellar's successor, had played the nation's
legitimate theaters with a full evening magic show for sixteen
years. Houdini's announcement that he would tour in the fall
with a competing mystery attraction inspired other magicians.
"As near as I can judge," Houdini wrote, "the following are
going to give a full evening's performance: Mysterious Smith,
Dunninger, Blackstone, Thurston, Dante. . . . Some of the
magicians thought I was going to use a lot of women in my
forthcoming show and they are trying to beat me to it. They
have been misinformed. I am going to specialize in Houdini
stuff."

Houdini planned to offer three shows in one—magic, escapes, and exposures of mediumistic phenomena. The escape
portion would feature his Water Cell. The spirit section would
include the most effective parts of his lecture and the routine
he had tested in vaudeville. The opening magic act was his
major problem.

A big show had been on his mind for many years, but the
project had been sidetracked by other activities. First his
passion for filmmaking, then his crusade to warn the public
about psychic racketeers. He wrote Karl Germain, a retired

illusionist who lived in Cleveland: "When I left England, July, 1920—I destroyed $25,000 worth of illusions I had bot[*sic*]— never used even a thought. I had the finest Noah's Ark [a production box] ever built, the Flying Moth, the original Vanishing Lady chair, etc., etc. I bot [*sic*] the entire illusion act of Hermalin in 1914—and paid about $1,000 in storage."

Crated in his storerooms were many wonders of other days. An automaton trapeze performer similar to one Robert-Houdin had used; Buatier de Kolta's expanding cube; Kellar's spirit cabinet; Psycho, Kellar's mechanical figure which played cards, an imitation of the device John Nevil Maskelyne had featured; and Dr. Lynn's "Paligenesia, or Taking a Living Man to Pieces and Restoring Him by Installments." He had first seen the Lynn illusion when his father had taken him to the British magician's performance in Milwaukee. Later, in England, he purchased the original equipment from Lynn's son. He decided to include it in his new production for sentimental reasons. Houdini bypassed the huge cabinet he had used to vanish an elephant. He had already reaped the maximum publicity from this. Besides, a live elephant would be too much of a nuisance on the road.

Bess was choosing the fabrics and colors for the show costumes. Collins, Vickery, and his other assistants were rehearsing the stage movements for the magic section of the production. There were almost daily conferences with L. Lawrence Weber, the impresario who would present the attraction. Routing, advance publicity, a new souvenir book, and other details were being worked out. Harry studied the list of cities to be played and made notes of firms which could challenge him with packing boxes, and mediums whose séances should be investigated.

Someone sent him an editorial from the August *American Brewer*. The publication suggested that he be made Prohibition Enforcement Administrator for New York: "Houdini's knowledge of spirits, cabinet mysteries and his presentation of unbelievable illusions make his qualifications second to none."

Houdini worked at his desk on the top floor of his house during the hot summer nights. A picture of his mother was hung so he could see it when he raised his eyes from his notes. New acquisitions for his library were stacked in heaps around him. Once he had haunted Second Avenue bookshops for bargains. Now he was the proud possessor of the finest collection of conjuring literature and memorabilia in the world.

He was not as suave as Thurston, as dignified as Kellar, or as amusing as Herrmann the Great. Yet in the numbered boxes in his office were clippings from around the world in which critics had proclaimed him a master showman. When he had presented a magic revue in England it had not been as well received as his escape act. Would the public accept him now with a full evening show?

THE BIG SHOW

Houdini's full evening show opened at the Shubert Alvin Theater in Pittsburgh the night of September 14, 1925. His audiences were never able to say, "It's up his sleeve." Harry ripped away the snap-fastened coat and shirt-sleeves moments after he appeared on stage and performed with his arms bare to the elbows.

Outstanding in his first act were the spectacular silks-from-fishbowl production he had introduced at the Hippodrome and Dr. Lynn's vivisection illusion. The Water Cell escape drew heavy applause in the second act. Most discussed afterward were his revelations of mediums' methods, which closed the show.

A daily Houdini column in the Pittsburgh *Press* answered queries from readers about spiritualists, clairvoyants, and crystal gazers. Why hadn't he attended Dr. Lee's séance? someone asked. Harry replied that he had challenged the medium from the Alvin stage and Dr. Lee had left town. The reader response was so great that he made arrangements to write similar columns in other cities on his route.

The Rev. Alice S. Dooley, of the Pittsburgh Church of Divine Healing, volunteered to be tested at the Alvin on September 17. Harry sealed three questions in as many envelopes and hung them on a string stretched across the stage. The psychic asked for music to put her in the mood to commune with her astral influences. The orchestra obliged with a dreamy waltz. She pointed to the first envelope. "All is well. March 30, 1894," she said. No vibrations were produced by the second query. Her answer to the third was, "It is possible." The committee of judges, three clergymen, opened the first envelope. The question was, "What Pittsburgh chief of police did I meet in Europe? When, how, and where?" The psychic's first statement had not answered any part of Houdini's question. The date she gave was meaningless. He had not gone to Europe until 1900. The third query was: "What was the name of the Hindu who taught me the East Indian Needle Trick? Where and what year and the circumstances?" "It is possible" was scarcely an enlightening answer.

The critic in Cincinnati's *Commercial Tribune* wrote that the show "was good fun from start to finish. . . . Houdini manages these magical shows just a bit better than anyone else. . . . There's one big difference between Houdini on a vaudeville bill and Houdini in his own show. In the latter instance there's more of him. Ergo, the show is better."

An addition to the program, started in Cincinnati at the Shubert Theater and repeated in other cities, was the introduction of five local members of the S.A.M. Each performed his favorite trick as Houdini sat in the audience and led the applause. The Cincinnati magicians surprised Bess with a bouquet as she finished the trunk illusion. After the performance the Houdinis were taken to a party where they were showered with confetti and compliments.

Two lines in the Dayton *Herald* review were underlined in Harry's clipping file: "Last season Thurston presented a remarkable entertainment. But Houdini captivated this reviewer in a much greater measure than his predecessor in magic."

Critics in Columbus, Indianapolis, and Syracuse wrote that the showman's personality made the show. Magicians wondered why Houdini didn't do more magic. The newspapers suggested he expand his spirit exposures. Herrmann, Kellar, and Thurston had performed excellent feats of conjuring but Houdini had something different to offer. He was, in the opinion of many editors, the only man in America qualified to expose psychic fraud.

Houdini was still a member of the *Scientific American* committee, though since the Margery case the committee had not been active. He also was a member of a new investigating group, appointed by the *Journal of Abnormal and Social Psychology*. The other members of the *Journal* committee were all Harvard men: Harlow Shapley, director of the Harvard Observatory; Theodore Lyman, professor of physics; Dr. Walter B. Cannon, professor of physiology; and Dr. C. C. Pratt, instructor in psychology. The *Journal* offered five thousand dollars to any medium who could produce phenomena under laboratory conditions.

In every city Houdini repeated his personal ten-thousand-dollar offer for spiritualistic manifestations which he couldn't duplicate or explain. Rose Mackenberg, a private detective he had hired in August, daily submitted voluminous reports on the séances she attended. During his performances, Harry reeled off the names of the most prominent local psychics and pleaded with them to come forward and claim his money. So many mediums had sued Houdini since he began his crusade that a stenographer now recorded every word that was said during this part of his show.

During the week in Syracuse, Julia Sawyer and Rose Mackenberg went on a special mission to Lily Dale, the famous spiritualist summer camp. At Lily Dale the curious could patronize clairvoyants, message-readers, and various phenomena-producers. Many believers spent their vacations there. In 1916 the Fox farmhouse had been moved to Lily Dale from Hydesville, where the first raps had been produced by the sisters, and similar sounds could still be heard when a medium presided at séances in the structure.

Julia masqueraded as a curious teen-ager, Rose as an elderly housewife. For three dollars each a medium named Pierre Keeler admitted them to a slate séance. Keeler produced a spirit message for Julia from a sister she never had, as well as communications from her mother and brother, who were said to be happy in the spirit world. This was a shock to Julia since both were alive. After the séance Keeler was taken to meet Julia's aged uncle, who slumped in a wheelchair under the care of a male nurse. Off came a set of fake whiskers. Harry jumped up and shouted that at last he had the goods on Keeler. The medium admitted his deceptions. He and Houdini, he said, were in the same business. "Not so!" Harry fired back. "I'm a legitimate entertainer, you're a cheat." The male nurse was an interested witness. He wasn't what he appeared to be either. He was a newspaper reporter from Syracuse.

That evening on the stage of the Weiting Opera House Houdini told how Keeler had been trapped. For the rest of the week most of his attacks were directed toward Keeler and Lily Dale.

Saturday night, after his last show, Harry intended to join the Syracuse magicians for a Chinese supper at the Asia Restaurant but he had a severe cold and a physician sent him to his hotel with instructions to stay in bed. Collins supervised the packing of equipment. Houdini's hotel was noisy that night. It was October 31. A Halloween party filled the corridors with shouting celebrants. Harry must have lain in bed thinking he might have gotten as much rest if he had gone to a party himself. Charles Eastman, one of the magicians who saw Houdini off at the railway station the next morning, said Harry was a very sick man.

Even so, the show with its star went on the following Monday in Cleveland as scheduled. No one noticed a letdown. Houdini was constantly revising and adding to the opening magic sequences. A vanishing chicken trick, purchased from Jack Gwynne in Pittsburgh, now was a part of the routine. He called the chicken Ponzi Gwynne (Charles Ponzi, a man then in the news, had swindled thousands of investors with his money-making schemes). Another Gwynne invention was getting a fine response. From a miniature Noah's Ark, Houdini produced a flock of pigeons.

Six days before the show opened in Baltimore, the *News* ran this eight-column headline on the front page of its second section: HOUDINI TO EXPOSE BALTIMORE FRAUDS. This was repeated the next day. On Thursday, November 5, the headline was changed to HOUDINI ON TRAIL OF BALTIMORE SEERS. Friday it read: HOUDINI TO ANSWER MEDIUM QUESTIONS. Photographs and stories about the "lieutenant in New York Police Reserves" appeared daily.

The Baltimore *Sun* caught the spirit of the show:

> Mr. Houdini appears and disappears in detachable shirt sleeves at the Academy of Music this week. He is supported by a capable cast of white rabbits, private detectives, pouter pigeons, furniture-movers and a brown leghorn rooster. The handcuff king fools all of his audience most of the time and most of his audience all of the time. Moreover he has $10,000 in negotiable bonds that he can unscrew the inscrutable when it comes to spiritualism.

> Legerdemain lovers lined up for half a block last night when it was time for the curtain, delaying Mr. Houdini's appearance and disappearance for almost twenty minutes. Inside they clapped and whistled just like the folks back home. Up went the curtain. Two of Mr. Houdini's flapper operatives in colonial disguise drew back a handsome

drapery by its tasseled cords. Behind stood Mr. Houdini's mechanical equipment, portable houses and uniformed scene shifters.

Out walked the whole show: Mr. Houdini in person, full dress and detachable shirt sleeves, which he detached immediately. He hushed the orchestra with a graceful gesture. "Ladies and gentlemen," he intoned in traditional fashion. The show was on.

The entertainment, like Mr. Houdini himself, is a vibrant testimonial to the fact that the hand is quicker than the eye. Now you see lamps, flower pots, and ladies of the harem. Now you don't.

He chopped a man to pieces and reassembled him. With feet encased in mahogany stocks, the magician was raised by block and tackle and dumped head first into a steel-lined tank of water and clamped inside like a roast in a pressure cooker. Write your own solution.

A brief lecture and working demonstration on departed spirits concludes a three-act performance. It is in this whirlwind finish that Mr. Houdini displays his roll and proves spiritualistic bell-ringers as bogus as the Wonderful Wizard of Oz.

Near the end of Houdini's week in Worcester, early in December 1925, a man in the audience interrupted his discourse on fraudulent mediums with a shouted: "You don't know what you're talking about." Harry invited the man to the stage. He refused and spoke from his seat. "History repeats itself," declared Armstrong LeVeyne, whose wife was a local medium. "Christ was persecuted and now we spiritualists are being persecuted. Some day, as in the case of Christ, we will be recognized. . . . The people some day will see the light."

"But Christ never robbed people of two dollars, did he?" Houdini challenged.

"Your tricks are frauds," LeVeyne retorted. "You are duping the public exactly as you claim spiritualists are."

"I studied years to do what I am doing," Harry answered. "The public knows that I am deceiving them. I give them optical illusions for entertainment, part of which is derived from their efforts to discover how I do it. I challenge you to come up here and duplicate my feat with the locked water tank or any other of my tricks."

The man ignored the offer. The audience hissed him. He spoke again: "Letty LeVeyne was my mother. She was a famous Australian vaudeville star—the greatest woman who ever lived. I loved my mother. I love my wife. I am here today to protect my wife—to protect her reputation.

"My wife is a member of the National Spiritualist Association and she is backed by it. She is backed by law. She is backed by the people and she is backed by the White House. She is backed as a teacher of spiritualism and she will give a demonstration at any time of her psychic ability, an endowment given her by the Deity. Let the public gather in our church and see her prove herself a divine medium."

This was the statement Houdini had been waiting for. "All right, let her perform here."

"This is not the place," LeVeyne answered. "We need a church."

Harry had heard this argument before. "What, do you mean to say this theater can't be converted into a church when so many theaters throughout the country are devoted to Lenten services? Aren't they regarded as churches then?"

"How can this be considered a church even for a few minutes when so many women appear on stage half dressed?" shouted LeVeyne. The audience laughed. Harry called Bess and Julia from the wings.

"Folks," he said with a smile, "this is my wife, Mrs. Houdini, to whom I have been married thirty-one years. And this is Miss Sawyer, my niece. Have you anything to say about their characters?"

"No," came voices from the audience, "they're all right."

Houdini pointed to Rose Mackenberg, one of his investigators, who was seated in a box near the stage dressed in black with a veil hiding her face. She, Harry said, was the Rev. Frances Raud. Take away the last six letters of the first name, add the remaining letters of the last name and the result was "Fraud."

"I am greater than you are. I own a church!" he asserted. "See, here are my certificates and my charter. Miss 'Raud' is its pastor."

Mrs. LeVeyne, the medium, shouted: "She stole it. . . . The state [spiritualist] association says she stole it."

Harry turned to his operative in the box. "Mrs. LeVeyne says you are a thief, that you stole this charter."

Mrs. LeVeyne screamed: "I did not say that. I never called her a thief."

"Yes, you did; yes, you did," chanted the audience.

The magician's black-garbed investigator said the charter for Worcester's Unity Spiritualist Church had been purchased from the Massachusetts State Association with thirteen dollars of Mr. Houdini's money. He had sat, in disguise, in the front row when she gave her first sermon denouncing the magician as spiritualism's most dangerous enemy.

She had visited the woman who called her a thief for a reading. "I have never been married and never had a child. Yet Mrs. LeVeyne told me that my husband and little girl were together in the next world and that they advocated my going into the business of spiritualism."

Mrs. LeVeyne jumped up. "I never saw that woman!"

"Sit down," hooted the audience.

Mr. LeVeyne entered the fray again. The spiritualists, he said, would hold an indignation meeting Sunday morning.

Houdini replied: "I drove out the fakes in California and I intend to drive them out in Massachusetts." The spectators cheered.

Mrs. LeVeyne yelled: "There are three mediums you haven't seen yet here." Harry replied he had not included them in his lists because they did not take money for their séances.

"I spent this afternoon speaking at Holy Cross College and after that dined with the faculty," Houdini continued. The spiritualists accused him of being in the pay of the Pope. Nothing could be further from the truth.

He reminded the LeVeynes that he had given ten thousand dollars in bonds to the mayor of Worcester. If they came to the stage and produced a single genuine manifestation, they could claim it. There was another thousand dollars if Mrs. LeVeyne could tell him the pet name his father called him.

"I expected Mr. or Mrs. LeVeyne to accept my challenge and take some of my money, but they are afraid. If you want me to show you how the mediums take the public, tell me." The audience cheered. With three volunteers from the audience helping, he closed the show with demonstrations of trumpet tricks, slate tests, and bell-box ringing, Margery-style.

When Houdini began his Broadway run at the 44th Street Theater, the year Walter, Margery's spirit voice, had given him to live was almost over. Only once—for a persistent cold on Halloween—had he been under a doctor's care. For a man approaching fifty-two he was in unusually good physical condition.

Blackstone was playing across the river at Werba's Theater in Brooklyn one week while Houdini was performing in Manhattan. A balloon anchored to a building on Broadway near Houdini's theater advertised the Blackstone show. Harry was tempted to shoot it down. He didn't. That would have publicized his competitor even more.

It was snowing when Houdini arrived in Hartford, Connecticut, for his engagement at Parson's Theater. He went directly from the train to talk before four hundred men at the Advertising Club, then to address a radio audience over WTIC. Hundreds were in line in front of the theater an hour before the show. Despite the storm, the house was sold out when the curtain went up.

During Houdini's three-week run in Philadelphia he took the night train to Washington. On the morning of February 26 he testified before a House of Representatives committee in support of a bill, H.R. 8989, which would ban fortune-telling in the District of Columbia. This bill and two similar ones, introduced in the Senate, had the magician's unqualified approval.

The spiritualists, their associations and publications were just as vehemently against them. The room where the Subcommittee on Judiciary of the Committee on the District of Columbia held their public hearing was filled, and among the spectators were many spiritualists as well as palm readers, crystal gazers, and clairvoyants.

"Please understand that, emphatically, I am not attacking a religion," Houdini said. "I respect every genuine believer in spiritualism or any other religion. . . . But this thing they call spiritualism wherein a medium intercommunicates with the dead, is a fraud from start to finish. There are only two kinds of mediums, those who are mental degenerates and who ought to be under observation, and those who are deliberate cheats and frauds. I would not believe a fraudulent medium under oath; perjury means nothing to them.

"How can you call it a religion when you get men and

women in a room together and they feel each other's hands and bodies? The inspirational mediums are not quite as bad as that. But they guess and by 'fishing' methods and by reading the obituary notices get the neurotics to believe that they hear voices and see forms. In thirty-five years I have never seen one genuine medium."

Washington abounded with fortune-tellers, lucky charm sellers, card readers, and mediums of every sort, Houdini claimed. For twenty-five dollars anyone could buy a clairvoyant license, then point to it and say: "If I were not genuine, I could not get a license."

Harry repeated his offer of ten thousand dollars for proof of mediumship. He took a telegram from his pocket, crumpled it, and threw it on a table. "Read that, you clairvoyant mediums, and show me up. Tell me the contents of that telegram." The spiritualists remained silent.

Representative Frank Reid, a Republican from Illinois, broke in: "I will tell you what it says: 'Please send more money.'"

Houdini replied: "You can make your own deductions. You are not a clairvoyant."

"Oh, yes, I am," Reid came back. This set off a round of laughter. Houdini wadded up another telegram.

"All right, if you are a clairvoyant, tell me what this wire is."

"It is asking if it didn't come," Reid answered.

"No, sir," Harry stated. "Everyone guesses at it."

The above quotations are from the stenographic report of the hearing. Newspapers gave varying accounts of these proceedings. The Associated Press dispatch quoted Reid as saying the telegram read, "I can't be there today." The Chicago *Tribune* described the congressman jumping to his feet and saying, "That's an invitation to you to appear before the committee this morning. I win the ten thousand dollars." International News Service reported Reid as having said, "Why, it's a request for money," and Houdini replying, "Right."

The New York *Morning Telegraph*'s account included an incident not mentioned elsewhere. When Houdini called on any one of the mediums in the hearing room to tell him the name his mother called him before he was born, a palmist, standing just outside the door, remarked: "She probably called him an incipient damn fool."

Mrs. Jane B. Coates, one of Washington's best-known mediums, took the stand. Chairman Clarence J. McLeod asked her to define the term mystic. "A mystic," she answered, "is a person who has evoluted certain senses within themselves which brings them knowledge from the world beyond." Was Houdini a mystic? the congressman inquired. "I think Mr. Houdini is one of the greatest mystics in the world today," Mrs. Coates replied. The hearings were adjourned until May 18.

When the session resumed, Houdini returned to Washington to act as a star witness for the bill. For three days he attacked the mediums and they lashed back at him when they took the stand. He showed how he could produce a "spirit" voice from a trumpet without moving his lips and cause a message to appear on a pair of blank slates. When the spiritualists called him "vile" and "crazy," he asked Bess to come forward.

"I want the chairman to see you. . . . On June 22, 1926, we celebrate our thirty-second anniversary. There are no medals and no ribbons on me, but when a girl will stick to a man for thirty-two years as she did, and when she will starve with me through thick and thin, it is a pretty good recommendation.

"Outside of my great mother, Mrs. Houdini has been my greatest friend. Have I ever shown traces of being crazy, unless it was about you?"

"No."

"Am I brutal to you or vile?"

"No."

"Am I a good boy?"

"Yes."

"Thank you, Mrs. Houdini."

The hearings ended May 21. Despite Houdini's testimony, no antifortune-telling bill was passed.

During the eight weeks Houdini performed at the Princess Theater in Chicago, his staff investigated more than forty mediums. Eight of nineteen sitters with Mrs. Minnie Reichart on Emerald Avenue one night were members of his team. In the blacked-out séance room spirit voices sang such divergent songs as "Yes, Sir, She's My Baby" and "Nearer, My God, to Thee" through Minnie's trumpet.

Aware that Houdini was in town, Mrs. Reichart pulled the floor plug for the only lamp in the room. Even if someone flicked the wall switch, no light would mar her performance. Her spirit control, Chief Blackhawk, was speaking through the trumpet in guttural tones when a flash illuminated the room. A Chicago *American* photographer had taken a picture. The team got into action. One man pulled up the shade and threw open a window. This was the quickest exit route. Then he and four other men jumped through to the lawn outside. There was pandemonium in the séance room. "Where's the outlet for the floor socket?" someone shouted. A feminine voice screamed: "Don't put on the lights. Do you want to kill our medium?"

Mrs. Reichart's supporters rushed the interlopers on the lawn. The medium's sister slapped the photographer, knocking off his hat, then clawed him. Another wallop sent the flash equipment from his left hand to the grass. He clutched his camera firmly with his right hand and fought his way to a waiting car. Lost in the battle—one hat, one camera case, and one flashgun.

In the newspaper darkroom the photographic plate was developed. The single shot had captured the plump mystic holding the trumpet to her lips with a handkerchief-wrapped hand—so no telltale fingerprints would appear on the metal surface. The photograph, four columns wide, titled "Picture Bares Fraud," appeared on the first page of the second section of the March 11 Chicago *American*.

The medium's sister was welcome to the photographer's hat and equipment, Houdini said in the accompanying story. "The picture is worth thousands of hats because it shows up one of the frauds who have been taking money from Chicagoans by pretending they could communicate with spirits."

A large signboard in front of the Princess Theater listed the names and addresses of mediums and repeated Houdini's ten-thousand-dollar challenge to them. This and the daily Houdini denunciations in the newspapers were too much for Herbert O. Breedlove, who ran the Mission of Love on Dearborn Street. He filed a criminal libel suit against Houdini, claiming that the magician's crusade was harassing his spirits. They weren't as communicative as they once had been. His patrons had stopped attending his meetings. Once he could expect at least thirty-five people each evening. Now there were only three or four.

Judge Francis Borelli heard the case in his South Clark Street courtroom. The crowd overflowed into the corridor outside. At one tense moment a gray-haired man collapsed and was carried from the room. Breedlove himself became so wrought up that he fell over in a faint and had to be lifted back into his chair.

The medium present testified that Breedlove's name had been on Houdini's challenge poster outside the theater. Houdini, the manager of the Princess, and the sign painters said it hadn't. In the course of the medium's testimony the judge asked him if he could summon spirits to the courtroom. Breedlove shook his head. "You see, the environment is not right."

Houdini took the stand. Fraudulent mediums were a menace to society, he said. He offered a thousand dollars to anyone present who could tell him the name his father used to call him. "I'm the only person now living who knows that name," he continued as he wrote it on a piece of paper.

The judge was interested. "Did you say a *thousand* dollars?" Houdini nodded solemnly. A calm descended on the courtroom. Breedlove stared at the ceiling. The late editions reported that Houdini had escaped again. This time from a libel charge.

The Chicago crusade produced one unexpected manifestation. Into Houdini's dressing room came an elderly couple, Mr. and Mrs. Ernest Benninghofen. They complimented Harry on his exposures. Mrs. Benninghofen said she had been known as Anna Clark, the "mother medium," because she had developed many young psychics, including Mrs. Cecil Cook, then a leading figure in the movement. Twenty years ago Mrs. Benninghofen had sold Mrs. Cook her northside apartment and her sucker list.

"When I reformed I had no intention of going before the public and showing how the tricks were done. I will come any time or place to help you, as I now see the great good that is being done."

Harry was almost overwhelmed. He had an ally, ordained by the National Spiritualist Association, who would stand up before an audience, confess her sins, and demonstrate the feats that had fooled her followers! He arranged a press conference at the Sherman Hotel. He promised the greatest revelation since the Fox sisters explained their raps.

By coincidence, the twenty-seventh annual convention of the Illinois State Spiritualist Association was in progress on the west side of the city. There, John Slater, who was said to have made a million dollars with his séances, ridiculed Houdini's stage exposures.

At the Sherman Hotel Houdini was busy introducing the "mother medium" to the press. Mrs. Benninghofen, he said, would go through her complete repertoire. The lights were switched off. There was prayer and song. "In the Sweet Bye and Bye" ushered in the phenomena. Trumpets rose and floated in the dark room. Ghostly hands appeared and disappeared. Spirits talked through the trumpets in the air—a shrill little Rosie, a deep-voice Uncle John, a dulcet-toned Aunt Susan. Even a whooping, shouting Indian guide, Chief Big Elk, put in a special appearance.

"If a trumpet strikes you on the head you should say, 'Thank you, Spirit,'" the medium instructed. Someone forgot her instructions. When the metal horn banged him on the forehead, he said, "Ouch!"

Mrs. Benninghofen began her exposures. Voices came at distances far beyond a trumpet length. She showed how she had attached two trumpets, mouthpiece to mouthpiece, in the dark. She whispered in the large end of one trumpet and her voice came from the far end of the other. She exhibited her vocal range. Like an accomplished ventriloquist, she could speak in many voices, many tones, from that of a child to a blustering Indian chieftain.

Houdini helped her unveil the secret of the ghostly hands. A glove coated with luminous paint was glued to a piece of black cardboard. When the luminous side was toward the spectators, the hand appeared in the dark; when it was turned away, the hand vanished. By moving the cardboard quickly from one area to another, he produced what seemed to be two hands at different places. Mrs. Benninghofen said she concealed the hand-producing device under her skirt.

She demonstrated the technique of freeing one hand in the dark, while the sitters on either side of her believed her to be under control. She released her right hand momentarily "to brush back her hair," then clasped hands again with the man on her right. Only this time she clasped his hand with her left hand—which was held at the wrist by a man to her left. Neither sitter realized that one hand was being "controlled," rather than two. With her free hand the medium swung trumpets in the air, fitted them mouthpiece to mouthpiece, and tapped people's heads at a distance with the large end of the far trumpet. It was, as Houdini had announced, a news-making session.

"I really believed in spiritualism all the time I was prac-ticing it," Mrs. Benninghofen explained, "but I thought I was justified in helping the spirits out. They couldn't float a trum-pet around the room, I did it for them. They couldn't speak, so I spoke for them. I thought I was justified in trickery because through trickery I could get more converts to what I thought was a good and beautiful religion. When people asked me if the spirits really moved the trumpets, I told them to judge for themselves. So while I acted a lie, I didn't tell one."

Houdini's first session on the road with his new show ended on May 5 in Harrisburg, Pennsylvania. He had been accepted by both press and public as a legitimate theater attraction equal to his predecessors—Herrmann, Kellar, and Thurston. Even with the heavy initial production costs, adver-tising, salaries of his thirteen assistants, and his corps of psychic investigators, the profits were more than he had anticipated—"36 weeks," he noted, "and all O.K."

BURIED ALIVE

Hereward Carrington, the only *Scientific American* committee-man to endorse Margery as a genuine medium, introduced a new wonder-worker to the American public in May 1926 at the Selwyn Theater on Broadway.

Rahman Bey, a twenty-six-year-old "Egyptian Miracle Man," demonstrated the power of mind over body by thrusting steel needles through his cheeks, impaling a thin knife in the skin of his neck, and pushing skewers through the flesh of his chest. Carrington provided a running commentary for the act.

Bey stretched flat on a bed of nails while an assistant stood on his midsection, walked blindfolded along a chalk line scrawled on the stage by a volunteer, and increased the pulse rate of one wrist while slowing down the other. A stone slab was hammered to pieces on Bey's midsection as he rested rigidly with the back of his neck on one sword blade, his heels on another.

For a climax, he threw himself into a trance and was buried in a coffin under a mound of sand. Carrington lectured for ten minutes on suspended animation and living burials, then the sand was shoveled away and the fakir was removed from the coffin. He revived himself enough to walk unsteadily to the footlights and accept his applause and curtain calls.

In July, Bey announced a dramatic twist to the living burial feat. Instead of being buried in sand, the coffin would be immersed in the Hudson River—and Bey would attempt to stay in it for an entire hour. Two doctors took his pulse count, measured his heartbeat. Bey pressed his fingertips to his temples, shut his eyes, and lowered his head. He swayed, fell backward into the hands of two assistants. They lifted him into a bronze coffin. The inner lid was bolted, the outer cover was soldered.

The coffin, lifted by a hoist, was swung over the water. Before it was lowered into the Hudson, an electric alarm bell rang. The bell was part of a safety device controlled from the inside of the box. The hoist brought the coffin back. Workmen feverishly hacked at the cover, tearing away the lid with chisels, hammers, and shears.

Nineteen minutes after Rahman Bey had been sealed, he was lifted out. His body was covered with perspiration, his face was contorted. After emerging from his trance, he explained, through an interpreter, that he had not rung the bell. Someone offered the theory that when the coffin was raised by the hoist, his body had rolled on the push button and triggered the alarm. Thirteen days later Rahman Bey was ready to try his underwater survival test again. This time his coffin was lowered into the placid waters of the Dalton swimming pool on 59th Street. He stayed, sealed in place, for a full hour.

The Egyptian mystic's most vocal critic was Houdini. Harry was familiar with most of the man's tests as a result of his dime museum days. There was nothing supernormal about them. Knowledge and practice were the secrets. He could do them all himself—except the buried alive stunt. Houdini had been buried beneath the ground once in California, and he had been imprisoned countless times in boxes or coffins that were lowered into the water, but his aim had always been to free himself as rapidly as possible.

Near the end of the month Rahman Bey's manager publicly challenged Houdini to duplicate the underwater endurance feat. Never one to shy away from a dare, Harry approached the problem with the same logic which had brought him renown as an escapologist.

He had read that a container the size of Rahman Bey's held enough air for a man to breathe three or four minutes at the most. Was this true? Houdini ordered a galvanized-iron box, six feet six inches long, twenty-two inches wide, and twenty-two inches high. He installed a telephone as well as a safety bell inside. If he ran into a snag, he could tell his assistant precisely how to handle it over the phone.

His practice runs were made in the basement of his house—out of water, but with the lid sealed. He was ready to risk a public demonstration by August 5. Rahman Bey claimed a trance state was necessary for the feat. Hereward Carrington pontifically reported that the fakir's circulation and respiration had almost stopped during his burials—but Bey offered no scientific proof that this was true.

"If I die, it will be the will of God and my own foolishness," Houdini said before being sealed in his metal box at the Hotel Shelton pool. "I am going to prove that the copybook maxims are wrong when they say a man can live but three minutes without air, and I am not going to pretend to be in a cataleptic state either."

The fifty-two-year-old magician, wearing a pair of black swimming trunks, hopped inside the metal container. The cover was swiftly soldered in place. Caps were screwed on two air vents in the lid. If an emergency arose, they could be unfastened long before the lid could be removed.

Weights were attached to the box and it was lowered under the surface of the pool. Men in bathing suits stood on the lid to keep it level below the waterline. Periodically they were replaced with fresh teams. After thirty minutes one of the men lost his foothold and fell off. The others, their balance jarred, toppled too. The box surged up above the waterline. In seconds, the swimmers pushed it back down under the water.

Collins, on the telephone, explained the reason for the sudden jolt. He assured Houdini that everything was under control. The official timekeeper, Joseph Rinn, announced the passage of each five-minute period for an hour. When Houdini exceeded Rahman Bey's record, Rinn called off each minute. After an hour and a quarter, Houdini told Collins the box had sprung a leak. There was no immediate danger. It was only a tiny trickle. Rinn boomed out the time every thirty seconds now. Just past the hour-and-a-half mark Houdini phoned Collins to bring him up. In two minutes the box was out of the water. One of the air-vent caps was unscrewed. Houdini thrust up an arm. Dr. W. J. McConnell took his pulse. It had been eighty-four at the time of entry; now it hammered at one hundred forty-two. Four tinsmiths ripped away enough of the lid for Harry to climb out. He was wringing wet and appeared to be drained of all but his last ounce of energy. Dr. McConnell gave him a cursory examination. His blood pressure was forty-two, compared with eighty-four when he went down. The thermometer in the metal box was checked. It had reached 99.2 degrees. Houdini said he was slightly dizzy as he stepped from the container. The ordeal left him with no other noticeable physical effects.

In answer to reporters' questions, Houdini said he had taken a series of very deep breaths of air before the lid was soldered. He used the same system of breathing on the stage prior to being lowered in his Water Torture Cell. He made a minimum of body movements in the box. He had relaxed, breathed rhythmically, with short intakes of air. He thought his demonstration would enable trapped coal miners and imperiled deep-sea divers to survive far longer than had previously been thought possible. He stressed that self-possession was vital. Panic would increase the air intake of the body.

Joseph Rinn, Hereward Carrington, and other witnesses at the pool discounted Houdini's controlled-breathing explanation. They believed, never having attempted the feat themselves, that a trick had been used to supply oxygen—either a false compartment in the box or a secret flow through the telephone lines. They were wrong.

Houdini wrote James S. Harto, a veteran Indianapolis magician and a friend from his circus days: "There is a rumor going around that there is a gimmick to the thing. I pledge my word of honor there isn't a thing to it excepting to lie down and keep quiet.

"I trained for three weeks in water to get my lungs accustomed to battle without air, and after one hour, did have to struggle and believe only due to the training was I able to stay so long. Rest assured there is no gimmick, no trick at all —simply lying on your back and breathing shallow breaths is all you do. Did it twice in a coffin with a glass top to test myself. There is no doubt in my mind that anyone can do it."

Houdini's explanation was validated in 1958 when James Randi demonstrated on British television his ability to survive under similar circumstances. Randi was younger and weighed far less than Houdini. The box he used was the same size. He stayed submerged for two hours and three minutes.

Having been successful with the makeshift iron box, Houdini bought a $2,500 bronze casket—Rahman Bey had used a bronze casket—and planned to perform the survival feat as an exploitation attraction on his fall tour. A new lithograph was printed to herald the feat: "Buried Alive! Egyptian Fakirs Outdone. Master Mystifier Houdini 'The Greatest Necromancer of the Age—Perhaps of All Time,'" his favorite quote from the *Literary Digest*. A coffin, with a cutaway section which shows Houdini tied inside, rests against the buttress of an Egyptian burial chamber. To the right is the Sphinx and above it, in a swirl of vapor, is the magician's face.

The magic portion of Houdini's road show had been expanded while the production was on tour the previous season. "The Flight of Time" was one of the most effective new tricks. Alarm clocks were cupped, one by one, in his hands, then hurled invisibly across the stage where they appeared, ringing at the ends of suspended ribbons. "Radio of 1950" purported to be a glimpse of the future. A girl materialized in an empty giant broadcast receiver. During the summer holiday Harry rehearsed a new version of the sawing-in-two feat—"Slicing a Woman," in which eight blades seemingly chopped a girl's body in sections. One of the most pleasing production effects began when an empty circular canopy was raised above the stage. Houdini fired a pistol, the canopy dropped, disclosing a girl seated in the arc of a new moon as silver confetti showered around her.

After a break-in weekend September 2–4 at the Lyceum Theater in Paterson, New Jersey, the Houdini show opened September 13 at the Majestic Theater in Boston. He announced his tour would take him from coast to coast in the United States and then around the world. On his arrival in Boston, he inevitably became embroiled again in the Margery controversy.

Repercussions from the *Scientific American*'s Margery report had radically affected the lives of two men. Dr. Walter Franklin Prince was no longer chief research officer of the American Society for Psychical Research. The governing body had disagreed with his skepticism about Margery. Prince was now expressing his doubts for a rival organization, the Boston Society for Psychical Research. His place with A.S.P.R. had been taken over by J. Malcolm Bird, who in a 518-page book, *"Margery" the Medium,* boosted her as a genuine psychic. The former associate editor of the *Scientific American* was as critical of Houdini as the magician had been of him in his 40-page pamphlet.

Hudson Hoagland, a graduate student who had tested Margery at Harvard as a member of a group which included Dr. Harlow Shapley, the astronomer, wrote an unfavorable appraisal of Mrs. Crandon's mediumship in the November 1925 *Atlantic Monthly.* Dr. Crandon and four of his friends retaliated with a 109-page rebuttal, *Margery, Harvard, Veritas.*

Near the end of Houdini's first week in Boston, Dr. Henry Clay McComas, professor of experimental psychology at Princeton, visited him backstage. Dr. McComas, with two professors from Johns Hopkins University, Drs. Robert W. Wood and Knight Dunlap, had investigated Margery earlier in the year for the American Society for Psychical Research. They had not been impressed. Dr. Wood squeezed the "tele-plasmic rod" which emanated from Margery's body in the dark. Dr. Crandon claimed the "psychic structure" was extremely sensitive, yet neither Margery nor the Walter voice objected. More than forty minutes later, one of the doctors suggested that Margery and the cabinet should be examined.

"When Mrs. Crandon heard this she began to gag as though ill. She bent forward as though vomiting and hurried from the room," Dr. McComas wrote in his report on the séance. "An examination showed nothing upon the floor and the stomach performance seemed simulated." Dr. Dunlap concluded that the "teleplasmic rod" was nothing more than the intestine of an animal, filled with cotton and wired to make it rigid. The men agreed that Margery gave an entertaining show, but thought her mediumship "unworthy of any serious consideration." Their report, submitted to the A.S.P.R. the following year, was not published.

Dr. McComas urged Houdini to see Margery's latest feats. The Crandons were quite willing to have Houdini attend a séance. Sessions were scheduled for Saturday and Sunday evenings and, Dr. McComas reported, Dr. Crandon himself had invited Houdini to attend the one on Sunday. Houdini agreed to go. As Dr. McComas understood their plan, he was to attend the Saturday night séance and make a full report on it to Houdini. Then the magician would go to the house on Lime Street on Sunday night and duplicate Margery's manifestations.

Houdini's intention, as set forth on September 18 in a letter to McComas, was somewhat different: "I would ask that I be permitted to take three or four college professors with me . . . she can do her stuff in my presence and I will go right in and duplicate them, or if you wish, I will stop her from doing anything by having her controlled properly. Or I will go into the séance room, make notes of the tests and the next day prevent her from doing anything (by keeping her properly under control) . . . the lady is subtle and changes her methods like any dexterous sleight-of-hand performer or any medium I have examined. Also give me ample time to make all arrangements during my stay in Boston."

Sunday afternoon Dr. McComas met Houdini at the Adams House Hotel and described in detail what had happened the night before. The séance was one of the best Margery had ever given. She was wired, hands, feet, and neck in a glass-sided cabinet which looked somewhat like an oversized phone booth. Her hands extended through holes on either side of the enclosure. Wires attached to her wrists were fastened to rings on the outside, but the wires allowed enough leeway for her to bring her hands into the cabinet. Walter's voice identified four wooden letters of the alphabet which were put in a basket and placed inside her enclosure. The letters were then hurled out of the cabinet in the direction of the sitters Walter specified. The basket rolled along a shelf in front of the cabinet as though motivated by an invisible force. A luminous cardboard "doughnut" rose vertically in the air inside the cabinet. A luminous basket floated up between Margery and the suspended "doughnut." A large basket, not luminous, was heard knocking about inside the enclosure, and eventually it was thrown out toward the sitters.

As Houdini listened to Dr. McComas' story, he realized Margery had perfected new techniques since he had attended more than a year before. None of the feats he had exposed in his pamphlet were in her current routine. It would be difficult to duplicate the new manifestations on the basis of an oral description; special equipment might be needed. If someone had slipped a collapsible reaching rod into Margery's right hand, wired at the wrist though it was, she could have used it to lift the basket. Once the basket was in the air, it would slide down the rod to her hand. She could hold the far end of the rod between her teeth, the handle of the basket over her wrist as her fingers identified the cutout letters by their shapes. She could have thrown them forward. The dual risings of the "doughnut" and the basket would indicate the use of two reaching rods—or perhaps a single instrument could do the job. He would be foolish to attempt to reproduce these feats until he had seen them himself. And even then, he probably would need confederates. If Dr. McComas' account was correct, certainly someone had secretly aided Margery—by giving a reaching device to her, then taking it away later.

Houdini didn't attend the Sunday night séance. Instead, he wrote Dr. Crandon, asking his permission to come to a séance later in the week. Houdini needed time to test his theories and practice the moves. It could be most embarrassing for him if he attended the Sunday séance without proper preparation—a fact that Dr. Crandon undoubtedly appreciated. Replying to Houdini, Dr. Crandon wrote:

"The only value which could possibly be attached to your presence at Lime Street would be because it would afford amusement to watch your attempts to duplicate these phenomena." If Houdini insisted on attending another séance, Margery's husband added, he could write to Dr. McComas; but by then Dr. McComas had returned to Princeton. The Houdini show went on to Worcester, without another Margery-Houdini confrontation.

"GRIT"

Houdini called Bess his good luck charm. He said that he had never been a success until he met her; that his best break came when he married her. He never forgot his wife's birthday or their wedding anniversary. He wrote her affectionate notes not only on the rare occasions when they were apart, but also at home and when they were together on the road. Invariably Harry was up hours before Bess awakened. Often she would find a tiny piece of paper propped up on the breakfast table or lying by her pillow. "Adorable Sun Shine of my life. I have had my coffee, have washed out this glass and am on my way to business. Houdini. My darling I love you." Or "Honey lamb, sweetheart. It is 8 a.m. No one pays any attention to me. So even though you do get a 'tantrum' and give me hell, I'd rather have you with me." Sometimes he would add "Who-dee-knee," "Houdinisky," or "none genuine without this signature."

He was frantic when she awoke nauseated and feverish one morning during their week at the Providence Opera House in October 1926. Houdini, who never consulted a doctor himself unless Bess cried and threatened to leave him, had a physician by her bedside in minutes. Ptomaine poisoning was the diagnosis. Rest and constant care were ordered. Houdini put in a hurried call to New York to summon Sophie Rosenblatt, a nurse who had attended his wife in the past. One of the girls in the show filled in for her on stage. On Friday evening Bess' temperature rose. Harry sat with her throughout the night.

On Saturday morning the fever abated. He snatched a few hours of restless sleep between the matinee and evening performance. After the last show Houdini saw Bess, her nurse, and his troupe off for Albany at the railroad station, then boarded the last train for New York. He dozed occasionally in his coach seat, but the jarring vibrations when the train stopped and started at stations along the way kept him awake

251

most of the journey. Always a light sleeper, in recent years he had worn a black bandage over his eyes in bed and slept with a small pillow under his side. The kidney injured during a strapped bag escape in Detroit still sometimes ached.

Houdini had an appointment with B. M. L. Ernst, his lawyer, in New York. The Ernsts weren't expected back from an overnight trip until later in the day, their maid informed him. He lay back on a sofa in the living room and fell asleep. It seemed to him that he had scarcely closed his eyes when he heard the family arrive.

In Bernard Ernst's study they discussed the strategy for handling the many libel suits which irate spiritualists had instigated against him. In Chicago: C. A. Burgess, $100,000; Mrs. Ben Haigh, $50,000, and Anna Wardell $50,000. In Boston: Frederick A. Wiggin, $10,000 or was it $100,000? Harry's mind wasn't as alert as usual. He had had little sleep since Bess became ill. The overall total was more than a million dollars. He told Ernst he had sworn statements from his investigators describing the trickery used in every instance. He could reproduce it publicly in the courtroom.

Houdini was equally concerned over another threat to his reputation. Since his clash with Clinton Burgess over the Elliott book, Burgess had continued to attack him in magic circles here and abroad. Harry Leat, a London magic dealer, supported Burgess and printed snide, deprecatory remarks about Houdini in his *Leat's Leaflets*. He wrote that he had "proof that Mr. Carloete of 194 Salt Street, Bradford, Yorkshire, England, invented the Water Escape and sold it to Houdini in 1911." This was a deliberate lie, Harry charged. He had affidavits from the men who made his equipment confirming that the ideas were his alone. Couldn't action be taken to stop Leat's slander? Ernst pointed out that the pamphlets were not sold. They went only to the dealer's customers and the words "For Private Circulation" were printed on the cover. British law protected the writer of such private opinions from libel charges.

Harry called Albany. Miss Rosenblatt reported his wife's condition was unchanged. There was a meeting with Frank Ducrot, who now owned the Martinka magic shop. Houdini needed several pieces of apparatus for his show. He phoned Albany again. The nurse advised him not to worry; she assured him she would stay with Bess during the night.

Houdini took the early morning train to Albany, again staying awake most of the trip. Bess was better when he arrived at the hotel, but still not well enough to leave her bed. He managed a brief nap before the opening night performance on October 11. There were rumors that Governor Al Smith was in the theater. Houdini peeked through the curtains, but didn't see him. Once Harry heard his introductory music and the curtains opened, he walked out with a happy smile—not at all like a man who had missed three nights' rest in a row.

In the second act, after his needle-swallowing feat, he changed into a blue bathing suit and sat on the floor as Collins and Vickery closed the bulky mahogany stocks tightly around his ankles, readying him for the Water Cell escape. He lifted his body so the heavy metal frame, which would hold the stocks in place, could be passed over him. He signaled to his assistants to pull the lines attached to the frame and haul him, feet first, into the air. The massive frame jerked suddenly as he was being lifted. A sharp pain shot through his left ankle. He winced, called to be lowered. The frame and stocks were swiftly removed. Houdini tried to stand, but couldn't—only his right foot would support him. Collins helped him up. He shrugged and forced a smile. He told the audience his foot had been injured. Was there a doctor present? Harry sat in a chair in the wings as a man, who introduced himself as Dr. Brannock, probed his ankle. A bone had been fractured. Dr. Brannock advised Houdini to go to a hospital immediately for an X ray. Harry promised he would—after the show. He limped back to the footlights. Give him time to change into his evening clothes for the third act, he said, and the show would go on. The audience cheered lustily.

There was a minimum of exertion in the last act as Harry lambasted the mediums with his usual verve. He sat during much of this part of the show. Fortunately, it was his right foot that rang a bell under the table, shook the tambourine, and wrote with chalk on the slate.

X rays at Memorial Hospital that night confirmed Dr. Brannock's diagnosis. Bandages and a splint were applied. At the hotel Houdini fashioned a leg brace which enabled him to get through the remaining two days in Albany and the next three in Schenectady. The day after the accident an editorial in the

Albany *Journal* saluted his courage under the title "Grit." New York papers printed a dispatch headed "Houdini Seriously Hurt Doing Trick in Water Tank." The story predicted that the injury "may keep him off the stage for some time to come."

The newspapers underestimated Harry's stamina and drive. It would take more than a broken bone to halt a Houdini tour. From Schenectady he traveled to Montreal, where on Monday, October 18, he opened at the Princess Theatre. A Canadian doctor, a friend of Dr. Brannock, examined his ankle. Keep off your feet and the bone will knit, was his advice to the magician. Houdini reacted by lecturing for the police on Tuesday morning and filling a long-standing afternoon date at McGill University. He arrived just before four o'clock leaning on Nurse Rosenblatt's shoulder. Bess, still ill, remained behind at the hotel. Harry waved the nurse away when Dr. William D. Tait, the psychology professor, came to escort him to the platform.

His scathing denunciation of spirit fraud was warmly received. He said he had been a member of the committee formed by the *Journal of Abnormal and Social Psychology* to investigate spiritualism in 1925. He was still a member of the *Scientific American* committee. Any medium who could demonstrate psychic phenomena under test conditions could become wealthy overnight. His friend Joseph P. Rinn offered $10,000; Dr. J. Allen Gilbert, $500. The two *Scientific American* prizes totaled $5,000 and he would pay $10,000. That was an aggregate of $25,500. He had been invited to speak at the Clark University symposium on spiritualism in December. He and two college professors had planned the program almost a year earlier.

He told how he had duplicated Margery's darkroom wonders, trapped the Cleveland medium Renner "black-handed." He displayed the photograph of Chicago's Minnie Reichart holding a trumpet to her lips. In New York, he said, he had gone to the West 84th Street séance room of Mrs. Cecil Cook in disguise. She produced the voice of his son Albert—a son he never had. A shaft of light from his flashlight caught Mrs. Cook speaking through the trumpet, and she was arrested by a New York police officer who had accompanied Houdini to the séance. The medium was tried, found guilty, and fined one hundred dollars. In Philadelphia he had defied John Slater, "the millionaire medium," during the Pennsylvania State Spiritualist Association Convention. Slater refused to accept his ten-thousand-dollar challenge to read five sealed questions.

In response to a query about Rahman Bey, the "Egyptian Miracle Man," he said he doubted that the fakir had ever seen the land of the pyramids. He demonstrated how Bey had thrust a long steel pin through his cheek. He asked a student to grasp the end of the pin firmly, then to draw it out with a quick pull. He turned his head to show there was no blood or other evidence of injury.

After the lecture the magician sat in one of the two chairs on the platform as he shook hands with faculty members and students who surged forward to meet him. One young man showed Houdini a sketch he had made while the magician talked. Harry termed it an excellent likeness. He autographed the drawing and invited the artist to make a close-up portrait later in the week backstage at the theater. Following his show, at 11 p.m. he went to a radio station for an interview.

On Friday, October 22, the McGill artist, Samuel J. Smiley, and Jack Price, a fellow student and friend, met Houdini in the Princess Theatre lobby an hour before noon. There was a crowd at the ticket window. Harry arrived with Bess, the nurse, and a secretary.

Sophie Rosenblatt suggested they have lunch. Houdini agreed it was time to eat. He extracted a frankfurter in a roll from the hat of a thoroughly startled woman bystander, then escorted the students to his dressing room.

Harry hung up his hat and overcoat, took off his jacket, rolled up his sleeves, removed his tie, opened his shirt collar, and leaned back on a couch as he picked up several letters from the heap on his dressing room table. Instead of slitting or tearing the ends of the envelopes, Houdini used thumb pressure to peel open the flaps. He talked about his career in show business as Smiley began to block out the lines for a portrait.

After a knock on the door, Houdini's secretary brought in another man and left. The newcomer was returning a book he had borrowed from the magician. He was more than six feet tall, with a reddish complexion and thinning hair. Harry introduced his visitor as J. Gordon Whitehead and said he also was studying at McGill. Whitehead questioned Houdini about biblical miracles. Houdini seemed preoccupied with his mail and in no mood for theological conversation. He did wonder musingly what the reaction of the people of that time would have been to his own seemingly impossible wonders.

Whitehead asked if it was true that Houdini could sustain punches to his midsection without injury. Harry raised his powerful arms and invited the student to feel the muscles. Whitehead was impressed. He asked if he could take a few trial punchs. Houdini, relaxed on the couch and idling through his mail, gave his permission. Whitehead struck him almost immediately, then gave him three more quick jabs with full force. Smiley and Price were horrified. They thought the fellow had gone berserk and were about to pull him away when Harry indicated that the battery should stop.

The three students left shortly after noon. Houdini complimented Smiley on the portrait he had made and asked him to sign it. Later in the day the magician became increasingly conscious of a persistent pain in his stomach. He hadn't had time to brace himself before Whitehead struck his first blow. Harry pulled up his shirt and pressed his fingertips to his abdomen. It was sore—tender to the touch.

Every move he made during the show that night intensified the pain in the broken ankle and his burning stomach. It was a good house and he played it well—adroitly masking his suffering. He kept up the pretense when he went back to the hotel and arranged an impromptu champagne party in his room for Bess. He invited Julia Sawyer and the nurse to share the wine with her.

By the time the Houdinis went to bed, the pain in his abdomen was so terrible that he couldn't sleep. About 2 a.m. he told Bess he thought he had a cramp or a strained muscle. She massaged his stomach. He pretended he was better and reassured her by saying her soothing touch had cured him. She fell asleep, while he rolled and tossed in agony through the night.

In the morning Bess found a note: "Champagne Coquette— I'll be at the theater at 12:00 p.m. H. H. Fall Guy."

Between shows Houdini writhed on his dressing room couch with the door closed. He sat up quickly when his secretary came in and he dictated two letters. Both were short. To

Oscar Teale, he said he was "getting together a number of mathematical problems and tricks. Have you any? If so, please let me have them." He added a penciled note asking about Mrs. Teale, but forgot to sign his name. A similar note was sent to Will Goldston in London. On this he scrawled: "Broke a bone in my left leg." There was no mention of the new injury.

The Houdini show closed Saturday, October 23, in Montreal. It was scheduled to open the next night at the Garrick Theater in Detroit for a two-week run. Still playing the superman, Harry didn't admit he was suffering until he was aboard the train and the pain became too intense to hide. Bess, who had barely recovered from her ptomaine poisoning, collapsed when she heard that a student had struck him four times in the stomach.

A telegram was hurriedly dispatched to George H. Atkinson, the show's advance man in Detroit, when the train made a brief stop at London, Ontario. He was instructed to have the best doctor in the city ready to give Houdini a thorough examination before the opening. Nurse Rosenblatt took Houdini's temperature. It was 102 degrees.

The Montreal train arrived late. Collins doubted they could truck the equipment to the theater, hang scenery, and get the magical apparatus uncrated and assembled before curtain time. Rather than check in at their hotels, the entire company went directly to the theater. There was no doctor waiting at the Garrick despite the urgent wire. Houdini pitched in and helped the stagehands and his assistants set up the heavy gear.

Dr. Leo Dretzka and the show's advance man paced the lobby at the Statler Hotel. The doctor had to leave for a medical convention that night, but he had promised to examine the ailing escape artist first. After asking a dozen times at the desk if Houdini had checked in, Atkinson finally phoned the theater.

There was no cot in Harry's dressing room at the Garrick. He stripped off his clothes and stretched out on the floor. Dr. Dretzka knelt and touched the inflamed stomach. Bess didn't hear the doctor say that an ambulance should be called immediately, that Houdini was suffering from acute appendicitis. Had she known the danger her husband was in, there would have been no performance that night.

Harry dressed for the show. The theater manager had

stopped by to say the house was sold out and standees were lined outside waiting to get in. "They're here to see me," Harry explained as the worried doctor rushed away to make his train. "I won't disappoint them."

DETROIT '26

Unaware of the drama backstage, the capacity audience in the Garrick Theater stomped, whistled, and clapped as they waited thirty minutes for the show to begin. Then an offstage clock tolled twelve—the signal for Houdini's opening music. Two girls in Colonial costume took the tassels at the center of the curtains and pulled them open. To the stirring "Pomp and Circumstance," Houdini, the master magician, walked briskly to the footlights.

"We have just made a thousand-mile journey from Montreal," he said, "and we are tired." He ripped off his sleeves, smiled, and began his magic. The silver coins vanished from his fingertips, dropped with a tinkling sound into the swinging crystal box. A pretty girl vanished and a flower bush appeared in her place. "Here I am," she shouted from the back of the theater and came running down the aisle. The alarm clocks disappeared one by one between his cupped hands, passed invisibly through the air and arrived on the far side of the stage, ringing shrilly, at the ends of pale blue ribbons.

Houdini's assistants opened the front and back doors of a large cabinet. He was about to dash through it as he usually did to prove there was nothing concealed inside. As he lifted his right foot, the weight on his broken ankle and the pain in his abdomen made him turn aside. Jim Collins took the unspoken cue. He stepped through the cabinet, then swiftly helped to close the doors. Houdini fired a pistol. The doors burst open. Four girls stepped out.

Harry manipulated playing cards. They vanished at his fingertips. He showed his right hand empty, back and front, plucked cards one by one from nowhere. A skeptical spectator tossed his own pack of cards to the stage and shouted for Houdini to do his tricks with them. Collins picked up the deck, passed it to the magician. Harry repeated his sleights with the unfamiliar cards. The audience shouted its approval.

"The Whirlwind of Colors" finished the hour-long opening

259

act. Houdini pulled the first silk streamer from the liquid-filled glass bowl. The movement of his hand as he tugged the streamers sent flames of pain through his stomach. Houdini stepped aside. Collins understood. He whipped out the hundreds of yards of silk, sent it spinning in the air, and finally yanked out the long string of flags for the spectacular finale.

When the curtains closed, Houdini staggered and fell. He was taken to his dressing room. His temperature was 104 degrees. Perspiration streamed down his face and body. He wiped away as much as he could, touched up his grease paint.

How he completed the rest of the show only he knew. Some extra reserve of willpower and iron determination must have provided the drive. He spoke faster than usual in the act exposing fraudulent mediums. Sometimes sentences ended abruptly—uncompleted. His good right foot slipped from its shoe and rang the bell under the table. His denunciation of fakers stirred controversy as it always did. He defined the mediums of Detroit. He answered questions fired by the audience.

After he took his bows and the curtains closed, Houdini collapsed again, but still he obstinately refused to give up and follow the doctor's orders. He changed his clothes and went to his room at the Statler Hotel. There was only one way Bess could handle him when he was in a stubborn mood. She had hysterics. Dr. Daniel E. Cohn, the hotel physician, was called. He phoned a surgeon. Dr. Charles S. Kennedy arrived at 3 a.m. on Monday. Kennedy said the magician was in a desperate condition; he must be rushed to a hospital. Still Harry delayed. He put in a long-distance call to his family physician, Dr. William Stone, in New York.

Stone consulted with the doctors in the hotel room, then asked for Houdini to be put back on the wire. What he said no one knows, but when Houdini put down the receiver, his resistance was gone. He was taken to Grace Hospital, where he was admitted under the care of Drs. Kennedy, Cohn, John Taylor Watkins, and Herbert H. Hewitt. That afternoon Houdini's ruptured appendix was removed. For three days the poison had seeped through his bloodstream.

The physicians in attendance telegraphed Dr. George Le-Fevre, a specialist in postoperative technique, who was in Montreal attending the convention of the American College of Surgeons. Bess, in near state of shock, was assigned a room at the hospital. Sophie Rosenblatt was never more than a few moments from her side. Mrs. Houdini was told that her condition was more serious than her husband's. Houdini's brothers, Theo and Nat, and his sister, Gladys, arrived from New York Tuesday afternoon and Dr. LeFevre came from Canada in the evening. He immediately made an examination and consulted with the other doctors.

Each day Miss Rosenblatt brought Bess to Harry's room for a visit. Pale, haggard, with dark circles under his eyes, he seemed to be in good spirits. He told Hardeen and his other relatives they had made an unnecessary trip. He would be up and around in no time. He complimented the doctors. They were doing something worthwhile for mankind. He once thought he should have been a surgeon himself. His nurses said he was a cooperative patient.

Houdini was to have been the guest of honor at a banquet given by the Detroit Assembly of the Society of American Magicians on Thursday night. Bess sent a message that he had looked forward to the evening and regretted he could not attend.

Twice a day Grace Hospital released bulletins on his condition. Front-page items on the magician's progress were carried by newspapers across the country. Early reports that he had been assaulted by a student in the McGill building after his lecture were denied by Dr. Tait, the professor who had introduced him. Tait told reporters he had seen Houdini leave the hall with the nurse, Miss Rosenblatt, and that no such incident had occurred.

On Friday morning the magician had a relapse. Streptococcus peritonitis had developed. A second operation was performed that afternoon. By Saturday the doctors described his condition as "less than favorable." They waited for the crisis. Sunday morning Harry weakly whispered to Theo: "I'm tired of fighting. . . . I guess this thing is going to get me." Later Bess leaned over and put her arms around him. His eyes, which had been closed, opened. He saw her tears. Then his eyes slowly closed again. At 1:26 p.m. on October 31, 1926, Houdini died.

Though his equipment had been crated at the Garrick Theater and shipped back to New York the day he was taken to the hospital, one piece had been mislaid and was still in the Detroit Transfer Company warehouse—the bronze coffin he had purchased to outdo the feats of Rahman Bey. It was not, as one newspaper reported, the "coffin" in which he had been buried underwater in the Shelton pool in New York. That had been a galvanized-iron box.

A special Pullman car attached to the Detroiter brought the body in the bronze coffin to Grand Central Terminal in New York. The papers had said the great mystifier would lie in state on the stage of the New York Hippodrome or at the National Vaudeville Artists Club. Someone at the Elks Club remembered that Houdini had left a sealed envelope, to be opened only after his death, in their safe ten years before. It was opened. The master showman was still in charge. The letter gave specific instructions for his funeral. The services were to be conducted in the vast Elks Lodge ballroom on West 43d Street, just off Broadway.

Two thousand people jammed into the Elks Club for the two-hour ritual. Even at the end Houdini drew a standing-room-only audience. "He possessed a wondrous power which he never understood and which he never revealed to anyone in life," Rabbi Bernard Drachman said in his eulogy. "He was one of the truly great men of our age." Added Rabbi B. A. Tintner: "He was exceptional, a unique personality, and besides that, he was one of the noblest and sweetest of men."

Francis Werner, a past president of the Society of American Magicians and one of Houdini's closest friends, broke a cedarwood wand in half as members of the society chanted: "The curtain has at last been rung down. The wand is broken. God touched him with a wondrous gift and our brother made use of it. Now the wand is broken." Until Houdini's death, the S.A.M. had no funeral rites. The ritual was written especially for the occasion, and since then, in modified form, has become part of the society's tradition.

There were tributes from Henry Chesterfield of the National Vaudeville Artists and Lonney Haskell, who spoke for the Jewish Theatrical Guild, and rites by the St. Cecile Masonic Lodge, the Mount Zion Congregation, and the Elks.

Bess, in a black silk dress and heavily veiled, sat through the long service with her nurse and Houdini's family—Theo, Nat, and Gladys. When the bronze lid of the coffin was hermetically sealed, she broke down. As the twenty-five cars in the funeral procession drove through the Broadway area, thousands stood silently on the sidewalks to mourn one of their favorite stars. Hundreds of men removed their hats in tribute.

At the Machpelah Cemetery in Brooklyn, Houdini's assistants, James Collins, James Vickery, Frank Williamson, John Ardon, Bepo Vittorelli, and Elliott Sandford, lowered the coffin into the grave by the side of his mother. Houdini's instructions had specified this burial spot. Cecilia's letters were in a black bag under his head.

Doubts about the accidental nature of Houdini's death were dispelled by the investigation of the New York Life Insurance Company. After getting signed statements from the student who hit Houdini in the dressing room of the Montreal theater, the two students who witnessed the act, and the five Detroit doctors who treated the magician, New York Life paid double indemnity on the policies he carried with them— $50,000. B. M. L. Ernst, Houdini's lawyer, estimated Mrs. Houdini would receive a half-million dollars in insurance payments. Later the Union Central Life Insurance Company of Cincinnati said Houdini's combined policies paid out approximately $160,000. Union's check to the widow was for $25,394.26.

For years Houdini had been one of the highest paid performers in the theater. When his will was filed, liabilities exceeded assets by several thousand dollars. Listed in the plus column: cash—$2,871.95; personal effects, books, etc.—$34,356; notes and mortgages—$3,118.46; stocks and bonds—$29,608.75. Many of the notes, bonds, and stocks were worthless. Charged against the $69,995.16 gross was $30,024.19 for the funeral and administration of the estate; $46,367.33 in debts, and a $693.99 commission to the executrix. Mrs. Houdini claimed she had advanced her husband $5,771.39 to pay his insurance premiums. His real estate, including the house on West 113th Street, was in her name and therefore excluded in this official reckoning.

The thousands upon thousands of dollars Houdini made in show business had been invested in his collection or lost in such ventures as the Houdini Picture Corporation and the Film Development Corporation. He also spent lavishly on the support of elderly people.

The Houdini collection on spiritualism originally had been willed to the American Society for Psychical Research. A codicil added when J. Malcolm Bird became the research officer of the society revoked this provision and the volumes went with his conjuring books to the Library of Congress. Houdini's will named Bess as the executor of his estate. She was to do what she wished with the dramatic collection. Eventually it was sold for a reported fifty thousand dollars to Messmore Kendall, a New York theater owner. With it went the long black boxes filled with his choicest magic treasures— the programs of Robert-Houdin, Doebler, Anderson, and other great prestidigitators of the past.

Before the books were crated, and while Bess was still numb with grief, many of the rare items were presented to or claimed by Houdini's friends. The dramatic collection, acquired from the Kendall estate, is housed at the University of Texas at Austin. Neither collection is complete. Thousands of important documents, playbills, books, letters, posters, and other memorabilia, once a part of this magnificent hoard, are in the hands of private collectors.

Houdini's magic apparatus was willed to his brother Theo. Some of it also was given to or claimed by others. Though the will specified that all of the equipment was to be destroyed after Hardeen died, much of it still survives in private collections.

Bess went to Atlantic City to recuperate after the funeral. Harry had given her everything—but a sense of self-reliance, she said. When she returned to New York, she supervised the crating of the books. A reporter asked if the house on West 113th Street had any secrets. She mentioned only one. During prohibition days, Houdini, who was a teetotaler, had purchased a six-gallon jug of whiskey. He kept it hidden in the basement. When a member of the family was ill, he went down with an empty bottle and came back with it filled. She hadn't found the jug. She thought he might have buried it.

Houdini's safe contained some surprises. One small package was labeled to "my beloved wife Beatrice Houdini." Inside were photographic negatives and a note: "Darling Wife and Loved One. In case you feel so disposed, destroy all of these negatives. I am not important or interesting enough for the world in general and so it's just as well you destroy them— unless you yourself either have a book written or write it yourself . . . otherwise destroy all film. Burn them. Your devoted husband, Houdini." It was dated August 20, 1926. A little more than two months before he died.

Bess called in a writer, Harold Kellock, to go through Houdini's scrapbooks. Kellock knew nothing of magic, but with the scrapbooks, diaries, and Bess' remembrances he wrote a fascinating biography. It was serialized in the *American* magazine, then published as a book in 1928.

Something else in the safe intrigued Bess—a thick packet of letters from women who had fallen in love with her husband. Though he hadn't reciprocated their advances, the letters apparently had appealed sufficiently to his vanity that he kept them. Months later Bess gave a tea party. Most of the guests had never been invited to the Houdini home before. After a pleasant afternoon, Bess stood at the door and gave each of the departing ladies a present tied in a ribbon. Inside were that woman's letters to Houdini.

There were too many haunting memories in the house on West 113th Street. Bess sold it and moved to 67 Payson Avenue. Theo Hardeen, who had been away from the stage managing Houdini's Film Development Corporation, returned to vaudeville three months after his brother died. Advertised as "The Legal Successor of Houdini," he pulled off his sleeves, threw invisible coins toward the swinging crystal box, produced and vanished a rooster, "hurled" alarm clocks across the stage, and performed the trunk substitution feat and other mysteries from the Houdini program. He owned, but never escaped from, the Water Torture Cell. Not that he didn't know the secret; he was too tall to fit inside it. Eventually he too became a president of the Society of American Magicians.

In December 1927 Bess announced plans to tour with a Houdini mystery never before presented on any stage: "Freezing a Man in a Cake of Ice," the feat with which Harry had experimented many years earlier in England. There was a showing for the press in a storeroom on West 53d Street. An Indian in a rubber suit was lowered into a metal container. A ton-and-a-half block of ice was frozen around him, using a carbon-dioxide and cold-water mixture. The sides of the cabinet were stripped away. The ice was chopped so the Indian's face could be seen inside. The top then was chipped off and he was lifted out of his icy confinement. It took forty minutes plus to freeze the ice, twenty more minutes to hack away the top to release the human ice cube. Vaudeville demanded a faster pace. A feature writer from the *Daily Graphic* was present at another demonstration a month later. He reported that Bess had been overcome by the fumes from the freezing solution. She was taken to a doctor, while "the Indian looked for a hot fire."

The act played a trial date at the Broadway Theater in Long Branch, New Jersey. It was the first time Bess had appeared on stage without Harry. She was nervous. Another showing date was set in New York. Though the trade papers reported Bess had signed for the Palace on Broadway and a follow-up Loew tour, nothing ever came of the act.

Stories of Houdini's careful arrangements to contact Bess after death—if such proved possible—circulated widely. He was said to have signed compacts with friends as well as with Bess, promising to try to send messages from the Great Beyond. She offered ten thousand dollars for proof of communication with the other world. Hundreds of spiritualists wrote that Houdini had appeared in their séance rooms. The messages they forwarded to Bess had no meaning for her.

Friends of an enterprising young medium, the Rev. Arthur Ford, pastor of the First Spiritualist Church of New York, let Bess know that Houdini's mother's voice had spoken through him while he was entranced on February 8, 1928. Mrs. Weiss had a message for Bess. It included the word Houdini had longed to hear in a séance room—"forgive." Bess, the spirit voice said, knew the word and Bess alone.

Contrary to *The Houdini Messages,* a booklet by Francis R. Fast, which Ford still gives to his friends, Bess did not confirm his entire message as correct. Bess wrote that Mrs. Weiss would never have called her son "Harry." He was always "Ehrich" to her. She did say the Ford message was the only one she had been sent "which has any appearance of truth."

Houdini had yearned to hear his long-dead mother say "forgive." When his brother Nat's wife, Sadie, had abandoned him to marry another brother, Dr. Leopold Weiss, Houdini had been scandalized. The once close-knit harmony of the Weiss family had been destroyed. He could not bring himself to forgive Leopold unless his mother told him to. She died before he could discuss the family crisis with her. This was one reason he searched so tirelessly for a genuine medium and was so infuriated when he encountered charlatans.

How could Ford have learned the one word that would

have changed Houdini's relationship with his brother, unless from the spirit world? There are at least two distinctly earthly explanations. In a letter dated December 16, 1926, Bess wrote Sir Arthur Conan Doyle about Harry's restless nights as he wakened with the words, "Mama, are you here?" on his lips. She said he never stopped hoping to hear the word "forgive" from his mother.

In his autobiography, *Nothing So Strange,* Ford tells of his visit to England in 1927, during which he talked with Sir Arthur several times. Did Doyle show Ford Bess' letter? Or in reminiscing about Houdini, did Doyle mention the key word? There is another even more obvious possibility. The Brooklyn *Eagle* of March 13, 1927, quoted Bess as saying that any authentic communication from Mrs. Weiss would have to include the word "forgive." This was nearly a year before the Ford message.

Two years after Houdini's death, Bess canceled her standing offer of ten thousand dollars for a true message from her husband. A news item in the December 1, 1928, *Billboard* reported that Mrs. Houdini had announced a week earlier "that she had been advised by spiritualists that they could get in touch with the spirit of Houdini more easily if the reward was withdrawn."

THE MESSAGE

On New Year's Day, 1929, Bess, who had been ill with influenza, fainted and fell down a flight of stairs in her home on Payson Avenue. Two days later a story by Rea Jaure, headed: "Widow Ill, Communes With Houdini," appeared in the New York *Evening Graphic*. It reported that Bess, while in a "semidelirium," had called out: "Harry, dear, why don't you come to me from the other side?" Then, extending her arms as though to grasp him, she cried: "I knew you would come back to me, my dear." Since the accident, which injured her spine, she had blacked out frequently and "was under constant care of physicians."

Shortly past noon on January 8, a séance was held in Mrs. Houdini's living room. The Rev. Arthur Ford arranged the tapestry-backed chairs in a semicircle around the French gilt sofa on which Bess, her head wrapped in bandages, lay covered with sheets and a blanket. Eleven months before, Ford had succeeded in getting the word "forgive" from Houdini's mother in the spirit world. On January 5, just three days before the séance and—by the strangest of coincidences—just two days after the story in the *Graphic* appeared, Ford had received another message, this one consisting of ten words in code, "from Houdini." After being shown a letter containing the ten words, Bess agreed to participate in a séance to be held in her home.

As Ford lowered the blinds to shut out the noonday sun, three of his followers—John W. Stafford, an associate editor of the *Scientific American;* Mrs. Stafford; and Francis R. Fast, a broker—took their seats along with reporters Rea Jaure, of the *Graphic,* and Harry R. Zander, of the United Press. Mrs. Houdini's press agent, Charles Williams, and her old friend Mrs. Minnie Chester, who had been acting as her nurse, were also present.

Ford slumped back in his chair, relaxed, and seemed to fall asleep. He began speaking in a voice that identified itself as

Fletcher, his spirit guide. The Fletcher voice, like Ford's, was soft, Southern, and slightly lisping. Then the Fletcher voice gave way to another voice, which identified itself as that of Houdini, although it too spoke in the same manner as Ford and Fletcher. Soon the new voice gave the ten code words: "Rosabelle, answer, tell, pray, answer, look, tell, answer, answer, tell." Then the Houdini voice asked if they were correct.

"Yes," Bess replied in a whisper.

"Thank you, sweetheart," the voice replied. "Now take off your wedding ring and tell them what 'Rosabelle' means."

Bess forced herself up on one elbow and tugged off her wedding ring. Inside the extra-wide gold band was engraved a portrait of her husband and the words of a song. She began to sing:

> "Rosabelle, sweet Rosabelle,
> I love you more than I can tell.
> Over me you cast a spell.
> I love you, my sweet Rosabelle."

Her voice broke on the last notes.

"I thank you, darling," Houdini said through Ford. "That was the first song I ever heard you sing. You sang it in our first show, remember?—What do you say now?"

Bess took the cue: *"Je tire le rideau comme ça."* She had learned this line—"I draw the curtain so"—when they played in France. It was what she said as she moved the cloth cabinet forward to hide the locked-and-roped trunk from the audience's view.

Fletcher was now speaking through Ford: "The message is a single word from Houdini. The word is 'believe.'"

But the séance was not over; the Houdini voice had a closing speech through the medium's lips:

"Spare no time or money to undo my attitude of doubt while on earth. Now that I have found my way back I can come often, sweetheart. Give yourself to placing the truth before all those who have lost the faith and want to take hold again.

"Believe me, life is continuous. Tell the world there is no death. I will be close to you. I expect to use this instrument

[Ford] many times in the future. Tell the world, sweetheart, that Harry Houdini lives and will prove it a thousand times."

The story broke in the afternoon edition of the *Graphic* that same day, January 8, and was flashed around the world. It also appeared that day in the Brooklyn *Daily Times,* but every dispatch this writer has seen quotes Rea Jaure from the *Graphic* and ignores the unsigned Brooklyn account. The *Graphic* story explained that the first word of the message was "Rosabelle." The other nine words spelled out "believe" in a code that the Houdinis had used in their act. The code was a relatively simple one, involving only ten key words or phrases, each of which stood for a number, which in turn represented the position of a letter in the alphabet. The word "pray" stood for "1"; "answer" for "2"; "say" for "3"; "now" for "4"; "tell" for "5"; "please" for "6"; "speak" for "7"; "quickly" for "8"; "look" for "9"; and "be quick" for "10." To convey B, the second letter of the alphabet, the speaker said "answer." For E, the fifth letter, the code was "tell." And for L, the twelfth letter, the cue words were "pray answer." Thus, the Ford message produced the word "believe": answer = B; tell = E; pray answer = L; look = I; tell = E; answer answer = V; tell = E.

Newsmen hurried to Payson Avenue for more details. Bess said that she had never met Ford before and that she had fainted after the message had come through. Only two people, her husband and herself, had known the code, she declared. There was only one copy of the message in existence. It was locked in a vault at the Manufacturers Bank on Fifth Avenue. When her "sick brain" was better, she would go to the bank and prove her statement.

Apparently overlooked in the furor of the moment—and by late researchers as well—is a statement she made in the January 9 *World:* "I had no idea what combination of words Harry would use and when he sent 'believe' it was a surprise."

Margery, the medium, was quoted in a story from Boston: "Harry Houdini, in death, has furnished the world with evidence which conclusively refutes the theories which he so vigorously defended in life."

Theo Hardeen, Houdini's brother, denounced the séance as a frame-up, an imposition on the public. Joseph Dunninger, then as now a great showman, went to Payson Avenue. He reminded Mrs. Houdini that the code had been printed on page 105 of the Kellock biography of Houdini, for which she had supplied the information. Bess had forgotten it was there. She told Dunninger that stagehands who had seen their act repeated time and again had known the words too.

Bess assured reporters that the safety-deposit box in the bank vault contained copies of two other messages, one which Houdini had said he would send to Sir Arthur Conan Doyle; the other was intended for Remigius Weiss, his friend in Philadelphia. Neither Doyle nor Weiss ever received messages, and Doyle said at the time that Houdini never mentioned that he would try to send him one. Nor were the three messages ever taken from the bank and shown to reporters.

On January 10, two days after the séance, a *Graphic* headline proclaimed: HOUDINI MESSAGE A BIG HOAX! According to this story, Rea Jaure had invited Ford to her apartment the previous evening. Because Ford had a lecture date in Newark, he did not arrive until 11:20 p.m. In the course of their conversation, Miss Jaure asked Ford if he recalled a party he had attended the previous month at Rockwell Palace in upper Manhattan. "Indeed I do," Ford answered. "My, it was funny, wasn't it? Bess and I had a great time, didn't we?" When Miss Jaure asked if Ford was going on a lecture tour with Mrs. Houdini, the medium said he was, and when asked who was financing the tour, he replied: "I am. Mrs. Houdini supplied the code as her part of the bargain."

William Plummer, the managing editor of the *Graphic*, and writer Edward Churchill signed affidavits that they had been hidden in another room of the Jaure apartment and had written down every word of the conversation.

The *Graphic* said that Ford had known Mrs. Houdini long before the Payson Avenue séance. The paper had letters he had written to her, including one sent from England, dated April 10, 1928.

Ford, in the company of his attorney, asserted that the *Graphic* story constituted a "blackmail attempt." He admitted having received Rea Jaure's invitation, but denied everything else in her story. According to Ford, his friend Francis Fast had advised him not to meet Miss Jaure. Instead of going to her apartment, he had joined a friend for a late evening meal after returning from Newark. The reporter, Ford continued, telephoned him shortly after midnight and asked why he had not come to her apartment.

Ford even produced a motive for Miss Jaure's attempt. He said the reporter was furious because Mrs. Houdini had refused to turn over to her the letters in which Charles Chapin, former city editor of the New York *World,* told why he had murdered his wife. Bess, in fact, met Chapin, who was serving a life sentence at Sing Sing, when she visited the prison two years previously to inspect the arrangements which had been made to house the criminology collection her husband had willed to Warden Lewis E. Lawes. Chapin had acted as Mrs. Houdini's guide and subsequently had written her frequently. Rea Jaure learned of these letters and realized that they might provide material for a sensational article. Bess became incensed when Miss Jaure broached the idea to her and told the reporter to leave her house. Ford said that Rea Jaure had threatened to expose his séance as a fraud if he didn't get the Chapin letters for her. According to Ford, his final words to her, before he slammed down the phone, were: "Well, you can go to hell."

Bess, still ill, was perplexed by the controversy the séance had stirred. She wrote a long letter to Walter Winchell, the *Graphic* columnist. He printed it twelve days after the séance. It said, in part:

> I want to let Houdini's old friends know that I did not betray his trust. I am writing you this personally because I wish to tell you emphatically that I was no party to any fraud. . . . When the real message, THE message that Houdini and I had agreed upon, came to me, and I accepted it as the truth, I was greeted by jeers. Why? Those who denounced the entire thing as a fraud claim that I had given Mr. Arthur Ford the message. If Mr. Ford said this I brand him as a liar. Mr. Ford has stoutly denied saying this ugly thing, and knowing the reporter as well as I do I prefer to believe Mr. Ford. . . . However, when anyone accuses me of GIVING the words that my husband and I labored so long to convince ourselves of the truth of communication, then I will fight and fight until the breath leaves my body.

Ford's troubles mounted. On January 25, the New York *Sun* reported that he had been expelled from the United Spiritualist League of New York. February 19 the executive council of the league and the governing board of his First Spiritualist Church met at the Martinique Hotel to decide whether or not he should be ousted from his post at the church for "conduct unbecoming a spiritualist minister." Plummer, Churchill, and Jaure of the *Graphic* presented sworn statements at the meeting, and James Lawlor, the doorman of the Jaure apartment building, identified Ford as a man he had seen enter and leave on the night in question. Ford's attorney introduced witnesses who said they had seen the medium elsewhere at the time. Four days earlier a man had been found who said, under oath, that he had impersonated Arthur Ford that night. He was annoyed because he had received only part payment for his work.

After six hours of heated debate, the hearing adjourned at 2 a.m. The executive council pondered the case for nearly a week, then cleared Ford "on the ground of insufficient proof." According to the February 25 New York *Telegram:* "Ford said that the authenticity of the message had not been questioned and maintained only his personal honesty had been challenged. Until the message was proved false, he would consider the Houdini matter closed."

This writer met Ford in Philadelphia before his name was on the front pages again with the story of the communication he relayed to Bishop James Pike from his dead son. Ford was not in the mood to talk about the 1929 séance on Payson Avenue. He said he had been in a trance and had to take the word of the people present as to what happened. He autographed a copy of Francis R. Fast's booklet *The Houdini Messages,* seventh edition, which tells the spiritualist version of the story. Under his name Ford wrote, "I have had no contact with Houdini since."

After Bess recovered from her illness, she no longer believed that the message came from her husband. In hundreds of later interviews she maintained unswervingly that she had never received a communication from Houdini. For a time she was president of The Happiness Club, a social group which met Sunday nights. Then she opened Mrs. Harry Houdini's Rendezvous, a restaurant at 64 West 49th Street. The enterprise interested her for a few months; then, bored with the details of management, she closed it.

In 1933, after Bess recovered from a heart attack, she made a personal appearance at the Houdini Temple of Magic, which Theo Hardeen opened on an Atlantic City pier. In the theater proper Hardeen escaped from Houdini's Water Can. Daily he went to the end of the pier where he was shackled, nailed in a wooden box, and lowered into the Atlantic Ocean. As Houdini had done in the past, he made a rapid underwater escape.

A year later Bess moved to Hollywood. There, under the wing of Dr. Edward Saint, a wiry little man with a goatee and a waxed moustache, she began a new life. Saint had been a crystal gazer. He could talk Bess' language and, as a showman himself, he shared her admiration for Houdini. Saint became her manager and almost constant companion. He was the first to suggest that Halloween, the day Houdini died, should be called National Magic Day. He tried to interest the movie studios in a film biography of the great magician, he arranged for Bess to appear at public events, and filled countless scrapbooks with the newspaper and magazine articles that continued to appear about Houdini.

At fifty-eight, Mrs. Houdini's hair was snow white. A large photograph of her husband dominated her living room, by it burned an "eternal light." Each October 31 she would sit quietly, just in case a true message should come through.

On the tenth anniversary of Houdini's death, Dr. Saint staged a final séance on the roof of the Hollywood Knickerbocker Hotel. A recording of Houdini's "Pomp and Circumstance" opening music was played. Dr. Saint pleaded for the ghost of the great magician to manifest itself and lift a spirit trumpet. The trumpet remained motionless. He implored the shade of the escape king to open a pair of locked handcuffs, or ring a bell, or bang a tambourine. Nothing happened.

"Houdini hasn't come," Bess said sadly. "I don't believe he will come." She turned off the light by his portrait.

She died February 11, 1943, aboard a train bound from Los Angeles to the East. Critically ill, she wished to spend her last days in New York. She had been taken to the railway station on a hospital cot, under the care of a physician, then she was put in an oxygen tent in her car. She died as the train reached Needles, California. In a way the spiritualists could say that was significant. The "East Indian Needle Feat" had always been called "Needles" when they spoke of it during his show.

Before her death, Bess told friends that if a medium ever announced a message from her it would be a fraud. "When I go," she said, "I'll be gone for good. I won't even try to come back."

POSTSCRIPT

It is now more than forty years since Houdini with almost superhuman effort completed his final performance on the stage of the Garrick Theater in Detroit.

Many years ago, as a young member of the Magicians Club of Baltimore, I sat in a dark hotel room on the anniversary of his death. A medium twisted in her chair and announced she had a message from the great magician for someone in the room. I was startled when letter by letter she spelled out my first name and added: "Houdini says, 'Carry on!' " Since then I have performed in many theaters here and abroad that were once filled with cheers for his exploits. I have talked with many people who knew him well, collected more than a thousand of his letters and stacks of his programs, manuscripts, books, and notes. Finally, one hot August afternoon I went to Cypress Hills in Brooklyn.

My first view of Machpelah Cemetery, through the arched entryway, was dominated by the life-size marble bust of Houdini at the top of the twenty-thousand-dollar exedra he had dedicated to his parents. A showman to the end, his instructions specified exactly where the sculpture was to be placed.

On the central column is a replica of the seal of the Society of American Magicians and the words "M.I. President 1917–1926." Once the final "6" had been a "7." The society had changed the final digit when someone realized that although Houdini had been re-elected for the 1926–27 term, he had not been alive in 1927. I wondered how many people were baffled by the "M.I." It's an abbreviation for Most Illustrious. The annual fee for taking care of the plot is paid by the S.A.M., a repayment, in a sense, of the fees Houdini paid in his lifetime for the upkeep of the graves of other famous magicians.

The stone nearest to the exedra is "Grandmother 1821–1887." This was Cecilia's mother. "Herman 1863–1885" is to the right of Rabbi Weiss' marker. I remembered a Houdini note that his brother had been moved to the family plot.

"Willie 1872–1925" is to the right of Herman and closer to the monument.

Nathan and Leopold are far apart, at opposite ends of the area. This is logical. After Nathan's wife had left him for Leopold, they hadn't spoken to each other. Sister Gladys is next to Leopold. Theo Hardeen is close to the marble monument.

To the left of Mayer Samuel Weiss is Cecilia and by his mother's side is Houdini. I bent to read the stone. "Houdini 1874–1926 and his beloved wife Wilhelmina Beatrice 1876–19—." Two raised oblongs remain where the final two digits were to have been hewn.

Although Bess had specified that she was to be buried beside her husband, this was not done. Her sister, Marie Hinson, had been with her on that final train ride. She said that Bess had embraced Catholicism again before she died. So Mrs. Houdini was not cremated as she had planned to be. Jim Collins, Harry's old assistant, was to have taken her ashes to Machpelah. But Jim died before Bess and so did Dr. Saint, her closest friend through the last years. Mrs. Houdini was given a proper Catholic burial in a proper Catholic cemetery in Westchester.

I wondered what Houdini would have thought of that— and of the legends that had arisen through the years. One man claimed Houdini had built a submerged aquariumlike chamber in order to accomplish the under-ice escape—a feat that he never actually performed. Another revealed that Harry carried his escape tools under a false dental plate. Still another told in great detail a ridiculous story about Houdini having a "skin pocket" under his knee. He said a surgeon had cut it as a hiding place for release gimmicks.

And I thought how delighted the great crusader would have been had he lived until the day when it was revealed that Walter's fingerprints which Margery claimed to have materialized in wax were proven to be those of her Boston dentist!

Ghostly forms and floating trumpets rarely appear in séance rooms these days. Houdini's campaign all but obliterated that phase of fraudulent mediumship. How he would have laughed just a few years ago when a true believer took an infrared photograph in a dark room which clearly indicated that the ghosts were flesh and blood!

Houdini had hoped to establish a permanent Temple of

Magic in New York, but this was not to be. On June 6, 1968, a Houdini Magical Hall of Fame opened in Niagara Falls, Ontario. I flew up to speak at the official reception. Klieg lights, newspaper and TV cameramen, and an orange Houdini banner high in the air, suspended by a balloon, jammed Centre Street with the curious. Inside the museum, life-size figures of the great escapologist portrayed him wriggling free of a strait-jacket, sitting, handcuffed and chained, in a jail cell. There were films of his flights in Germany and an underwater escape from a packing box. Cases of manacles and locks which once had been on display in the lobbies of theaters around the world were again on view. The next day I drove by the falls, where the most exciting scene of his film *The Man from Beyond* had been staged.

Houdini is still the best-known name in magic. Scarcely a day goes by without it appearing somewhere in the press of the world. Anyone who does something remarkable is labeled a Houdini, whether he escapes from a famous prison or makes a fantastic catch during a ball game. No other mystery worker has ever appealed so much to the public's imagination.

Many years ago a Washington dramatic critic showed me an unopened envelope in which a letter he had written to Houdini on October 30, 1926, the day before he died, had been returned. To the printed "Houdini on Tour" in the upper left-hand corner, Bess had added a single word—"Forever."

SOURCES AND
ACKNOWLEDGMENTS

Were it not for Clayton Rawson, who almost eleven years ago began prodding me to put my research into print, this book would still be unfinished. Since I made my first notes many who contributed important information have died: Theodore Hardeen, Mrs. Houdini, James Collins, Will Goldston, Bernard M. L. Ernst, Frank Ducrot, Frederick Eugene Powell, Dr. Henry Ridgely Evans, Howard Thurston, Dante (Harry Jansen), Fred Keating, Horace Goldin, Jean Hugard, Okito (Theodore Bamberg), Fulton Oursler, Harry Blackstone, Samuel Margules, Joseph F. Rinn, Messmore Kendall, Willard Greene, John J. McManus, Jean Irving, Lester Grimes, and William Lindsay Gresham.

I am indebted to Mrs. Roberta Ernst, Joseph Dunninger, John Mulholland, Clarence Hubbard, Dr. Boris Zola, Al Flosso, Arthur Lloyd, Amedeo Vacca, Dr. and Mrs. Victor Trask, Dai Vernon, Jack Gwynne, Theo Doré, Fred Beckman, Walter B. Gibson, Clarence Blair, Carroll Bish, Edgar Heyl, C. B. Yohe, Loring Campbell, George Boston, Art Ronnie, Michael Miller, John Daniel, Arnold Furst, Bernard Rind, Arnold Belais, the Rev. William C. Rauscher, and Albert Green for their recollections or helpful suggestions.

I am grateful to fellow collectors in this country who gave me access to their material: George Pfisterer, Sidney Hollis Radner, H. Adrian Smith, Tad Ware, Stanley Palm, Dr. Morris N. Young, Dr. Joseph H. Fries, Pat Culliton, Manuel Weltman, Robert Lund, Larry Weeks, Stuart Cramer, Dr. John Henry Grossman, John Booth, Lloyd E. Jones, John Daniel, Philip T. Thomas, Fred Rickard, Al Guenther, David J. Lustig, and George McAthy.

Equally cooperative were the late Agosta-Meynier and the late Dr. Jules Dhotel in Paris, Robelly in Orléans (Loire), the late Dr. Kurt Volkmann in Düsseldorf, Leo Leslie Clemmensen and Peter and Jorgen Borsch in Copenhagen, George

Armstrong and Stanley Thomas in London, Roland Winder in Leeds, and James B. Findlay in Shanklin, Isle of Wight.

Thanks also to Herbert E. Pratt and Arthur Ivey at the Magic Circle Collection, London; A. H. Wesencraft, Harry Price Collection, University of London; Paul Meyers, New York Public Library Theatre Collection; the late Dr. William Van Lennep, Harvard Theatre Collection; and Richard Hart at the Enoch Pratt Library in Baltimore.

Much of the source material for this biography is in my collection in New York: 1,003 letters written by Houdini from September 1900 to October 1926; Houdini scrapbooks, programs, playbills, and heralds; lithographs, photographs, newspaper, magazine, and film accounts of his exploits; annotated volumes he once studied; books, pamphlets, and unpublished manuscripts he wrote.

There are hundreds of letters written to or about him by Harry Kellar, Will Goldston, Mrs. Houdini, Hardeen, B. M. L. Ernst, Oscar Teale, Clinton Burgess, Harry Leat, and Rose Mackenberg; and scrapbooks of Hardeen, Goldin, Thurston, Teale, Goldston, and Servais LeRoy. There are also files of the magic periodicals of Houdini's time: *Mahatma, The Sphinx, The Magical World, The Magic World, The Wizard, The Magic Wand, Magic, The Magician, The Magazine of Magic, The Escape Artist, Edwards' Monthly, Leat's Leaflets, The Magic Circular, M-U-M, Conjurers' Monthly Magazine, Die Zauberwelt, Der Zauberspiegel, L'Illusionniste;* and the library includes more than seven thousand books on conjuring, spiritualism, witchcraft, and psychic fraud.

BIBLIOGRAPHY OF WORKS
BY HOUDINI

Magic Made Easy. New York, 1898; Chicago, 1899, published by author.

Between 1900 and 1924 souvenir booklets were published in England, the United States, and Russia bearing such titles as *America's Sensational Perplexer; Houdini; The Famous Houdini; The Original Jail Breaker and Handcuff King; Life, History and Handcuff Secrets of Houdini; Handcuff Tricks Exposed;* and *Houdini, the Adventurous Life of a Versatile Artist.* There are nine examples in the Christopher Collection.

The Right Way to Do Wrong. An Exposé of Successful Criminals. Boston, 1906, published by author.

Editor, publisher, *Conjurers' Monthly Magazine.* New York, September 1906–August 1908.

The Unmasking of Robert-Houdin. New York, Publishers Printing Co., 1908.

The Unmasking of Robert-Houdin Together With a Treatise on Handcuff Secrets. London, George Routledge & Sons, Ltd., 1909.

Mein Training und meine Tricks. Leipzig, Berlin, München, Paris, Grethlein & Co., 1909.

Handcuff Secrets. London, George Routledge & Sons, Ltd., 1910.

The Marvelous Adventures of Houdini, the Justly Celebrated Elusive American. Brooklyn, N.Y., 1917, published by author.

Editor, *M-U-M.* The Society of American Magicians Monthly. New York, 1917–1926.

Miracle Mongers and Their Methods. New York, E. P. Dutton & Co., 1920.

Magical Rope Ties and Escapes. London, Will Goldston, Ltd., 1921.

Mysterious Mr. Yu or Haldane of the Secret Service. New York, 1921, published by author.

Yar, the Primeval Man. New York, 1921, published by author.

Il Mistero di Osiris or the Mystery of the Jewel (Talisman); Mystery Tale of Old Egypt by "Giovanni Deadota." New York, 1921; published by author.

Houdini's Paper Magic. New York, E. P. Dutton & Co., 1922.

Editor, *Elliott's Last Legacy, Secrets of the King of All Kard Kings,* by Dr. James William Elliott. Compiled by Clinton Burgess. New York, Adams Press Print, 1923.

A Magician Among the Spirits. New York, Harper & Brothers, 1924.

Houdini Exposes the Tricks Used by the Boston Medium Margery. . . . Also a Complete Exposure of Argamasilla. . . . New York, Adams Press Publishers, 1924.

Editor, "Red Magic." The New York *World* Sunday Supplement (also syndicated as "Home Magic"), 1924–1926.

Houdini Souvenir Program. New York, 1925.

"Conjuring," *Encyclopaedia Britannica,* 13th ed., 1926.

Houdini Souvenir Program Coast to Coast Tour. Season 1926–27. New York, 1926.

Houdini's Book of Magic and Party Pastimes. New York, Stoll & Evans Co., Inc., 1927.

Houdini's Big Little Book of Magic. Racine, Wisc., Whitman Publishing Company, 1927.

In addition to writing hundreds of articles for newspapers, conjuring periodicals, and theatrical journals, Houdini contributed to many magazines; among them: *Collier's, Popular Science, Vanity Fair, Hearst's, Popular Radio, The American Magazine,* and *Weird Tales.*

A Houdini bibliography by Manuel Weltman, listing more than two hundred items, was published in *Genii,* the magic monthly, in October, November, December 1967, and January 1968. Mr. Weltman plans to add to it in the future.

GENERAL BIBLIOGRAPHY

Abbot, Anthony (Fulton Oursler). *These Are Strange Tales.* Philadelphia, The John C. Winston Company, 1948.

Anonymous. *Secret of the Great Handcuff Trick.* Boston, Mutual Book Company, 1907.

————. *The Davenport Brothers, the World-Renowned Spiritual Mediums.* Boston, William White and Company, 1869.

Bird, J. Malcolm. *"Margery" the Medium.* Boston, Small, Maynard & Co., 1925.

Boston, George L., with Robert Parrish. *Inside Magic.* New York, The Beechhurst Press, 1947.

Cannell, J. C. *The Secrets of Houdini.* London, Hutchinson & Co., Ltd., 1932.

Carrington, Hereward. *The Physical Phenomena of Spiritualism.* Boston, Small, Maynard & Co., 1907.

————. *Handcuff Tricks.* Kansas City, Mo., A. M. Wilson, 1913.

Christopher, Milbourne. *Panorama of Prestidigitators.* New York, The Christopher Collection, 1956.

————. *Panorama of Magic.* New York, Dover Publications, Inc., 1962.

Clarke, Sidney W. *The Annals of Conjuring.* London, George Johnson, 1929; also published serially in *The Magic Wand,* 1924–1928.

Clempert, John. *Thrilling Episodes of John Clempert. The Shining Star of the Realms of Mystery.* England, 1909, published by author.

Courtney, Charles, in collaboration with Tom Johnson. *Unlocking Adventure.* New York, Whittlesey House, 1942.

Crandon, L. R. G. *The Margery Mediumship. Unofficial Sittings at the Laboratory of the Society for Psychical Research, London, December 6, 7 and 8, 1929.* Boston, 1930, published by author.

Crawford, W. J. *The Psychic Structures at the Goligher Circle.* London, John M. Watkins, 1921.

Cunningham, Robert. *Cunning "The Jail Breaker." Jail Breaking a Science.* U.S.A., published by author, 1907.

Curry, Paul. *Magician's Magic.* New York, Franklin Watts, Inc., 1965.

Davenport, Reuben Briggs. *The Death-Blow to Spiritualism.* New York, C. W. Dillingham, 1888.

Day, J. *Secrets of the Handcuff Trick.* Birmingham, England, n. d.

Dexter, Will. *This Is Magic.* London, Arco Publications, Ltd., 1958.

Doerr, H. R. *The Secrets of Houdini's Feats Explained.* Philadelphia, published by author, n. d.

Doyle, Arthur Conan. *The Edge of the Unknown.* New York, G. P. Putnam's Sons, 1930.

Dunninger, Joseph. *Houdini's Spirit Exposés.* Ed., Joseph H. Kraus, New York, Experimenter Publishing Co., Inc. 1928.

———. *Inside the Medium's Cabinet.* New York, David Kemp and Company, 1935.

———. *100 Houdini Tricks You Can Do.* New York, Arco Publishing Company, Inc., 1954.

Ernst, Bernard M. L., and Hereward Carrington. *Houdini and Conan Doyle: The Story of a Strange Friendship.* New York, Albert and Charles Boni, Inc., 1932.

Evans, Henry Ridgely. *The Old and the New Magic.* Chicago, The Open Court Publishing Company, 1906; 2d ed., revised and enlarged, 1909.

———. *Adventures in Magic.* New York, Leo Rullman. 1927.

———. *History of Conjuring and Magic.* Kenton, Ohio, International Brotherhood of Magicians, 1928; new and rev. ed. (abridged). Kenton, Ohio, W. W. Durbin, 1930.

———. *A Master of Modern Magic. The Life and Adventures of Robert-Houdin.* New York, Macoy Publishing Company, 1932.

Fast, Francis R. *The Houdini Messages.* New York, published by author, n.d.

Finger Print Demonstrations by E. E. Dudley, Arthur Goadby, Hereward Carrington. Boston Society for Psychic Research. Bulletin XVIII, October 1932.

Ford, Arthur, in collaboration with Marguerite Harmon Bro. *Nothing So Strange.* New York, Harper & Brothers, 1958.

Fortune Telling, Hearings before the Subcommittee on Judiciary of the Committee on the District of Columbia House of Representatives Sixty-Ninth Congress, First Session, on H.R. 8989, February 26, May 18, 20, and 21, 1924. Washington, Government Printing Office, 1924.

Frikell, Samri (Fulton Oursler). *Spirit Mediums Exposed.* New York, New Metropolitan Fiction, Inc., 1930.

Furst, Arnold. *Great Magic Shows.* Los Angeles, The Genii Publishing Company, 1968.

Gibson, Walter B. *Houdini's Escapes.* New York, Harcourt, Brace & Company, 1930.

————. *Houdini's Magic.* New York, Harcourt, Brace & Company, 1932.

————. *Houdini's Magic and Escapes.* (The two books in one volume.) New York, Blue Ribbon Books, Inc., n.d.

————, and Morris N. Young (eds. and comps.). *Houdini on Magic.* New York, Dover Publications, Inc., 1953.

————, and Morris N. Young. *Houdini's Fabulous Magic.* Philadelphia and New York, Chilton Company, 1961.

————. *The Master Magicians.* Garden City, N.Y., Doubleday & Company, Inc., 1966.

Goldston, Will. *Secrets of Magic.* Liverpool, England, The 'Mahatma' Magical Company, 1903.

————, (ed.). *The Magician Annual 1909–10.* London, A. W. Gamage, Ltd.

————. *Exclusive Magical Secrets.* London, The Magician Ltd., 1912.

————. *Further Exclusive Magical Secrets.* London, Will Goldston, Ltd., 1927.

————. *Sensational Tales of Mystery Men.* London, Will Goldston, Ltd., 1929.

————. *Great Magicians' Tricks.* London, Will Goldston, Ltd., 1931.

————. *A Magician's Swan Song.* London, John Long, Ltd., n.d.

Gresham, William Lindsay. *Houdini, the Man Who Walked Through Walls.* New York, Henry Holt & Company, Inc., 1959.

Hammond, William Elliott. *Houdini Unmasked.* Ca. 1926, published by author.

Hardeen, Theodore (comp.). *Life and History of Hardeen. Ca.* 1926, published by author.

———. *Houdini, His Life and Work in Prose and Picture.* 1927, published by author.

Hugard, Jean. *Houdini's "Unmasking"; Fact vs Fiction.* With an *Introduction and Supplementary Chapter by Milbourne Christopher.* Printed in book form, with a title page dated 1957, as part of *Hugard's Magic Monthly* (Brooklyn), June 1957—January 1959.

Hull, Burling. *The Challenge Handcuff Act.* New York, 1916, published by author.

———. *Thirty-three Rope Ties and Chain Releases.* New York, American Magic Corporation, 1915.

Hunt, Douglas, and Kari Hunt. *The Art of Magic.* New York, Atheneum, 1967.

Kellock, Harold. *Houdini, His Life-Story, by Harold Kellock from the Recollections and Documents of Beatrice Houdini.* New York, Harcourt, Brace & Company, 1928.

Kendall, Lace. *Houdini, Master of Escape.* Philadelphia, Macrae Smith Co., 1960.

Leat, Harry. *Forty Years in and Around Magic.* London, 1923, published by author.

McComas, Henry C. *Ghosts I Have Talked With.* Baltimore, Williams & Wilkins Company, 1935.

McKenzie, J. Hewat. *Spirit Intercourse, Its Theory and Practice.* London, Simpkin, Marshall, Hamilton Kent & Co., Ltd., 1916.

Margery Mediumship, The. Proceedings of the American Society for Psychical Research. New York, 1928, 1933; 3 vols.

Mulholland, John. *Quicker Than the Eye.* Indianapolis, The Bobbs-Merrill Company, 1932.

———. *The Story of Magic.* New York, Loring & Mussey, 1935.

———. *Beware Familiar Spirits.* New York, Charles Scribner's Sons, 1938.

Murchison, Carl (ed.). *The Case For and Against Psychical Belief.* Worcester, Mass., Clark University, 1927.

Pressing, R. G. (comp.). *Houdini Unmasked.* Lily Dale, N.Y., *Dale News,* 1947.

Reeve, Arthur B., and John W. Grey. *The Master Mystery from Scenarios.* New York, Grosset & Dunlap, 1919.

Richardson, Mark, . . . L. R. G. Crandon. *Margery, Harvard, Veritas: A Study in Psychics.* Boston, Blanchard Printing, 1925.

Rinn, Joseph F. *Sixty Years of Psychical Research.* New York, The Truth Seeker Company, 1950.

Robert-Houdin, Jean Eugène. *Memoirs of Robert-Houdin, King of the Conjurers.* New Introduction and Notes by Milbourne Christopher. New York, Dover Publications, Inc., 1964.

Sardina, Maurice. *Where Houdini Was Wrong.* Tr. and ed. with Notes by Victor Farelli. London, George Armstrong, 1950.

Seldow, Michel. *Les Illusionnistes et Leur Secrets.* Paris, Librairie Arthème Fayard, 1959.

Severn, Bill. *Magic and Magicians.* New York, David McKay Company, Inc., 1958.

Sharpe, S. H. *Introducing Houdini versus Robert-Houdin: The Whole Truth.* Reighton, England, published by author, 1955.

Stanyon, Ellis. *Great Handcuff Secrets.* London, Stanyon & Co., 1904.

Truesdell, John W. *The Bottom Facts Concerning the Science of Spiritualism.* New York, G. W. Carleton & Co., 1883.

Williams, Beryl, and Samuel Epstein. *The Great Houdini.* New York, Julian Messner, Inc., 1950.

Wilsmann, Alyos Christof. *Die Zersägte Jungfrau.* Berlin, Verlag Scherl, 1938.

INDEX